German Paratroops in Scandinavia

German Paratroops in Scandinavia

Fallschirmjäger in Denmark and Norway April - June 1940

Óscar González López

Schiffer Military History
Atglen, PA

To Raquel, Nicolás, and Marcos, with undying affection.
For Albert, in memory...

Cover: *Leutnant* Becker encouraging his men gathered at the Bjørnfjell station May 14, 1940.

Book translation by Martin John Houghton

Book Design by Ian Robertson.

Library of Congress Control Number: 2008941237

Printed in China.
ISBN: 978-0-7643-3241-8

This book was originally published in Spanish under the title *Fallschirmjäger en Escandinavia - Paracaidistas Alemanes en la Invasión de Dinamarca y Noruega Abril - Junio 1940* by Galland Books

Published by Schiffer Publishing Ltd.
4880 Lower Valley Road
Atglen, PA 19310
Phone: (610) 593-1777
FAX: (610) 593-2002
E-mail: Info@schifferbooks.com.
Visit our web site at: www.schifferbooks.com
Please write for a free catalog.
This book may be purchased from the publisher.
Please include $5.00 postage.
Try your bookstore first.

In Europe, Schiffer books are distributed by:
Bushwood Books
6 Marksbury Avenue
Kew Gardens
Surrey TW9 4JF, England
Phone: 44 (0) 20 8392-8585
FAX: 44 (0) 20 8392-9876
E-mail: Info@bushwoodbooks.co.uk.
Visit our website at: www.bushwoodbooks.co.uk

Contents

Oberfeldwebel Alexander Uhlig
Ritterkreuz am 29.10.1944 als Führer der 16. /Fsch.Jg.Rgt. 6

Prologue

This book is a study centered on the operations carried out by German paratroops in Denmark and Norway from April to June 1940. In response to a request from the Author as one of the few remaining living witnesses to the events described, I will try to write a few lines by way of a prologue.

During the Norwegian campaign at the beginning of 1940 I was a NCO (*Feldwebel*), and commanded a section in the first company of the 1st Parachute Regiment (1./FJR 1). It was with this unit that I took part in the operations in Oslo, Dombås, and Narvik. These operations were not directed against Norway, but rather against Great Britain.

Germany and Britain had been at war since Autumn 1939, and according to Churchill the only objective as far as he was concerned was the destruction of Germany. The British deployment in Norway began in April 1940, with the clear objective of cutting the supply of minerals from Narvik to Germany. The British military presence also supposed another threat to German interests, as it left the country open to an Allied attack on its Norwegian flank. Germany's military operations there were designed to put an end to this situation, which they succeeded in doing, as the Allies evacuated Norway in June 1940.

Both the *Fallschirmjäger* and the other troops of the *Wehrmacht* did our duty as soldiers in order to protect our country. This was our objective. We did not fight blindly following a party or a personality.

During the last four years I have tried to answer all the questions put to me by Óscar González López regarding these operations. I hope and trust that the results of his research manage to resolve and clarify all aspects pertaining to the involvement of German airborne troops in Scandinavia (to date, many pages have been written that have lacked truth and dishonoured the *Fallschirmjäger*).

My memories are for those of my fallen comrades who did their duty as soldiers. My only hope is that future generations will be spared the experience of war, which can bring nothing but pain and cruelty, and that they can live in peace and freedom. This is the heartfelt wish of this veteran paratrooper. Good Luck (*Gluck ab*).

Alexander Uhlig.
Fallschirmjäger awarded the Knight's Cross
on 29 October 1944
December 2007

"*War supposes a complete alteration from what we consider normality. All wars consist of the same: the face of horror and the death of the soldier. This is not heroic, it is sordid and miserable. All my words are a denunciation of war.*"

(Albert Valjeur, in a letter to the Author)

Introduction

The conquest of Denmark and Norway presents an interesting case of joint strategy which deserves closer study and analysis. Many of the lessons learned from this campaign are still applicable today, when complex large-scale operations, executed over great distances, have become the norm in regards to military strategy. Although the conditions and available technology have changed redically—and continue to change—present campaigns and operations show significant similarities to Operation "*Weserübung*."[1]

The Germans, for example, placed great emphasis on mobility, speed, and rhythm. Simply put, their pholosophy was one of "be the first to arrive with the maximum means available." The German system guaranteed the highest level of independence to its officers, insisting that what was fundamental was that they kept faith with achieving the assigned objectives. While the Allies advanced with caution, the Germans fought with fluidity, concentrating on defeating the enemy rather than "holding" ground. The Allies, however, showed a greater predilection for a "methodical" approach to battle, and it would have been impossible to imagine them "moving" isolated detachments of troops along a coastline hundreds of miles long, confident in joining up with them at a later date, all in the face of a powerful enemy fleet, bad weather preventing aircraft from flying, and large-scale amphibious counter-attacks.

The German plan hinged to a great extent on quickly interrupting the mobilisation of Norwegian troops, as well as seizing all those areas which were susceptible to being used for hypothetical Allied disembarkations. The German obsession, therefore, was not precisely one of guarding flanks and establishing a front.

With this strategy the Germans concentrated their "power" (speed, rhythm, air power, and superior tactical ability) against an enemy with less resolve and with a faltering "will to win." Although casualties on both sides were similar (even significantly higher in the *Kriegsmarine* and *Luftwaffe)*, German morale remained high throughout the campaign.

As a laborotory for future operations, the German invasion of Norway faced a new challenge in the history of warfare. One of the lessons was in inter-service cooperation, an essential condition for victory. Operation "*Weserübung*" required the total integration of air, land, and maritime forces, and each service responded with total resolution. This was the first operation of its type that had a unified command.

The *Kriegsmarine*, which was slightly weaker than the *Royal Navy*, suffered considerable losses but achieved its objective, successfully landing troops and covering their deployment.

The *Luftwaffe* undoubtedly conducted one of the best planned and innovative air operations of the time, flying great distances in adverse conditions. The German pilots carried the responsibility for providing strategic mobility, as well as supporting the ground forces (who lacked heavy artillery). Their contribution was decisive.

However, the *Luftwaffe* did not only supply pilots and aircraft of different types, but also a force of paratroops who were undoubtedly the spearpoint of the German attack, surprising both friend and foe alike.

The German parachute troops (*Fallschirmjäger*) can be considered as elite soldiers within the German armed forces during World War II, mainly due to their successes during the first years of the war. They fought better than the average German soldier, and the different actions in which they were engaged during the invasion of Norway support this thesis.

Certainly, the *Fallschirmjäger* of 1940 was a well trained, highly motivated individual, both physically and psychologically fit, always alert and with personal initiative, and aware of the necessity to act no sooner than he reached the ground. Other important features of his training were the ability to adapt to circumstances, weapons handling (his own and those of his enemy), and preparedness for hand to hand combat. A special mention can be made of the fact that officers were perfectly trained in the tactics of ground warfare.

Sadly, in some respects the *Fallschirmjäger* were their own worst enemy. Their hard earned reputation went against them. They were assigned missions for which they were not properly prepared. In the case of Norway, their first jump behind enemy lines—one of the first in combat of the war—was highly improvised and badly prepared. The paratroops were sent to Dombås against much better equipped Norwegian troops. They were left to their luck, and were completely vulnerable without adequate weapons and equipment for their mission.

This is a case that will be analysed in more detail because it shares some common features with other German airborne operations (Holland and Crete, to give two examples). These parachute drops were to have their "price," despite achieving their objectives (at the cost of serious losses). The isolation of several *Fallschirmjäger* units hastily or incorrectly dropped on their targets and subjected to heavy attacks—such as occurred in Norway and later on in Holland, Crete, and the Ardennes—revealed serious errors in planning and a weak point in the strategical use of paratroops.

The study of German airborne operations in Norway allows us to analyse the different uses of the *Fallschirmjäger*. To some degree, the campaign makes a perfect summary of the strategies employed throughout the war.

In the first place, the drop was made on an objective located well behind enemy lines, holding the position until contact was made with ground forces, even though this was done in strength against limited but vital targets (airports), as had been done in earlier operations with airborne troops. In both cases the preferred method was to drop paratroops directly onto the target in order to increase the factor of surprise, something the "lightly armed" *Fallschirmjäger* must have taken into account.

A second method employed specifically on large-scale operations, such as Crete, was hardly ever used in Norway. Only at Dombås did the Germans use what their strategists called "oil stains," that is to say, several drop zones intended to form a ring around the target.

Finally, in operation "*Weserübung*" the *Fallschirmjäger* were used as infantry, although deployed behind enemy lines and taking maximum advantage of surprise, supporting the infantry and losing their "status" as specialist troops. This last method was only justified in an emergency situation.

Historical research has dedicated few lines to analysing in detail the actions of the German airborne troops in the occupation of Denmark and Norway. Furthermore, what has been written is short on accuracy, and above all, criticicism. This last mentioned aspect is essential. Narration goes hand in hand with the analysis. Reading about the paratroop operations gives cause for serious reflection. Therefore, the aim of this book is to offer a critical look at all aspects of the German strategy, which was to mark the actions of the *Fallschirmjäger* throughout the rest of the war.

The purpose of this work is to offer a chronology of the actions of the *Fallschirmjäger* during operation "*Weserübung*." Chronology, because the idea is to present a coherent, precise, and objective narrative of the outstanding role played by this elite unit. A combat jump by paratroops had never been made before April 1940, so if only for this reason the event is worth a closer look.

The testimony of those who took part in the battles (Norwegians and Germans) and the use of primary sources has provided the "backbone" to this work. Contact, either direct or through correspondence with the veterans who participated in the fighting in Norway has been both a challenge and an honour. There is no doubt that listening to their personal accounts 67 years after the events took place has been a primary motivating factor for a lover of history. I have experienced something similar to that which the great writer Josep Pla alluded to when he stated "*what interests me is history, living history, getting inside history.*" Ernst Mössinger (+), Albert Valjeur (+), Alexander Uhlig, Gerhard Broder, Wilhelm Metscher, Heinz Kluge, Friedrich Heinrich Ungeheuer and Per Waaler allowed the Author to "get inside history" every time they offered more of their invaluable "treasure": their memories.

This work can also be said to have gravitated arround the research undertaken by the historians Karl-Heinz Golla, Cato Guhnfeldt, Andreas Hauge, and Øivind Solvik. Having their guidance and advice has been a genuine privilege. Also, the gracious help of Arne Gunnar Løvlund of the "*Dombås krigsminneforening*" museum, and of Jan Lehre was essential to my almost obsessive search for accuracy. Essential, too, was the collaboration of Richard Kloes, Arnold Wesenberg, Paul Ullmann, Eugen Siffermann, Ingeborg von Hove, Tor Schye (who placed the extremely interesting archive of his father, Kristian Fredrik Schye, at my disposal), Øyvind Holt, Hans-Joachim Oehler (of "*Der Deutsche Fallschirmjäger*," always disposed to attend to our consultations), Günter Schalich, Ian Tannahill, and Lucas Molina, who I have never thanked enough for his confidence and dedicated support in enabling this work to see the "light of day."

Eric Queen, Simon Orchard, Bart Jansen, Erik Ettrup, Ramon Boronda, Andreas Hauge, and Kristian Hosar kindly allowed me to use photographs from their collections, and Iñaki Merino masterfully drew "the impossible." The patience—once again—and knowledge of Josu Otxoa, given through his valuable suggestions, helped guide my work along the right track. Lastly is the recognition that down to the smallest, this book is touched with the "*patient and loving presence*" of Raquel. To all of them I offer my most sincere thanks.

Finally, their remains one last reflection, for the wish, that is in no way trifling for its brevity: peace. Seen from the perspective of a historian, one must be at least guided by the experiences of those who fought in and survived these events. In this sense, the book opens with the revealing words of Albert Valjeur, *Fallschirmjäger* and friend, who died before the publication of this book. His motto is also ours: "*all my words are a denunciation of war*."

1 Cf. Hooke, R. and Coglianese, C. (1993), pp. 100-101.

1

The Precedents

Finland

The initial armed confrontation in Scandinavia did not involve Germany but the Soviet Union. Nevertheless, it is well known that the Soviet attack on Finland[2] was followed with special interest by Germany. The difficulties confronted by the Russians in their Finnish incursion led Hitler to believe that his "ally" lacked a resolute army, incapable of conducting a "lightning" war. This perception undoubtedly influenced the decision to attack the USSR in June 1941.

On the other hand, the "Winter War," as it became known, mobilised the Allies. In this context, the invasion of Denmark and Norway, apart from making it obvious that the war would inevitably extend throughout Europe, was the second "assault" on an area "appealing" for its strategic location (control of the North Sea or the Baltic) and its resources (Swedish iron ore, for example).

Reviewing the troops in Finland before going to the Front.

Finnish soldiers at the Front.

On Wednesday, 29 November 1939 the Soviet Union attacked Finland. The Russian leader, Stalin, had already agreed with the German foreign minister, von Ribbentrop, that the Baltic states of Lithuania, Estonia, and Latvia would remain within the Soviet sphere of influence. In October 1939 a "mutual assistance pact" was signed between the Soviet Union and Latvia. In June 1940, while the world contemplated the German invasion of Western Europe, the Soviet Union easily annexed the three weak Baltic States.

However, Finland was a very different country to the Baltic States. Stalin saw that the proximity of the Finnish frontier to Leningrad, the USSR's second city, was a serious threat. Following the same strategy he would use to annex the Baltic States, he offered the Finns a mutual assistance treaty and at the same time demanded that Finland cede areas of the Karelia Isthmus, near Leningrad. Finland rejected both proposals and was then immediately invaded by the USSR.

Finland possessed an army of barely 30.000 men grouped into nine divisions each composed of three infantry regiments. She had sixty obsolete tanks, one hundred and fifty aircraft, and twenty-two anti-aircraft batteries.

During the hard winter of 39/40, reserves were mobilised and fifteen Finnish divisions faced forty-five Soviet divisions, inflicting heavy casualties on the Russians. In Suomussalmi (Karelia), on 5 January 1940 Finnish ski troops of the 9th Division, under the command of Colonel Siilasvuo, counter-attacked the Soviet 163rd and 44th Divisions, destroyoing them. The Russians lost 27,000 men killed in action or frozen to death and 50 tanks, as well as artillery and vehicles. Finnish casualties were 900 dead and 1,770 wounded.

On the "Mannerheim Line" the Soviet 10th and 20th Armoured Divisions also suffered heavy losses. The heavy T-28 tanks could make no headway against the (few in number) Finnish anti-tank troops.

All these events were being followed closely in Germany. The staff officers in the High Command noted the incompetance demonstrated by the Soviet Divisions engaged in combat, as well as the serious deficiencies in their arms and equipment.

In February 1940 the Allies, seeing that the Soviets were significantly reinforcing their forces, decided to send an expeditionary force of 50,000 men to support Finland.

Despite the serious losses incurred between 1 and 13 February, the heavily reinforced Soviet Northwest Front under the command of General Timoshenko, which was composed of the 7th Army (General Merestokov) and the 13th Army (General Grendal), broke through that part of the "Mannerheim Line" protecting the Carelia Isthmus to the north of Leningrad. Finland finally succumbed and capitulated on 12 March 1940. The Winter War had cost the Soviets some 200,000 men, almost 700 aircraft, and 1,600 tanks. The Finns had lost 25,000 men, and were forced to sign a treaty on 15 March ceding the city of Viborg and the Carelia Isthmus, as well as other territories.

The *Altmark* Crisis

What had been shown to be beyond doubt was that Scandinavia in general, and Norway in particular, was a focus of attention for both the Allies and Germany even before the invasion of Poland. Geographically, strategically, and economically it had undoubted value, and Germany depended to a great extent on this region for its supplies of minerals.

Norway remained neutral in 1940, although German ships used the port of Narvik, which was ice-free all year round, to transport Swedish iron-ore from Kiruna and Gällivare to the Ruhr. Germany imported about 11 million tons of Swedish iron-ore anually, which amounted to two thirds of its overall needs. Mineral supplies were also transported from the Swedish port of Luleå, in the Gulf of Bothnia, but this activity was paralysed by winter ice. Therefore, the vital importance of Narvik and Norway for the Germans was apparent.

Evacuation of German victims from the *Altmark*.

For this reason *Grossadmiral* Raeder had argued with his Staff (long before the actual invasion) for the occupation of Norway, at the same time looking to establish bases for his submarines and the High Seas Fleet in order to evade the British blockade. The British, together with the French, were perfectly aware of this situation, to the extent that they reinforced the blockade they had imposed on Germany since the beginning of war, even considering the pòssibility of disembarking troops in Norway themselves. Germany, for its part, began approaching the Norwegian pro-German politician, Vidkun Quisling, in an attempt to persuade him to take power following a *coup d'etat*. At the same time preparations were begun for invasion, although the first choice remained the "political option" with Quisling.

However, events were to take over. On 16 February 1940 a boarding party from the Royal Navy destroyer *HMS Cossack* freed 299 British merchant sailors who were being held prisoner aboard the German tanker *Altmark*, which was hiding in the Norwegian Jössing Fjord.

The *Altmark* had been an auxilliary ship to the pocket battleship *Graf Spee* during its foray into the South Atlantic until its sinking following the Battle of the River Plate. The *Altmark* was heading back to Germany via the Arctic route carrying officers and men of the British merchant navy, victims of the *Graf Spee*. After entering three nautical miles within Norwegian territorial waters it was spotted by British reconnaissance planes.

Chased by ships of the *Royal Navy*, it had sought refuge in Jössing Fjord guarded by two Norwegian Navy torpedo boats, where it was boarded by men from *HMS Cossack*, who freed the prisoners and caused six casualties amongst the German crew.

Although the Norwegian government protested the violation of neutrality, it did not do so energetically, which Germany interpreted as a sign of the good relations between the British and Norwegians. Moreover, the option involving Quisling was not producing the desired results.

Hitler was to respond to the British actions in two "directives" dated 26 February and 1 March. The preparation for the invasion of Norway, which by January was well under way, received the codename "Operation *Weserübung*" (across the Weser), a name that conjured up the idea of nothing more than a river crossing, rather than the occupation of a fair portion of Scandinavia. The date for starting operations was set at 20 March and contemplated the invasion of Denmark and Norway.

Preparations for Invasion

Denmark had a tiny army of no more than 14,000 men. The Royal Danish Navy consisted of 3,000 men and assorted submarines, torpedo boats, and two antequated sailing ships used in the coastal defense role: the *Niels* and the *Juel y Peder Skram*. The Danish Navy was also responsible for forts and other coastal defenses. As far as aircraft were concerned, the Danes possessed 89 combat planes (47 with the Army and 42 with the Navy), which were for the most part obsolete.

At 4:15 on 9 April 1940, two German motorised brigades belonging to the XXI Corps, commanded by *General* Kaupisch, crossed the frontier and quickly took control of the country. The effective collaboration of the *Fallschirmjäger* (paratroops) in the operation was significant, as we shall see later, as they were tasked with taking over airfields and the vital bridges linking the numerous Danish islands.

General Student[3] had made Hitler aware that he had been unhappy that his *Fallschirmjäger* had not been used in the Polish campaign of 1939. The *Führer* had responded by arguing that he had not wanted to prematurely reveal his new secret weapon. However, 1940 was to be the year chosen to show the first examples of what a well trained and highly motivated airborne force could achieve. Nevertheless, the initial idea had been to use them in the invasion of Holland and Belgium, not against Denmark and Norway. The decision to employ this "new weapon" was taken only two days before the start of "*Weserübung*," when it was decided that certain objectives were so important that it would be worth revealing the secret in order to obtain rapid success. Therefore, on the morning of 7 April Hitler and Jodl decided to deploy them.

So it was to be in April 1940 that the *Fallschirmjäger* were to take part in their first large-scale airborne operation. This would be based on the plans of the German High Command, the OKW (*Oberkommando der Wehrmacht*). Specifically, it would consist of a large-scale drop, rather than the commando-type operations favoured by the *Luftwaffe*. In short, an air assault supported by land and maritime forces. The airborne operations against Denmark and Norway were to be based on an assault force at the head of the German advance, used to capture airfields and bridges. The seizure of bridges was of vital importance, as it allowed the other units involved (above all armour) to advance rapidly into Denmark. On the other hand, the reasoning behind the occupation of airfields in southern Norway was to give the *Luftwaffe* the operational radius needed for future campaigns, which in turn would permit the deployment of reinforcements and supplies.

---

2 The following is a brief guide to rank equivalents: *Flieger/ Jäger* (Private); *Gefreiter* (Lance Corporal); *Obergefreiter* (Corporal); *Oberjäger/Obj./Unteroffizier* (sargeant); *Feldwebel/Fw.* (Warrant Officer), *Oberfeldwebel/OFw.* (Staff Sargeant); *Hauptfeldwebel* (Sargeant Major); *Leutnant/Ltn.* (2nd Lieutenant); *Oberleutnant* (Leiutenant); *Hauptmann* (Captain); Major (Major); *Oberstleutnant* (Lt Colonel); *Oberst* (colonel); *Generalmajor* (Brigadier General); *Generalleutnant* (Lieutenant General); *General der Flieger* (Air Force General); *Generaloberst* (General of the Army); *Generalfeldmarshall* (Field Marshal).

3 Golla, K.-H.: *Die deutsche Fallschirmtruppe 1936-1941*, Hamburg, Mittler & Sohn, 2006, p. 90.

The *Altmark* anchored in the Jössing fjord. (Museum Forsvarsmuseet)

2

The Invasion Begins

Paratroops in Denmark

The *Luftwaffe* was responsible for transporting the paratroops and ground troops of the Army (*Heer*) to Ålborg, in Denmark, and Oslo, Bergen, Stavanger, and Kristiansand, in Norway. It was also the *Luftwaffe's* mission to ensure that the landings from German ships were carried out unopposed. Finally, the Air Force was to support the ground forces in neutralising enemy resistance. Once the Danish and Norwegian airfields had been occupied anti-aircraft artillery batteries would be installed, and the *Luftwaffe* would then maintain the air space free from enemy threats. The remit would also extend to protecting Norwegian waters and the coast, defending against enemy action (submarines).

Fallschirmjäger about to make a training jump, taken before April 1940. The paratroops trained hard for operation *Weserübung*. Note the equipment: RZ 1 (*Rückenpackung Zwangauslosung 1) parachutes*, in service from 1936 to the end of 1939, although many paratroops jumped with this model during 1940, especially at Narvik (in the case of the *Gebirgsjäger*), and even in 1941 at Crete. It can be distinguished from the way the "static line" hangs vertically on the right of the parachute pack. The helmet, with double emblems, and the jump suit are the model M 38. (Óscar González)

Photograph of two *Fallschirmjäger*, probably taken between 1938 and 1939. The paratrooper on the left is wearing a jacket without the *Luftwaffe* eagle. The first *Fliegerblusen* were tailored that way, and with the branch of service color *(Waffenfarbe)* around the collar. Nevertheless, regulation n° 1,290, dated 14 October 1940, regulated for the use of the *Luftwaffe* emblem on the jacket. The *Fallschirmjäger* on the right is wearing the first type of boots (*Fallschirmschützen-Stiefel*), with the side lacing and the M 36 jump suit, with double vertical zip, the first to be worn by the paratroopers. It was manufactured by "*Karl Heisler*" of Berlin, and the legs were adjustable. Although substituted for the M 38, it continued in service during the invasion of Norway and Belgium. A container for arms and ammunition can be seen between the two soldiers (*Waffenbehälter*), along with its corresponding parachute (*Lastenfallschirm*). The lack of markings on the container is another indication that the photograph was taken before the war. (David J. Bunde)

Fighter and bomber squadrons were to be deployed at airfields in Jutland and Norway to oppose the Royal Air Force. There would also be transport aircraft available for the movement of infantry and paratroops.

The *Luftwaffe* was to be assigned, therefore, a role that until then had been considered theoretically, but never put into practice: direct cooperation with the *Heer* and the *Kriegsmarine*.

In command of the preparation and execution of the *Luftwaffe* contribution to the operation was the *General* commanding *X. Fliegerkorps*, *Generalleutnant Geisler*. The units to be deployed were as follows:

- *Kampfgeschwader* 4, 26, and 30.
- A Group from *Kampfgeschwader* 100.
- 3 *Flakabteilungen.*
- 1 *Fallschirmjäger battalion.*
- 7 air transport Groups, each with a land and maritime squadron.
- In order to organise the work on the ground *Luftgaustab zbV 300* was to deploy in Denmark and *Luftgaustab zbV 200* in Norway.
- 3 companies of the "*General Göring*" motorised regiment were given the task of carrying out the *Luftwaffe's* ground operations.
- Fuel for the aircraft, bombs, and the heavy anti-aircraft batteries were to be transported by the "Exportation squadron" (*Ausfuhrstaffel*) by sea to Narvik, Trondheim (sometimes referred to in German as Drontheim), and Stavanger, in Norway.

Orders were as follows:

"*The Lagerak crossing and the airfields at Ålborg are to be taken by the* Fallschirmjäger *and by air-transported troops pertaining to III./IR159. The 'X. Flieger Korps' will be in command of transport units and the paratroops (one company) (...). The landing of air-transported troops in Oslo-Fornebu, Stavanger, and Ålborg will first require the* Fallschirmjäger *to take control of these airfields.*"[3]

The transport units were given notice on 6 April, and also that day I./FJR1[4] was placed under the orders of "*X Flieger Korps*." The units charged with carrying the paratroops were activated on the 8th. That same day, at 0500 h, the paratroops were placed on standby and transported in the Ju 52s of II./KGr zbV 1, under the command of *Olt*. Drewes, from Stendal-Borstel to the different airfields assigned to each *Fallschirmjäger* unit:

- *Stab.* and 1./FJR1 (*Olt* Schmidt) together with 2./FJR1 (*Olt* Gröschke), to Schleswig.
- 3./FJR1 (*Olt* Von Brandis) to Uetersen.
- 4./FJR1 (*Hptm* Gericke), to Barth/Pommern.

Finally, zero hour for the attack on Denmark was set at 0515 h.

The first airborne attack in history commenced in the early hours of 9 April 1940. Its objective consisted of taking the unarmed fortress of Masnedø, as well as the important airfields around Ålborg, in northern Jutland, and the bridges at Storstrøm. The operation at Masnedø was not included in the original orders issued to "*Gruppe XXI*." In an article written after the war,[5] Gericke related how on 8 April, in Hamburg, he had been asked by members of the Army's High Command if he would be capable of taking intact and

Fallschirmjäger on the Danish coast. ("Falschirmjäger Hier und Da")

holding the bridges at Masnedø and Vordingborg. After answering yes, his 4th Company was taken out of I./FJR1 and received "*Special orders from above.*" It is also very likely that *Hauptmann* Walther[6] was also informed of the nature of these new orders issued to the 4th Company, which was to come directly under the orders of the higher "*Kommando XXXI*". Along with the new orders came an alteration in the place from which they were to deploy: Uetersen, instead of Barth. Gericke describes the events in detail:

"*I remeber it was a Sunday, around mid-day. I sat drinking coffee with my family on the balcony of my house in the barracks at Stendal, when a liason officer appeared and handed me a telegram* '*Hauptmann* Gericke to report immediately to Hamburg to receive an important communication. Transport aircraft will arrive today in Stendal for an urgent flight.' *I hurriedly packed my bags and boarded a 'Condor' for Hamburg.*

The meeting took place in the Hotel Esplanade, where I was staying. They wanted to know if my Company was capable of landing on the bridge joining Falster and Seeland (Sjælland), *securing it and holding the position until relieved by the infantry, which would be disembarked in Gedser. I assured them that as far as I was concerned there would be no problem. It would mean the first action for our young soldiers. On receiving the affirmetive, the relief of the Generals surrounding me was palpable. The securing of this 3.5 km long bridge was vital to the success of our operations in Denmark.*

I quickly returned to Stendal with some very brief information on the target: a postcard of the island of Masnedø, in which it was possible to see the bridge; a tourist brochure of the city of Vordingborg and a few maps. In Stendal the order for my company to 'separate' from the rest of the Battalion so as to carry out a direct order from 'above' had already arrived.

The parachutes were packed, the ammunition supplied, and the weapons placed in their containers. 12 Ju 52s [sic][7] *were waiting on the runway ready to take off. Everything took place quickly but at the same time secretly, like a commando action, under the cover of an 'alert exercise.' The atmosphere was not tense, but rather ordered and tranquil. Activity on the runway was unceasing: trucks were supplying the planes,* Fallschirmjäger *with their parachutes ready were awaiting orders, and engines were being checked. More aircraft arrived:* Stukas *and bombers. Finally the paratroops boarded the aircraft, and these began to move on the runway. The squadron captain reported that his unit was going to make a 'practice flight over the sea.'*

The airfield was buzzing with activity, and everyone was at his post. The support and air defense were essential. The atmosphere was noticably tense. The canteens were packed, and songs and marches could be heard everywhere. Only the platoon commanders, together with their company commander, remained waiting in the barracks; they knew the truth about the 'exercise.' *They also knew that once they received the codeword they could discuss the mission assigned to them. This did not take long in coming. That same afternoon orders were given to the troops. The Sargeant Major gathered the Company. The men listened attentively to their commander:* "The Führer has decided to attack Denmark and Norway in order to protect the Reich. We have received the order to occupy Denmark tomorrow at 0600 h."

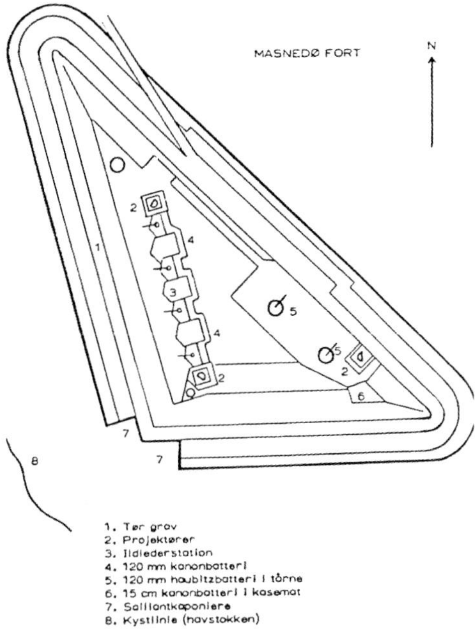

Plan of the Danish fort at Masnedø, taken by Gericke and his *Fallschirmjäger* of 4./FJR 1.

In the early hours of the morning at 0530 h (0430 h in Denmark), 9 Ju 52/3ms belonging to 8./KGr zbV 1 (the 8th company of the fighter squadron for special purposes 1) took off from Uetersen airfield, northeast of Hamburg, and headed towards Masnedø. The planes were carrying the 4th Company of the 1st Parachute Regiment (4./FJR1) minus one of its platoons; the group was formed of two platoons, one of which was machine-guns, in total about 108 paratroopers. At the front of the formation were the commander, *Hauptmann* Walter Gericke, and his platoon commanders *Leutnant* Alkmar von Hove and *Oberleutnant* Karl (Tyczka) Tannert, among others. The company commander was using a road map and a few postcards! Their orders were the following:

"*The 4th Company will jump on the island of Masnedø, take the bridge joining Falster with Seeland* (Sjælland) *intact, and hold it until the infantry arrive. The remaining platoon will take the airfields at Ålborg (East and West), which are of vital importance for later operations against Norway, and will also hold them until relieved by the infantry.*"

In less than an hour the fort at Masnedø and the bridges at Storstrøm (3,199 m long and built between 1933 and 1937) that joined the island of Falster with that of Masnedø, and the one at *Vordingborg*, which in turn connected Masnedø with Sjælland, were in German hands. This left the way open for the motorized units of the third battalion, 305th Infantry Regiment (III./IR 305), commanded by *Oberst* Buck, to advance without difficulty into the interior of Sjælland (Seeland).

We will leave it to Gericke to narrate the moments prior to the drop and the development of the action:

"Everything was ready to go in the early morning. The ground crews had prepared the aircraft. The engines had been repeatedly checked. The soldiers moved like shadows on the runway. Slowly, almost imperceptably, the night gave way to the dawn, which brought a sense of relief to the captain of the transport squadron. The sun would be up in an hour. The light at this time of day made it almost impossible to distinguish sky from sea in the mix of cloud and darkness... Then we received the order: 'pick up the parachutes and board the plane!' *We took off soon after, sheltered within the grey darkness of the morning. The Danish coast appeared like a shining strip. The anti-aircraft fire shone too. The sun appeared like a gigantic red ball above the horizon. Below us were large houses which appeared empty and asleep (...), the sea was spread around us, occasionally dotted with small boats. Suddenly, the large bridge appeared, joining Falster with Seeland. A huge construction, we were upon it in no time. The aircraft continued ascending and we saw land again, the island of Masnedø. We could also see the road, as well as the railway line which crossed the island; soon after a factory chimney appeared. Finally we got the signal: Jump!"*

Once over the target, at approximately 0635 h (twenty minutes later than planned) the drop was made from 150 meters. Important coastal batteries were located here (4 armoured cupulas) which required immediate neutralisation. Gericke, leading the first group of

Above and opposite: The island of Masnedø and the Storstrøm bridge, 3,199 m long and constructed between 1933 and 1937, connecting the islands of Falster and Masnedø. ("Fallschirmjäger Hier und Da")

paratroops, landed here, while the rest landed 100 meters from the fort. Gericke continues to detail events:

"In a matter of seconds the planes emptied and the paratroopers glided to earth. Hardly had we touched the ground than we collected our weapons. Our chutes remained on the ground like large white dots. I located myself on the railway platform to observe the fort through my binoculars. I could soon make out the four concrete cupulas above the highest walls. It appeared that the garrison were unaware of our presence because everything remained silent. More men began to jump from the Ju 52s, landing only 100 m from the fort. Once on the ground they attacked with their pistols and grenades, without waiting to collect their weapons from the containers, protected by a machine-gun we had set up on the platform. The sentries were completely surprised and offered no resistance. The rest of the guard were sleeping and were immediately overpowered. The Danish sailors came out with their hands up and their legs shaking, surprise and fear written on their faces. Before they realized what was hgappening the German flag was flying over the Danish fort. Its four guns, an anti-aircraft battery, and several grenades had fallen into our hands."

However, Gericke does not record how many frightened, surprised Danes surrendered. In fact, the fort was in the custody of no more than three men (and only two of them were soldiers): Henry Schmidt, the civilian responsible for the fort; plus the soldiers Adolf Kernwein and Olaf Jensen. To top it all they only possessed one rifle between them, an obsolete "*Remington M/1867*" without ammunition. The *Fallschirmjäger* had assaulted the fort with pistols and grenades (the weapons they had jumped with), covered by machine-guns mounted next to the railway platform.[8]

Following a brief interrogation, in which the Danes gave all kinds of information, the Germans came to the conclusion that the fort was not operational. It appeared that the Danish government had not wanted to "invest" in defense, to the point that the fort had been "dismantled" and its guns and radios taken and stored in Copenhagen.

Heinrich Heun, born 29 September 1916, took part in the capture of the Masnedø fort and later in the fighting at Narvik (he wears the Narvik Shield on his left arm). (Heun Archive)

Once the fort had been quickly occupied, the *Fallschirmjäger* made the pre-arranged signal (a green light) to indicate to the covering force of Me-110 fighter-bombers to abort their attack. Next, the paratroopers requisitioned several bicycles from nearby farms and occupied the Storstrøm bridge, meeting no resistance from the surprised Danish guards. In the words of Gericke:

"*The Danes were completely astonished to see all the paratroops on the ground, as well as those that continued to fall from the sky.*"

The paratroops also prepared to meet a possible counter-attack from the troops stationed in nearby Vordingborg. The garrison there consisted of the 5th Regiment, made up mainly of recruits, under the command of Colonel Harrel, who gave the order to "*repel any enemy attack*." After about 30 minutes they could expect to be supported by the 19th Battalion, which had orders to head to the southwest of Vordingborg along Highway Nº 2 and the train station. However, before entering in combat the order arrived from Copenhagen to avoid any confrontation with German troops.

The *Fallschirmjäger* arrived at the outskirts of Vordingborg, occupying the bridge and the railway station. *Hauptmann* Gericke remembers:

"*The sirens were wailing and alerting the population, but it was already too late because the streets had been taken by our paratroops and all the communications interrupted, so no trains could circulate. Any boats attempting to leave were prevented from doing so by shots across their bows. The Vordingborg garrison surrendered immediately and were confined to their barracks.*"

With the bridges securely in their hands, the Germans then waited 20 minutes for the "*Pionieren*" of III./IR 305 commanded by *Oberst* Buck, who arrived from the south and crossed the Storstrøm bridge (although an advance guard of pioneers arrived in the town almost at the same time as the paratroops). This force of pioneers had been transported in the ships *Mecklenburg* and *Schwerin* and disembartked at Gjedser, in the south of Falster, with the mission of linking up with and supporting the paratroops. When it became apparent that there would be no attack from the Danish troops in Vordingborg they contiued to occupy the town, ready to penetrate deep into Sjælland, the island on which Copenhagen is located. The *Fallschirmjäger*, by then reinforced by a platoon of machine-guns and anti-tank guns, remained on the bridge and the railway station until 0920 h, when they were finally relieved by a company of sappers. The *Fallschirmjäger* returned to Warnemünde in trucks, and on the 9th to Stendal aboard Ju 52s:

"*We were transported to the ferry in commandeered Danish automobiles. Once in Warnemünde we boarded aircraft that were waiting for us, and we arrived at our barracks that afternnon, where I could again sit on my balcony, and recount the rapid action of my paratroops.*"[9]

A legend arose around this first action by the *Fallschirmjäger*, which suggested that the jump had been made due to an error from German intelligence. Before the invasion German officers dressed as civilians, posing as tourists and businessmen, had visited Vordingborg and the surrounding area. Their mission had been to gather information on installations and troops.

While in one of the city's bars they heard the comment that the fort was guarded by the "white italians." Believing this to be the cover name of some special force, the paratroops were used to make the attack. Later, it became apparent that the only "white italians"

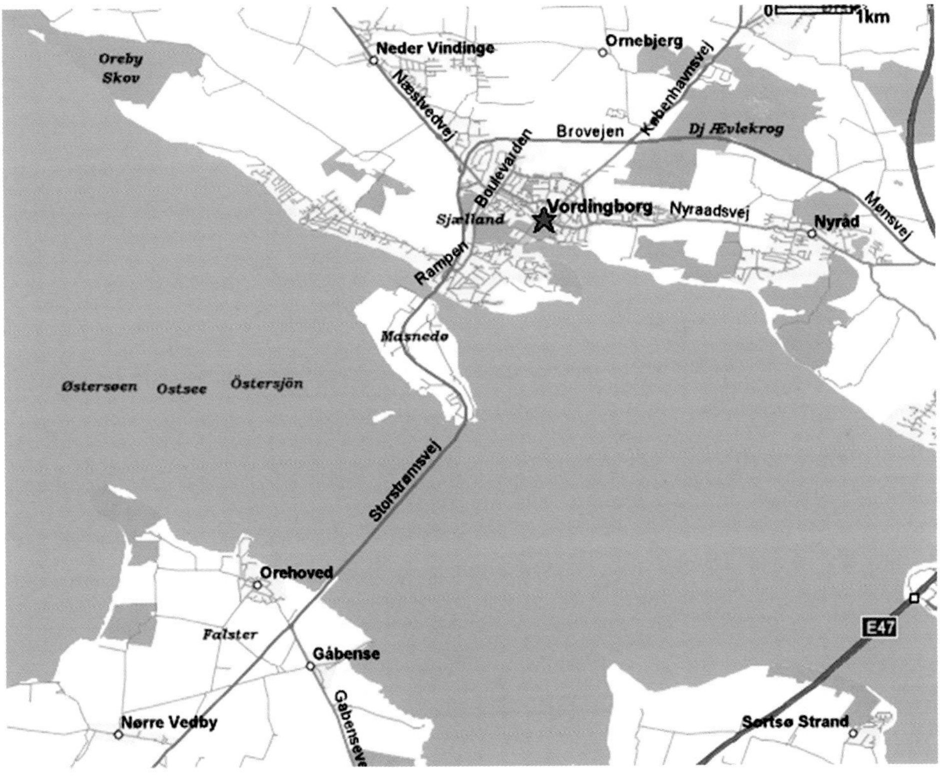

Modern map of the island of Masnedø and the Storstrøm bridge.

Storstrøm bridge today.

found at the fort were the chickens belonging to the civilian in charge of looking after fort Masnedø.

While German motorized units were making their way towards southern Jutland, the remaining *Fallschirmjäger* platoon of 4./FJR1 (the *III. Zug* commanded by *Oblt.* Eckleben, and composed of 36 men, the 3rd *Gruppen*, travelling aboard 3 Ju 52s of 8./KGr zbV 1) took part in another lightning raid. The men took off from Uetersen and seized the two airfields at Ålborg (East and West) in the north of the country at 0625 and 0700 h, as well as the bridge over the Lim fjord, without meeting any resistance. The Danes had ordered the aircraft stationed at the Vaerloese airfield, near Copenhagen, to move to Ålborg. This did not happen, as they were attacked on the ground by German planes from I./ZG 76 at 0545 h, which destroyed 11 of the aircraft and seriously damaged another 14 (the Danish air force had 48 aircraft).

This left the way open for 53 aircraft of *KGr zbV 1* to transport the next wave of the attack there: the third battalion of the 159th Infantry Regiment (III./IR 159[10]). These airfields were then converted into advanced bases which could be used in the attack on Norway (170,000 liters of fuel was transported to Ålborg together with the infantry). The third platoon of the 4th Parachute Company returned to Germany by train on the 9th.

At around 0600 h the Danish capital was in German hands. Other landings similar to the one at Copenhagen were also carried out successfully, resulting in the occupation of ports considered of high strategic value along the North Sea: Nyborg, Korsör, Gedser, Tyborin, and Middelfart. The Danish Armed Forces had only been able to offer weak resistance, which had left them with 13 dead and 24 wounded. The Germans had suffered 20 casualties. Following an ultimatum and the threat to bomb Copenhagen, Denmark capitulated on 10 April and was forced to accept the German occupation. However, the Danish government continued to carry out its functions with certain independence until 1943, which included competence in judicial and police matters, as well as controlling the Navy and Army. The King, Federick 9th, remained in the country.

The rapid occupation of Denmark ("*Weserübung-Süd*") was the step prior to the invasion Norway.

Plans for Norway

The invasion of Norway began (without any prior declaration of war) on 8/9 April 1940 with a combined air-sea operation. Seven divisions were disembarked, organized in six groups, in Narvik, Trondheim, Bergen, Kristiansand/Arendal, Egersund, and Oslo under the command of *General* Nikolaus von Falkenhorst.

Prior to this, on 1 March 1940 the German Army's 21st Corps was renamed Group XXI and was tasked with the invasion of Norway. This formation consisted of two mountain and five infantry divisions under the commander of "*XXI Korps*," General Nikolaus von Falkenhorst. The battle order for the invasion of Norway was as follows:

- **Corps Troops**

- 730th Heavy Artillery Battalion (mot) equipped with 100 mm pieces.
- 463rd Signals Battalion.
- 667th Engineers Regiment zbV (special purposes).

- **2nd Mountain Division**, *General der Gebirgstruppen* Valentin Feurstein.

- The Division fought in the center and north of Norway.
- Formed from the 136th and 137th Mountain Light Infantry regiment; the 111th Mountain Artillery Regiment, the 47th Mountain Anti-tank Battalion, the 67th Mountain Reconnaissance Battalion, the 82nd Mountain Engineers Battalion, and the 67th Mountain Signals Battalion.

- **3rd Mountain Division**, *Generalleutnant* Eduard Dietl.

- The majority of the Division arrived in Trondheim and Narvik on 9 April.
- 138th and 139th Mountain Light Infantry Regiments; 112th Mountain Artillery Regiment; 48th Mountain Anti-tank Battalion; 68th Mountain Reconnaissance Battalion; 83rd Mountain Engineers Battalion; and 68th Mountain Signals Battalion.

- **69th Infantry Division**, *Generalmajor der Artillerie* Hermann Karl Richard Eugen Tittel.

- Elements of the Division were transported to Bergen, Stavanger, and Oslo between the 9 and 15 April.
- Formed by the 159th, 193rd, and 236th Infantry Regiments; 169th Artillery Regiment; 169th Anti-tank Battalion; 169th Reconnaissance Battalion; 169th Engineers Battalion; and the 169th Signals Battalion.

- **163rd Infantry Division**, *Generalmajor der Artillerie* Erwin Engelbrecht.

- Elements of this Division arrived in Oslo, Kristiansand, Arendal, and Stavanger, on 9th April.
- 307th, 310th and 324th Infantry Regiments and the 234th Artillery Regiment. 234th Anti-tank Company; 234th Bicycle Squadron (Mobile Reconnaissance Unit); 234th Engineers Battalion; 234th Signals Battalion.

- **181st Infantry Division**, *Generalmajor* Kurt Woytasch.

- Around 15 April the Division was transported to Trondheim, mainly by air.
- 334th, 349th, and 359th Infantry Regiments and 222nd Artillery Regiment; 222nd Anti-tank Company; 222nd Bicycle Squadron (Mobile Reconnaissance Unit); 222nd Engineers Battalion; 222nd Signals Battalion.

- **196th Infantry Division**, *Generalleutnant* Richard Pellengahr.

- A large part of the Division was in Oslo on 15 April.
- The 340th, 345th, and 362nd Infantry Regiments; 233rd Artillery Regiment; 233rd Anti-tank Company; 233rd Bicycle Squadron (Mobile Reconnaissance Unit); 233rd Engineers Battalion; and 233rd Signals Battalion.

- **214th Infantry Division**, *Generalmajor* Max Horn.

- The 355th, 367th, and 388th Infantry Regiments; 214th Artillery Regiment; 214th Anti-tank Battalion; 214th Reconnaissance Battalion; 214th Engineers Battalion; and 214th Signals Battalion.
- Arrived in Kristiansand and Arendal on 17 and 18 April.

The *Fallschirmjäger* were given the task of occupying the airfields at Sola, in Stavanger, and Fornebu, in Oslo, which were key to the initial German deployment. The 10th Air Corps (*X Fliegerkorps*), under *Generalleutnant* Hans Ferdinand Geisler, was to provide air support with 290 bombers, 40 Stukas, 100 fighters, and 70 seaplanes. As well as this there were 500 Ju 52s to transport troops and supplies across the mountain ranges and fjords. The transport aircraft deployed were as follows:

"*Lufttransportgruppe Land*":

- KGr zbV 101–107, with Ju 52s and Ju 90s (the 107 with Ju 90s and Ju G38s), operating from Stade and Schlesswig, supported by four Fw 200 *Kondor* C-Os of KGr zbV 104 and the C-1s of *Stab* I./KG40, used to transport troops and materiel to Oslo. Another five Do 26s also participated.[11]
- The "Gebirgsjäger" and other infantry had been concentrating in Neumünster, Germany, since 2 April. From there, 10 aircraft of KGr zbV 102 took off and headed for Narvik on 13 April 1940. These planes had to land on a frozen lake; once on the ground the troops moved to secure the vital railway line which transported the iron-ore from Sweden. As far as casualties were concerned, two Ju 52s had to make an emergency landing no sooner had they taken off. The Ju G38s and four Ju 90s of KGr zbV 107 took their cargo of troops to Norway without any setbacks.

"*Lufttransportgruppe See*":

- KGr zbV I - III./108 (22 He 59s and several Ju 52 See from *F.d.L. West*)

"*Transportgeschwader*":

- KGr zbV 1 with 3 *Gr.* and 2 *Staffelen* Ju 52s for transporting the *Fallschirmjäger*.

The German government sent an official note to the government and King of Norway stating that their intention was to "*occupy the country peacefully*." This "peaceful" occupation turned out to be longer and more costly in casualties than had been first thought. Up to June 1940 almost 130,000 German troops were deployed in Norway. Facing them were 6 Norwegian divisions totalling 60,000 men. The Norwegians were supported by a further 35,000 British, French, and Polish troops (the last from exile), which landed on 14 April in Narvik, Namsos, and Åndalsnes.

The fighting in the far north of the country (Narvik) came to an end at the end of May. Before that, on 30 April, German troops from Oslo and Trondheim linked up in Dombås. The occupation of Denmark had undoubtedly given the Germans ideal airfields from which to support and resupply their troops in Norway. Finally, as a consequence of the start of the campaign in the Low Countries and France, Allied troops were withdrawn from Norway on 3 June.

This caused the pace of events to move rapidly. By order of King Håkon VII, in exile in London after fleeing Norway with his family and the country's gold reserves at the start of the invasion, the Norwegian armed forces capitulated on 10 June 1940. The occupation government, headed by *Reichskommissar* Josef Terboven, had been ready to take charge by the end of April.

German casualties in the campaign in Denmark and Norway reached 1,317 killed, 1,604 wounded, and 2,375 missing, the majority of whom had drowned at sea (the *Kriegsmarine* suffered most). The campaign was to cost the *Luftwaffe* 260 aircraft, including 86 transport planes, with 1,130 casualties among the crews, of which 341 were killed in action and 448 reported missing. The *Luftwaffe* destroyed 93 of the 169 aircraft lost by the British (43 planes were lost when the aircraft carrier *HMS Glorious* was sunk): 43 were lost in air combat, 24 due to anti-aircraft fire, and the rest on the ground.

The German battleship "*Blücher*"[12] was sunk by the Norwegians in Dröbak fjord, near Oslo, on 9 April, and the same fate befell two light cruisers, ten destroyers, a torpedo boat, and four U-boats during the weeks that followed. The destruction of these vessels and the damage sustained to others meant that the *Kriegsmarine* lost about a third of its strength in the campaign. The *Luftwaffe* lost 242 aircraft.

Allied losses were as follows: 1,896 British and 1,335 Norwegians, plus 530 French and Polish. Great Britain also lost two light cruisers, nine destroyers, and six submarines (2,500 dead in total).

The *Fallschirmjäger* were involved in operations in Norway from the very beginning to the final day of the campaign. The actions in which they participated were varied, ranging from the taking of airfields to lightning raids to penetrate enemy defenses, as well as supporting the ground troops. This variety of missions (worthy in itself of study) is what will be analyzed in this book, dealing with each case in an identical manner, with each event not only narrated in detail, but also critically examined.

This is one of many illustrations published after the invasion of Norway. It is done by illustrator Adolf Bock (Born in Berlin in 1890 and died in Sweden in 1968). It was printed by the publisher Erich Klinghammer, Berlin.

4 The German designations for Division, Regiment, Battalion, and Company are used. For example, 3rd Mountain Division (3.GJD), 1st Parachute Regiment (FJR1), 1st Battalion (I./), and 1st Company (1./).
5 Gericke, W.: *Stoßtrupp übers Meer,* DDF, Abril 1953, pp. 5 and 6. Also Gericke, W. (1941), p. 51. A ll his testimony in the text are from these two sources.
6 Without doubt one of the most charismatic *Fallschirmjäger*. Erich Walther was born on 5 August 1903. He led I./FJR1 in April 1940 during the invasion of Denmark and Norway, and in the invasion of Holland in May that same year. For the latter action he was decorated with the Knight's Cross on 24 May. He returned to Norway to lead the *Fallschirmjäger* around Narvik. He was promoted to *Major* on 19 June 1940. The following year, in Crete, still leading I./FJR1, he was later being transferred to the Russian front. From 1942 he commanded FJR 4, which fought the Allies in Sicily, southern Italy, and Cassino during the following years. He was awarded "Oak Leaves" to his Knight's Cross on 2 March 1944 and commanded *Divisionsgruppe Walther* in Arnhem in September that year. In the winter of 1944 he received command of *FschPzGrenDiv 2 "Hermann Göring"* fighting in Prusssia. At the beginning of 1945, on 1 February, he received the "Diamonds" to his Knight's Cross. After a period convalescing from wounds he returned to take charge of what was left of his Division. At the end of the war he was taken prisoner by the Russians, dying in Buchenwald on 26 December 1947.
7 Although Gericke mentioned 12 transport planes, only 9 were used to drop paratroops at Masnedø and 3 at Ålborg. All were from the same unit.
8 Even the "German surprise factor" was not so. It appears that they did not pass unseen as at 6:00 h, Fort Masnedø informed the Navy and the garrison of Vordingborg that "*German paratroops had landed on the dock near the railway line, next to the bridge and fort.*"
9 Gericke, W. (1953), p. 6.
10 According to Hubatsch (1952), p. 94.
11 Vázquez, J.: *"Weserübung Nord": assault on the fjords*. In "Revista de Historia Militar," nº 2, March-April 2000, p. 95.
12 During the invasion of Norway the *Kriegsmarine* experienced one of its darkest chapters. Among all the losses, the hardest was the loss of the heavy cruiser *Blücher*.
The *Blücher* was a cruiser of the *Admiral Hipper* class. It displaced 18,000 tons, and its main armament consisted of 4 double turrets with 203 mm guns. Launched in 1937, it was one of the most modern and powerful of the *Kriegsmarine's* ships. It was the flagship of *Gruppe 5*, assigned to the capture of Oslo, and apart from the crew it carried 800 passengers, including troops and civil servants to administer Norway once it had been conquered.
On the morning of 9 April 1940, while passing the town of Drovak en route to Oslo, two old *Krupp* 280 mm coastal batteries at the Oscarsborg fort (*Aarón and Moisés*, installed in 1893) opened fire on the *Blücher*, with one of the first shots hitting the ship's steering, leaving it practically unable to return fire. A second impact hit the hangar, setting fire to the fuel of the plane it was carrying and starting a fire that spread out of control.
The *Blücher* began to manoeuvre desperately to avoid the fire from the coastal defense batteries, which left it exposed to a new threat. The torpedo boat *Whitehead*, built in 1901, fired two torpedos at the cruiser that exploded in the engine room, leaving the ship adrift. At this moment the rest of the German fleet thought the *Blücher* had hit a mine, causing them to flee the area rapidly, leaving the cruiser to its fate. With the fires continuing to spread, the captain ordered the ship's torpedos to be fired towards the coast to avoid further explosions, and at 07:23 h, one hour after receiving the first impact, the *Blücher* sank. Of the 2,200 people on board 600 lost their lives. The survivors swam to the coast.
Had the German's been negligent? Had there been a terrible error in intelligence? The *Stukas* could have neutralized the antiquated coastal defense batteries; moreso, the *Blücher* itself could have knocked them out (the coastal defense batteries opened fire when the ship was at a range of 1,600 m). The *Blücher* could have easily dealt with them from 10,000 m.

3

The Stavanger-Sola Aerodrome

German airborne operations in Norway[13] were to be undertaken by the 1st Battalion of the 1st Parachute Regiment (I./FJR1[14]). This Regiment was commanded by 47-year-old *Oberst* Bruno Bräuer, one of the fathers of the "idea and strategy" of German parachute troops. In fact, he was the first to obtain the *Fallschirmjäger* qualification in 1936. Various units of the *Luftwaffe's* anti-aircraft artillery were deployed together with the paratroops: I./Flak-Regiment 32, II/Flak-Regiment 33, and I./Flak-Regiment 611.

The 3rd Company of the 1st Parachute Regiment (3./FJR1) was tasked with securing Sola airport, together with the city of Stavanger. This was the newest airport in Norway. Built in 1937, it was the only airport in the southwest of the country with concrete runways.

View of Sola airfield, next to the city of Stavanger. In April 1940 it was the newest and most up to date in Norway. Built in 1937, it was the only one in the southwest of the country with a concrete runway. (Erik Ettrup)

This was a high value objective in operation "*Weserübung*," as it could be used to attack Scotland, Scapa Flow, and southern Norway.

In command of this unit was the young Count *Oberleutnant* Henning Freiherr von Brandis, who was to die the following month on 10 May in the fighting for the bridges at Dordrecht, Holland.

The 3rd Company (135 *Fallschirmjäger*), aboard 12 Ju 52s belonging to 7./KGr zbV 1 commanded by *Hauptmann* Günter Capito, took off from the the airfield at Stade at 0530 h. Minutes later, another 53 Ju 52s of KGr zbV 104 took to the air carrying 4 companies of IR 193 and *Luftwaffe* ground personnel. The distance to Sola was some 590-600 km and an estimated three hours, twelve minutes flying time. The flight path avoided Denmark, given that it was also to be attacked once the flight had continued on.

Incidents began occurring as soon as they had taken off. The Ju 52 transporting the Company's 8th Group was unable to take off, and another aircraft caught fire during its take off, although everyone on board was able to evacuate the Junkers without injury. They later boarded a reserve plane and rejoined the formation.

Sola airfield is in German hands, and the Norwegian positions have been taken by the *Fallschirmjäger*. ("Fallschirmjäger Hier und Da")

At the same time a flight of 12 Junkers 88s belonging to 8 and 9/KG 4 took off from Lünebeck airfield. Their mission was to reach Sola at the same time as the paratroopers. Eight Messerschmitt Bf 110s (Me 110s) belonging to 3/ZG 76[15] (commanded by 27 year old *Oberleutnant* Gordon M. Gollob) left Sylt a little later. These aircraft were also tasked with providing air support. For these planes the journey was only to be "outgoing," as their fuel tanks did not give them sufficient range to return, so they were totally in the hands of the paratroopers.

On the flight to Sola, the 11 planes carrying the *Fallschirmjäger* ran into thick fog banks at Skagerrak. Although the crews had been trained in "flying by instruments," they had never done so in formation or over the sea. The most sensible course of action would have been to return, but they were well aware that if they didn't capture the airfield, the following waves would be in dire straits. Therefore, they decided to continue, and fortunately visibility returned some 100 km from the Norwegian coast. Once in flight the formation was deployed over a wide area, flying in a circle while waiting for those aircraft that had been delayed to catch up. However, only 9 aircraft reached the target: the 3rd Group had to land in Denmark, and the plane carrying the 9th Group was forced to return to Stade due to the fog. 108 *Fallschirmjäger* were available at the target.

The eight Me 110s had more serious problems. Two of the planes collided, and *Oberleutnant* Gollob decided to abort the mission. When they landed in Denmark only four aircraft remained. The other two had not received the radio message aborting the mission and continued to Sola.

Given the reports of bad weather, *General* Hans Geisler decided that all aircraft should return to their bases. The paratroopers heading for Oslo (less 3 planes) and Trondheim turned back, but the message was not received by the forces heading for Sola.

The planes carrying the *Fallschirmjäger* were running out of fuel. They were 45 minutes behind schedule and were not sure of their position. Suddenly, the two Me 110s that had not returned to base joined them and they continued to Sola. As they had rehearsed the mission using scale models back in Germany, *Hauptmann* Capito, the leader of the formation, knew exactly where to go.

Meanwhile, the 8 Junkers 88s had begun their attack at the airfield. Many of the Norwegian aircraft (4 Fokker CV-E biplanes, 2 Fokker CV-Ds, 2 De Havilland "Tiger Moths," and 4 Caproni Ca.310s[16]) were destroyed on the ground or abandoned by their crews. Very few escaped destruction. For example, of the Caproni Ca. 310 light bombers, one exploded on the ground, while the remaining three managed to flee. Next, the German planes reseived orders to aid a German merchantman under attack from a Norwegian destroyer. The two lone Me 110s strafed the runway, flying only 10 meters off the ground. The Norwegian troops were unable to respond.

Finally, it was time for the assault by the *Fallschirmjäger*. The Ju 52 approached Sola from the East. Around 110 men, led by Von Brandis, jumped from low altitude (70m) at approximately 10 AM. First *Kompanietrupp*, *I. Zug*, *II. Zug*, and *III.* (*schwerer*) *Zug* all reached the ground in seconds. At first the Norwegians thought they were being bombed and abandoned their positions near the runway. The paratroops regrouped and opened fire. The Norwegian commander gave the order to withdraw, with some of the troops escaping in the commander's own car. Norwegian resistance only continued on the eastern end of the runway; however, this was soon overcome by *Fallschirmjäger* of *I.* and *II. Zug* (sections).

A group of *Fallschirmjäger* from 3./FJR1 after being decorated with the EKII for the taking of Sola. They are seen here posing in their barracks at Stendal on 18 April 1940. All of them belong to *Gruppe Schmidt*, commanded by the then *Oberjäger* Leonhard Schmidt, kneeling on the right. Next to him is *Gefreiter* Bart. Standing from left to right are Beckmann (killed in Russia), Taschner, unknown, and *Gefreiters* Brock and Bardele. Leonhard Schmidt was born on 9 December 1916. He was awarded the Knight's Cross on 30 April 1945, by then a *Hauptmann* and commander of II./FJR1 in Italy. He took part in the fighting in Poland, Stavanger, Holland, Narvik, Crete, Russia, and Italy. He died on 9 August 2006. (Schmidt Family Archive)

In the South, *III. Zug* (which consisted of no more than a *Zugtrupp* and the 7th Group) was engaged.

The machine-gun fire coming from an anti-aircraft battery[17] and two bunkers (the only two concrete defensive positions at the airfield) became a serious threat to the paratroopers. It would appear that the majority of the German casualties were caused by a single soldier firing a machine-gun who belonged to an elite Ranger regiment stationed in Oslo.

The 7th Group soon dealt with the bunker located at the south of the airfield, taking 8 prisoners in the process. The Group was covered by machine-guns deployed by the leader of the 3rd Section, *Leutnant* Schmelz, who had been injured during the drop. With the covering fire provided by these guns, the 7th Group were able to take the house near the bunker, where they found a Norwegian officer and twenty-four men, whom they took prisoner.

The 1st Section had dropped onto the runway and was pinned down by the intense fire coming from the Norwegian defenders in the airfield's main buildings. To make matters worse, a *Fallschirmjäger* was killed by fire from the Me 110s, the pilots being convinced in the confusion that they were attacking Norwegian troops. This mistake also resulted in a further five men being wounded. In the end the Section was able to take three anti-aircraft positions (although without machine-guns). The airfield's second in command was captured in the attack and the buildings adjacent to the runway were occupied.

Obergefreiter Ludwig Benedikt was one of those killed during the taking of Sola. He was shot through the heart during the assault, killed before he hit the ground. From Ohlstadt, he was born on 5 June 1915 and was the youngest of 9 siblings. He moved to Grainau, near Garmisch-Panterkirchen, to work with his older brother. Before Norway, he took part in the annexation of the Sudetenland in October 1938 (on his chest are the ribbon and shield for the occupation of Prague) and the Polish campaign. Although not married, he was in a reletionship with a girl from Dresden, with whom he had a son. (Óscar González)

The 5th Group of the second Section immediately deployed against the machine-gun bunker on the eastern side of the airfield. Two men were killed and three wounded in the ensuing firefight. The rest of the Group, together with elements from the 4th under the command of the leader of the 5th, assaulted the position with grenades (given the seriousness of the situation they had little choice; they had not even had time to recover the weapons from the containers).

The group that had been formed from the Company HQ was able to secure the runway and clear away the barbed wire and parachutes. Once this had been done flags were laid out to mark the runway—all of this being done under fire. At the same time, the 5th Group—reinforced by men from other Groups—occupied a house located some 500 meters from the runway, from which they had received fire. Meanwhile, the 6th Group occupied a nearby hotel from where the Norwegian defenders had retreated, leaving their machine-guns behind.

What follows is a personal account by a paratrooper who was present during the action. It comes from fragments of an article written by *Obergefreiter* Theo Krupp titled "*Reichskriegsflagge über Stavanger–Sola*" (Battle Flags of the Reich over Stavanger-Sola). The article appeared in 1941 in the book—which was clearly propagandandistic—*Fallschirmjäger hier und da*[18] by Walter Gericke. In spite of the context and intention of the work, it provides an excellent description of events during the heat of the batle:

"The afternoon has arrived and our commander is still not with us. We are all anxious for news. Finally, the Company commander's [Oberleutnant von Brandis] *car draws near, but our hopes are dashed when we see him disappear into his office. For a time he remains poring over a large map, and we suppose that this means he will soon tell us where we are heading. His voice sounds assured, which is a good sign. We are all gathered with him. 'Men, let us sing one more time'—the hymn of the* Fallschirmjäger *breaks the silence. Then, we are all silent once more and listen attently as he communicates to us concisely and with pride what is our objective: 'The Company has been given the mission of taking the airfield at Stavanger-Sola.' An operation desired by all well-trained* Fallschirmjäger.

Following this announcement instructions are given to the individual sections. Our Section was given the mission to take, immediately following the assault, the anti-aircraft positions next to the airfield buildings. We all listened attentively in silence. The Major's voice rose again: 'We will fight to the last man in order to complete our mission.' The operation could begin. We were all enthusiastic, discussing the best way to take our objective. One considered it best to take the target from the rear, another stated philosophically that in the end anything could happen rather than that which was planned. And if he proved to be right?

The rest of the day was left to preparing the mission; we even worked through the night. Finally our Major said: 'This operation is going to be our calling card!'

At 04:00 h our hymn broke the silence of the dawn. Following a stormy Spring night the aircraft fired up their engines. We were all overcome by a powerful feeling. We all sat next

A contemporary aerial view of Sola airport. (Ettrup/Ritterbach/Schellenberger Archive)

to each other silently contemplating the mission ahead. I must make a humorous comment on one of my fellow paratroopers. During all the jumps we had made during peacetime he had had to assume a rather strange posture in order to 'hold onto' his stomach. However, on the day he was heading for the enemy target he had forgotten all about this....

We were flying over enemy territory and had been sitting for three hours. The weather was cold and unsettled. The fog refused to clear, and we felt as though we were inside a giant washing machine. The Lieutenant flying our plane did so with decision, like a guard dog seperated from the pack. We descended and came out of the fog. In the distance we could see land. The coast of Norway! The mountain peaks were capped with snow, the lakes all frozen over. The landscape was one of winter. We flew over small houses and gardens, and could clearly see people, some of whom gestured towards us while others threw themselves on the ground. I asked myself if we could expect to be received so pacifically.

At 10:00 h the siren sounded in the cabin. With relief we all stood up and hooked on the static lines of our parachutes. Below us was the Stavanger-Sola airfield, and we were received in a hail of bullets. The first Fallschirmjäger *were already on the ground, taking cover. The bullets were coming from all sides, and we could hear them whistling past our ears. The first paratroops to land began moving forward in short rushes. Next to me was Seppel. 'Chin up!' –I told him– 'we must move forward.' Hardly had I said this than we found ourselves once more with our noses in the sand. The fire was becoming more intense. Again we got up to advance, and I saw Sep fall to the ground. He had been hit. Where was the enemy fire coming from? It seemed to be from a small structure on the edge of the airfield. It was sure to be a camouflaged bunker. I reached Sep but he was already dead. His head lay on the runway with blood coming from his mouth. I had to keep advancing. After a few minutes my Section had regrouped. To our left was the anti-aircraft position. But first we had to clear the bunker.*

Our Section commander gave his final orders: we were to use grenades and explosives. Meanwhile the machine-gun located in the bunker tried desperately to halt our attack. We crawled over the cupula and inched our way towards one of the slits. We found ourselves in a blind spot, and felt sure we were safe from the enemy fire. Next we readied the grenades and explosive charges. We tied three grenades together and threw them and the gun fell silent. We then placed the explosive charges on the door and lit the fuse. Now protected, we waited for what seemed like minutes. After a few seconds there was an enormous explosion, and bits of iron flew into the air. The door had been blown off and we could enter. We threw in grenades and followed firing our pistols. The shock wave from the explosion had flung the occupants against the walls of the bunker and they lay mortally wounded, so we took them outside. The bunkers were finally neutralized. There were more explosions. We then moved on the anti-aircraft position. Our real mission was now underway.

The crew of the anti-aircraft gun tried in vain to turn it on us. Again we readied our grenades. In a few moments the Norwegian position was destroyed. Our Section leader, now assured we were back on plan, indicated that we throw our grenades. We jumped to the position ready to lob our grenades when we noticed the Norwegians were running. At first we were perplexed, not knowing what was happening. However, it seems that as they could not bring their gun to bear on us the crew had fled in terror. The position fell into our hands without a fight. In a few minutes we had everything under control, and we transformed ourselves into 'parachute artillery' using the Norwegian gun.

Little by little the shooting died down. The liaison had occupied the military buildings, and the flag of the Reich now flew over Stavanger. We regrouped, ready to receive new orders. We were to form assault groups in order to secure the nearby town. Positions in the hills next to the airfield were occupied. I myself carried my machine-gun onto the roof of a building to cover my comrades' assault. However, no serious resistance was encountered. A few isolated shots were heard, but not for long. The Norwegian troops were taken to the airfield, where they were informed of all relating to their retention. The airport buildings were inspected. Upon seeing the dining room it became clear with what surprise the attack had been received. The troops had been at breakfast and the food was still on the tables.

Our fallen comrades were laid out, wrapped in parachutes in the main airfield building, where we bid our last farewells. There were wounded Norwegians everywhere, and they were treated by our medic. Stavanger was in German hands after 35 minutes while fresh troops continued to land at the airfield. The operation was perfectly coordinated, everything going like clockwork. At mid-day we heard the German news: 'Norway has been occupied by German troops.' Nobody was aware it was us, the Fallschirmjäger, *who had been the first to engage the enemy.*

The radio operators were working furiously when a message from the British was received: 'The airfield must be returned to the Norwegians during the night, if not there would be a counterattack!' Of course, this did not worry us at all.

The night was cold and damp. It is 00:00 h, and there is no sign of the Norwegian counterattack. The sentries are especially alert, concentrating on any sounds they hear. The hours pass and we do not understand why the British do not come."

After half an hour of fighting, Sola was secured for the following waves of reinforcements from the 1st and 2nd Battalions of the 193rd Infantry Regiment (IR 193), commanded by *Oberst* v. Beeren. In fact, the first aircraft carrying men of the 1st Battalion landed 50 minutes after the start of the paratroops' assault (one of those aboard died as the

Image of a hangar constructed before 1940 and conserved at Sola airport. (Ettrup/Ritterbach/Schellenberger Archive)

result of another German mistake when a fighter opened fire on the plane). The runway had not been badly damaged, so reinforcements could be brought in unhindered. The Junkers 52s of KGr zbV 104, 106, and 107 were able to land without problems in the second wave (53 more Ju 52s had left Utersum at 08:00 h, transporting more men of IR 193, as well as arms, munitions, fuel, and other supplies), although the first planes to arrive received fire from isolated Norwegian positions.

The Ju 88 returned to Sola after sinking the Norwegian destroyer and silencing the few remaining weak points of resistance. The Norwegian commander in Sola surrendered the airfield when it became obvious he could not stop the waves of planes with rifles and machine guns.

German fire stopped when they saw the Norwegians fly the white flag. *Oberleutnant* Baron von Brandis went forward and saluted the Norwegian commander, who in turn handed over his pistol as a sign of surrender, although Brandis immediately returned it to him. 90 Norwegian soldiers were taken prisoner, and were ordered to clear the runway of obstacles to make ready for the incoming waves of troops. Finally, at around 13:00 h the Ju 52 carrying von Brandis's 9th Group, which had had problems during take off at Stade, landed.

The city of Stavanger was occupied without a fight. During the first day 2,000 German soldiers were brought to Sola, which included the *Stab*, I. and II./IR 193, part of *Luftgau-Stabs* zbV 200 and *Luftwaffe* ground personnel, as well as 180 bombers, transport planes, and fighters. The 3./FJR1 withdrew to Stade on 10 April sometime after 13:00 h, following the handover of the airfield to 1./IR 193, which also occupied the port and city. The dead and wounded had already been returned to Germany the day before. Once in Stade (they landed at 16:50 h) the unit returned to their base at Stendal-Borstel by train, arriving on 11 April.

German losses at Sola were 3 dead (among them *Obergefreiter* Ludwig Benedikt) and 8 wounded. The Norwegians lost 57 men and four officers wounded.[19]

13 Vázquez, J.: *"Weserübung Nord": asalto a los fiordos*, in "Revista de Historia Militar", nº 2, March-April 2000; nº 3, May-June 2000; nº 4, July-August 2000.

14 In operation *Weserübung* the companies of I./FJR1 were formed of 144 men each (*Kompanie Tupp* –HQ-, 12 men, three *Züge* –platoons-, each of 36 men, and a fourth platoon of 24 men. This was known as "heavy weapons" (machine-guns). It was transported by a *Staffel* (12 planes). *Kampfgruppe zbV* had 53 Ju 52s, so it could transport a battalion in the following way: *Stab* –HQ- (2 planes), Signals platoon (3 plane), and 4 companies (48 planes). At Narvik the composition was different, with variable formations formed "ad hoc."

15 The I *Gruppe* of *Zerstörergeschwader 76* (I./ZG 76), under *Hauptmann* Günther Reinecke, deployed two *Staffel* in the taking of the airfields at Oslo and Stavanger: the 1./ZG 76 at Fornebu and the 3./ZG 76 at Sola.

16 According to Vázquez (2000), nº 3, p.138. Less documented are the details from Dildy (2007), p. 23, stating that 4 *Ca.310s* and 8 *Fokker CV-Es* had been transferred from Kjeller to Sola

17 The Norwegians used two types of machine-gun: the 7.92 mm *Colt M/29* and the more obsolete *Hotchkiss M/1898*. The *Madsen* (*Rekytgevaer M 1903*) was the infantry LMG.

18 Gericke, W.: *Fallschirmjäger hier und da*, Berlin, Schützen Verlag, 1941, pp. 55-61

19 Data corroborated by Renisch and Golla. Although another version exists, that of *Leutnant* Hohenberger [in Gericke (1941)], stating 18 paratroops of 3./FJR1 were killed in action and around 30 wounded.

Regarding materiel losses, 2 Me 110s collided in midair; 2 Ju 52s from KG zbV 106 were lost over the Skagerrak; 1 He 59 crashed on landing; and 1 Ju 87 also crashed on landing, as did an He 111.

4

Fornebu-Oslo Airport

Fornebu[20] is located some 6 km from Oslo, the Norwegian capital. In April 1940, work on the construction of this airport was still incomplete. However, in spite of this, it was operational and well defended.

In the Spring of 1940 Fornebu was the base of the *Jagevingen*, the Norwegian Air Force's fighter unit. This consisted of a squadron of 10 *Gloucester Gladiators*, of which only 7 were operational on 9 April. On 8 April, the day German ships were to begin heading to Norway, there were only nine aircraft available (four Mk. I and six Mk. II). Of these only 5, at best, were operational. At midnight, following the urgent orders dictated by Captain Erling Munthe Dahl, 7 aircraft were made operational.[21] The other three, as well as 2 *Tiger Moths*, were lying camouflaged on the edge of the runway.

Defense of the runway was charged to the *Jagevingen's* ground troops. Three anti-aircraft machine-guns were located in pits on the eastern edge of the runway, while two more located to the north provided protection for Fornebu. Furthermore, a little way from the road was a searchlight section from the Oslo Air Defense Corps.

The Airborne Assault Plan

340 *Fallschirmjäger* belonging to I./FJR1 (1st and 2nd Companies, commanded by *Oberleutnant* Herbert Schmidt and *Hauptmann* Gröschke, respectively, as well as the Battalion HQ *Stab*), together with the commander of the same, *Hauptmann* Erich Walther, were to be dropped on Fornebu, transported from Schleswig by 29 Ju 52s belonging to the 5. and 6. *Staffel* of *Kampfgeschwader zbV 1*. This Group was an ordinary *Luftwaffe* transport unit that had been trained together with the paratroopers. This was the unit specifically assigned to transport the paratroops during operation *Weserübung*. The unit's commander was 44-year-old *Oberstleutnant* Karl Drewes. Among the 29 transport aircraft there was a Ju 52 specifically assigned to intelligence and communications tasks. These aircraft carried the paratroops from Stendal to Schleswig on 8 April. *Oberleutnant* Wilhelm Metscher was Drewes' adjutant, and describes the events leading up to the action as follows:

> "*On Monday 8 April our Ju 52 had been lying ready on the runway at Stendal since the early hours of that morning. I was Drewes' adjutant, and was the pilot of his aircraft, which would lead the formation. The* Fallschirmjäger *arrived with their parachutes and weapons containers at 07:30 h and began loading the planes. We took off at mid-day heading northwest, landing at our destination as planned. That night we received orders and repoirts regarding the action.*"

Page 44: Left, *Oberstleutnant* Karl Drewes, who gave the order for the Ju 52s transporting the *Fallschirmjäger* to turn back due to the bad weather conditions. Next to him is his adjutant, *Oberleutnant* Wilhelm Metscher. Metscher piloted the aircraft carrying Drewes and *Hauptmann* Erich Walter, who commanded the paratroops. The photograph was taken on the 15 April, after the crews that had carried the *Fallschirmjäger* to Dombås were decorated with the EKII. Drewes had also wanted to abort that mission, but Hitler had insisted the jump go ahead whatever the cost. Metscher was born on 1 September 1915. As a pilot, he had already participated in the occupation of Austria, the Sudetenland, and Poland, and always the role of transporting *Fallschirmjäger*. (Wilhelm Metscher)

Page 45 and above: Some views of Fornebu airfield. Some of the installations were undergoing work at the time of the attack, as is the case of the building next to the restaurant. These photographs were taken by the 1st Company just before leaving for Dombås on 14 April, 5 days after the start of the invasion. (Óscar González)

One of the paratroopers preparing for the mission was *Jäger* Friedrich Heinrich Ungeheuer. He also remebers how the operation began:

"*At that time I was still in training and had only completed four jumps. My fifth would be over Norway. Our Company commander,* Oberleutnant *Schmidt, briefed us on the coming operation. Everybody was occupied with the preparations. Many were thinking of their families. For my part I did not feel afraid, but I was worried about the conditions in which the drop was to be made. I had made my last training jump from 100 m, and we were expecting to jump from 80 at Fornebu.*"

At the same time, a flight of 8 Me 110s[22] (4 had been originally detailed) of 1./ZG 76, under the command of 29-year-old *Oberleutnant* Werner Hansen, were to fly in a supporting role at Fornebu (although the paratroops flew without escort to the drop zone). The plan was as follows:

"*The commander of I./FJR1 is to be in charge of the drop and capture of the aerodrome. The mission is to be carried out as specifically as possible. Soldiers are to be courteous and treat the Norwegians with respect. All Norwegian resistance is to be broken usng 'appropriate methods.' The Norwegians guarding the airfield are to be replaced and their arms and ammunition confiscated. If Fornebu is occupied either by our ground troops or*

Friedrich Heinrich Ungeheuer had only jumped on four occasions prior to 9 April 1940. This photograph, taken in 1944, shows him at the rank of *Feldwebel*. He is wearing several decorations, including the Narvik Shield on his left arm, the Crete ribbon on his left cuff, the Knight's Cross First Class (EKI) on his breast and the *Luftwaffe* Ground Combat badge. Ungeheuer joined the *Luftwaffe* in 1939. He was trained as a paratrooper at Wittstock in 1940. Ungeheuer jumped at Dombås on 14 April (in fact he was the last *Fallschirmjäger* firing—together with Gerhard Broder—before the surrender). He later jumped at Narvik and fought on Crete, Leningrad, Smolensk, and Monte Cassino. Wounded in 1945 and was taken prisoner, first by the Americans, and later the British. (Ungeheuer Archive)

naval forces, and our aircraft are able to land unmolested, then the Fallschirmjäger *will withdraw until further orders. Once the paratroops have completed their mission they will receive new orders. It is possible that they will be ordered to march to Kjeller in order to occupy the airfield there. If by 10 April they have not received new orders for a new mission, the* Fallschirmjäger *will return to Germany.*"[23]

The operation was due to commence at 05:30 h (German time) on the morning of 9 April.[24] However, the meteorological reports were not favourable. There were clouds and fog up to 600 m above sea level. Added to this was the fact that only half of the Junkers crews were well trained in flying by instruments, something that Drewes had repeatedly complained about during the preparation for the invasion. The demand for trained personnel was great due to the large number of aircraft to be employed against Norway.

Over the Skagerrak, the planes began to have problems maintaining visual contact. An aircraft at the rear of the formation reported that it had lost contact with those planes following it. The fear in the Junkers leading the operation was that the missing planes had collided in the clouds. Because of this, Drewes himself gave the order for the aircraft to return to base. The *Fallschirmjäger* commander, Walther, who was flying in the leading plane (piloted by Metscher),[25] protested energetically, as he did not consider the situation to be so desperate, but Drewes would not budge. It must be remembered that only half the crews were trained in flying by instruments. Wilhelm Metscher remembers:

"*At first light we were flying over Denmark. That country had decided not to resist. Nevertheless, we were heading to our first 'serious' combat action against Norway. Once over northern Jutland the weather worsened. We had to fly at low altitude so as not to lose sight of land. But as we were flying over the Skagerrak the clouds began to mix with fog, complicating things even further. We had to fly blind, using our instruments. The other two planes of my Group* (Kette) *stayed with me, so we had no problems. Our hope was that the clouds would disperse and the weather would improve once we were over Norway, because we could only carry out our mission with good visibility. One of the main problems was that approximately a quarter of the crews were untrained in flying by instruments. The cloud and fog was proving too much for them. The commander* [Drewes] *was with me, scanning the sky in the terrible fog (we only had 20 m visibility). I could see the tension in his face; he had to make a decision whether or not to continue the mission. A little later he received a radio message saying two aircraft had collided and crashed into the sea.* Oblt. *Drewes immediately gave the order to return to Ålborg, in Denmark.*"

So it was that with the Norwegian mountains already in sight, 26 aircraft turned for home at 08:30 h, while another 3 (a complete *Kette*) continued towards Oslo, unaware of the order to turn back. A message was sent to the commander in chief of the transport units at the General Headquarters in Hamburg: "*Kehre wegen Schlechtwetter um*" (turning back due to adverse weather conditions). Without doubt it was a controversial decision.

Leutnant Ernst Mössinger, aged 24, led the 36 paratroops of the 2nd Platoon of the 1st Company. They were flying in three planes towards Fornebu:

"I had received hardly any information on the target and did not have a map. The only photographs I had seen had been shown to me by Hauptmann *Walther during his meeting with the Group commanders. We had planned to jump from between 80 and 100 m. I would jump first as Group commander. My men were all aged between 18 and 20 years old; only a few of the officers were a little older. The 1st Company were the youngest in the Battalion. Nevertheless, they were all highly motivated, although thoughtful and withdrawn during the flight, but all were convinced that taking the aerodrome did not suppose any great risk. (...) I sat next to the cabin, on the left, next to the door, when a member of the crew approached me and told me they had received orders to turn back. We could not shake off our disappointment, as we could already see the snow-capped Norwegian mountains and the outline of the coast. I thought maybe Drewes and Walther's aircraft were in a fog bank."*

Regarding the two aircraft "presumably lost," there is no confirmation of the event. Everything would appear to indicate that the Ju 52 commanded by *Feldwebel* Theo Karl Brand (second in command to *Leutnant* Becker), a 23-year-old from Solingen, which was transporting the 12 *Fallschirmjäger* of the first Group of *I. Zug*, 1st Company,[26] was shot down, possibly by a British *Bristol Blenheim* fighter.[27] Other sources[28] state that it was shot down by Norwegian fighters. The Ju 52/3m (WNr. 6570) of 5. *Staffel*, II./KG zbV 1, was probably brought down by two *Gladiators* (nº 429 and nº 433) based in Fornebu and piloted by Rolf Thorbjørn Tradin and Finn Thorsager. *Feldwebel* Albert Meier, pilot, was killed, along with the rest of the crew: *Unteroffizier* Heinz Söhnel, *Oberfeldwebel* Franz Rose, and *Feldwebel* Paul Diegner, as well as the 12 paratroopers. The aircraft crashed at Torgskjær, in the outskirts of Høvik, to the north of the Oslo Fjord.

In two of the three planes continuing on to Oslo was the Battalion HQ; the third was the communications aircraft. It is curious to find that one of the three planes that did not receive the order to turn back was precisely that which was dedicated to communications, although another hypothesis is that it ignored the order due to its "special" mission.

The First Wave of Troop Transport

The troops following in the wake of the *Fallschirmjäger* formed the second wave of the attack. Specifically, they were being transported in 53 Ju 52s belonging to *Kampfgeschwader zbV 103*, commanded by *Hauptmann* Wagner. The planes were carrying the 2nd Battalion of the 324th Infantry Regiment (II./IR 324). This formation took off at 06:00 h, twenty minutes after the *Fallschirmjäger*, and flew at an altitude of 300 m until they ran into the fog over the Skagerrak, where they descended to sea level. All the crews were trained in flying by instruments, and therefore had no problems maintaining their course. The planes flew in groups of 3, although at intervals, due to the length of the flight.

Heinz Kluge was a mechanic and gunner aboard the first transport plane to land at Fornebu. During the months of April and May1940 he took part in numerous transport missions in Norway, mainly carrying fuel from Kastrup to Trondheim. During all this time he did not spend a single night in Norway (nor was he ever fired upon). At the end of May 1940 he resumed his job as a flying instructor, becoming a *Hauptmann* in 1943 and Technical Officer in the Flying by Instruments school in Sprottau, Silesia, where he remained until the end of the war (despite the fact that in 1944—for a short time—he was chosen to train as a Messerschmitt *Me 262* pilot in Leipheim). He was taken prisoner by the Americans and regained his freedom at the end of 1945. (Óscar González)

At 08:30 h these aircraft received the order to turn back. The message said: "*Return to Schleswig due to bad weather*," and was signed by *Fliegerkorps X*. But Wagner was not convinced by it, as it did not state to which unit the order was directed, nor was it signed by *Transporterchef Land* (the Transport Units commander), von Gablenz, who was responsible for KGr zbV 103. Therefore, he thought the message was directed at another formation or was even false. As he was very close to the target and the weather showed signs of improving, Wagner decided to ignore the order. However, some of the planes in the formation did return to base.

When Drewes' message was received in the General Headquarters of *Fliegerkorps X*, informing them that the *Fallschirmjäger* were turning back, the commander, Hans-Ferdinand Freiherr von Geisler, wanted to abandon the assault on Fornebu. However, the commander of the transport units, Von Gablenz, oposed the measure, arguing that his forces could take Fornebu without the paratroops, and it was worth letting them have the opportunity to do so. In the end, he proposed that the *Fallschirmjäger* decide themselves, once the target was reached. Geisler, who had received strict orders from Göring on the matter, would not be pressured, and so Von Gablenz had to abide by his decision. The hypothesis exists that it was Von Gablenz himself, obstinate and opposed to Geisler's order, who badly worded the order, concious of what he was doing, as is corroborated by Metscher:

"*The message 'return to base due to bad weather' was sent by the commander of the transport units, to be confirmed by the commander of* X. Fliegerkorps. *But the order was not backed up or confirmed by Von Gablenz, and was not sent to all the aircraft heading to Oslo. This caused terrible chaos, made worse by the presence of inexperienced pilots in the formation (young men who had recently joined the* Luftwaffe, *and even* Lufthansa *crews recycled to participate in wartime missions) and the bad communications we had with the ground from our aircraft (even communication between planes in the air was bad at that time).*"

It is clear is that the decision created a bad feeling among some of the German officers involved. Bruno Melchior was one of the paratroops heading towards Fornebu. He remembers the circumstances and consequences of the order to turn back:

"*I was in the 2nd Company, which took off from Schleswig for Fornebu. To be exact, I was a* Gefreiter *in the Group commanded by* Oberjäger *Biehl, who died later in action at Dordrecht, Holland, on 10 May. The commander of the 2nd Platoon,* Leutnant Graf *Blücher, was in my aircraft. The order to abort the mission was, logically, unknown to the soldiers travelling aboard the transport aircraft. Once back on the ground in Ålborg, at approximately 09:30 h, we left the aircraft carrying our parachutes. I observed that there was an argument taking place between the transport commander* [Drewes] *and the chief of our own I./FJR1,* Hauptmann *Walther.*[29] *I remember that the officers went into the airfield buildings. Later we received the order to take off our parachutes....*"[30]

Meanwhile, Wagner's Ju 52s, ignoring the order, continued north, meeting up with the planes carrying the paratroops which were on their way back to Germany. The pilots of these Ju 52s signaled to them by moving their wings in an attempt to indicate that the mission had been aborted, but Wagner and his men interpreted these movements as a greeting: "*We could make out lots of small dots heading towards us.*" After descending below the clouds they saw there were "*some 30 to 40 Ju 52s heading in the opposite direction to us,*" according to a later report.

Unteroffizier Heinz Kluge was a member of one of Wagner's crews:

"*We received the alert at around 5am. All the crews received a ten minute briefing. The paratroops were already on their way to the target. I was not surprised to be told the objective of our mission was Norway. We also were aware that the Norwegian government had decided to resist invasion. (…). Three of us formed the crew of my aircraft:* Unteroffizier *Hannes Andresen, from Schleswig, an expert pilot trained in flying by instruments; and myself as engineer and gunner. Although I had not graduated officially as a pilot, I knew enough to fly the Ju 52. Nearly all the crews had left their radio operators on the ground. However, unlike most of the crews transporting the paratroops, all of our pilots were trained in flying by instruments. Also with us was our superior officer,* Hauptmann *Ingenhoven. Our plane was carrying 12 infantrymen plus an* Unteroffizier *or* Feldwebel, *I do not remember exactly. What I do remember is that we were loaded with equipment and supplies. None of those men had flown before; they were all silent.* Hauptmann *Wagner was in the lead aircraft; mine was in the second group* (Kette), *behind him and to his right. (...) We continued north. The pilot took the plane down, and we descended beneath the clouds and found excellent weather. However, to our surprise there were only three or four aircraft of our formation.The rest had disappeared!*"

At 09:00 h some aircraft from Wagner's group (Kluge included) flew at low altitude over the Høytorp fort, near Mysen; this city was a point of reference on the route to Oslo. At the moment the planes found themselves flying in groups of three, widely dispersed, and the fort's anti-aircraft defenses (10 or 12 *Colt* 8mm machine-guns) opened fire. The garrison in the fort had been on alert for an hour. The Norwegians began to experience serious problems with their machine-guns; most likely they were not using the most appropriate ammunition. They only caused slight damage to the German planes, with just one suffering damage of importance to one of its engines.

At the same time other aircraft entered the Oslo fjord and flew over the Oscarsborg fort, in the same place the "*Blücher*" had been sunk. Here, too, the anti-aircraft defenses opened fire, again without inflicting serious damage. By now the German troops were sure they would meet serious resistance at Fornebu. Kluge continues:

"*We listened to the music coming from Radio Oslo.* Hauptmann *Ingenhoven took up the co-pilot's position. I took the machine-gun, keeping my eyes peeled for enemy aircraft. We did not continue along the fjord to Oslo. We were trying to avoid the anti-aircraft defenses, especially those at Kjeller airfield.*"

The Norwegian Fighter Squadron (*Jagevingen*) at Fornebu

Following a night of alarms and reports of engagements between foreign naval units and the forts along the Oslo, the *Jagevingen* were placed on alert at 05:00 h.[31] The weather was cloudy, although as the morning continued it became clearer around Fornebu. The clouds were more persistant over the Oslo fjord.

At 6am, two of the Squadron's *Gloucester Gladiators* started to patrol. One of the *Gladiators* intercepted and attacked a *Dornier*, probably a Do 17, although the German plane managed to escape into the clouds. More *Gladiators* began to patrol the area, although without intercepting any German aircraft.

Following a report from Malmö, some 500 km south of Fornebu in neutral Sweden, confirming that "*15 heading north at 07:18 hours*," the *Jagevingen* Squadron was put on standby. They calculated the time these aircraft would reach Oslo and decided to send the *Gladiators* up to intercept them, in case the capital was the target. At 08:05 h five *Gladiators* took off from Fornebu, flying south and patrolling the Dröbak area. Half an hour later they were joined by two more fighters.

At 08:35 h the Norwegian patrol, flying at 1,800 m, spotted 8 Me 110 fighter-bombers heading north below them at 500/600 m. This formation was 1./ZG 76, led by *Oberleutnant* Werner Hansen, which had the mission of protecting and supporting the *Fallschirmjäger* at Fornebu and the following air-lift operation. These aircraft had taken off at 06:50 h. Estimating their time of arrival in Fornebu at the same time as the *Fallschirmjäger* at 08:45 h, their surprise can be imagined when on their way to Oslo they saw some of the aircraft carrying the paratroopers on the horizon heading back in the opposite direction. Even so, Hansen's group did not change course.

Having spotted German planes, Lieutenant Tradin, leading the Norwegian patrol, ordered his men to break formation and attack. The air war began with a result in the Norwegian's favour. It appears that 2 Me 110s, 2 Heinkel He 111s, and a Norwegian *Gladiator* were shot down, the latter having to make an emergency landing (nº 427, piloted

Kristian Fredrik Schye in the cockpit of his aircraft during his time in Canada. After being shot down on 9 April while at the controls of *Gloucester Gladiator* Nº 427, and following the treatment of his wounds, he tried to make his own way back to his parents' house in the outskirts of Oslo, but he was warned that the Germans were looking for him. Given the circumstances he tried to escape, first to Sweden and later to Britain. Following a brief period spent in the British Isles, he was sent to "*Little Norway*" in Canada as an instructor, in order to train Norwegians as pilots. When the base closed in 1945 he was sent back to the south of England, where he continued to serve as an RAF instructor. Schye became a doctor after the war. He died on 28 October 2003. (Tor Schye)

by Schye), while two more were destroyed on the ground at Fornebu by Me 110s while they were having their guns reloaded. Because of this the remaining Norwegian planes were oredered not to land there to rearm.

Following this aerial combat, it was the turn of the anti-aircraft defenses. The crews of the unprotected machine-guns located at the north of the runway were quickly put out of action, with one of the soldiers wounded. However, the Messerschmitt 110s were unable to silence the three machine-guns on the east and extreme north of the runway. Per Waaler, pilot of *Gladiator* nº 425, recalls:

"I landed to refuel, but my plane had been hit by the Heinkel I had just shot down. In fact the engine broke down. Suddenly somebody shouted 'Look!' We saw a Me 110 coming towards us, firing at my plane, which burst into flames as it was hit, as well as Lütken's [nº 419]. *We ran for shelter. Nearby (in the restaurant area) were three anti-aircraft machine-guns (there were two more in the open on the runway). We fired back at the Germans as they gained height. Luckily, almost miraculously, there were no casualties amongst the machine-gunners."*

The caption accompanying this photograph in the *Luftwaffe* magazine "*Der Adler*" was: "*The sign of the German commandants buiding at Fornebu airfield.*" *Hauptmann* Buchard Flakowski was given command directly by the German military attaché in Oslo; Spiller was one of the "directors" on the ground of the German deployment. (Óscar González)

A few of the Messerschmitts finally managed to reach the target area (although not at the planned time, but a few minutes before 09:00 h). However, they found no sign of the planes carrying the paratroops. The planned assault by the *Fallschirmjäger* did not materialize, which then caused the leader of the Messerschmitts to fly back and forth anxiously over the airfield looking for the transport planes, ignoring the fact that the majority had turned back. Finally, at 09:19 h a Ju 52 appeared, which instead of dropping its paratroops, proceded to circle the airfield and begin to descend to land.

The reason for this manoeuvre was that this was not one of the planes transporting the *Fallschirmjäger*, but rather one of the aircraft from the second wave (belonging to *Kampfgeschwader zbV 103*).[32] In the plane was *Hauptmann* Wagner, who had assumed that the objective had by then been secured and had decided to land. He would pay for this decision, as he and four other soldiers died in a hail of bullets from the Norwegian machine-guns on the east of the airfield. Heinz Kluge was at the controls of the aircraft that followed Wagner's plane:

"*We approached from the east. As soon as we arrived at the objective we were joined by other planes from our formation. The weather had improved; although there were still clouds, visibility was good. Then we started to receive fire. I could make out the machine-guns on the ground. We were flying at about 600 to 700 m, crossing Oslo from the east and heading directly for Fornebu. Our intention was to begin the landing procedure from the south on the runway that crossed the airfield from north to south. Wagner's plane landed first at 09:19 h. The defenders concentrated their fire on this aircraft. Wagner, meanwhile, was positioned in the opening to the cabin, preparing the machine-gun. No sooner had*

An aerial view from north to south of Fornebu airfield. Several civilian aircraft can be seen among the Ju 52s; these planes were already at the airfield before the attack began. At bottom left is a Ju 52 belonging to "*British Airways*," and next to the runway, a DC 3 of the Dutch company "*KLM*." (Bundesarchiv Koblenz)

his plane touched down than he was hit twice in the heart, dying almost instantly. Four other soldiers aboard the plane were also killed and three more wounded. The pilot, Oberfeldwebel *Sievert, had sufficient wits about him to abort the landing and head back to Ålborg, in Denmark. When the plane landed 52 bullet holes were found in the fuselage.*"

Metscher also remebers the tragic series of events:

"*My memories of the jouirney back to Denmark are less dramatic than those I have of the outward trip. My only concern was keeping visual contact with the other planes in my formation, given the thick fog. When we arrived in Ålborg the* Fallschirmjäger *were waiting for us; they had taken the airfield hardly without firing a shot a few hours earlier. Once we had landed we had nothing else to do apart from wait for the weather to improve so we could head back to Oslo. The proof of the confusion surrounding the order to return became apparent as other Ju 52s arrived at the Danish airfield (they had flown by instruments, having been piloted by expert crews). These had momentarily touched down in Fornebu, but had had to abort the landing after coming under heavy Norwegian fire. As later became apparent, some of our planes had crashed on the runway or burst into flames. One of the Junkers was carrying the body of the commander,* Hauptmann *Wagner. We were also informed that our military attaché at the embassy had fallen, something we later found out to be untrue.*"

Kluge's Ju 52, immediately behind Wagner, had landed at 09:20 h but with better luck, as none of the occupants were injured. The plane was carrying Wagner's second in command, *Hauptmann* Peter Ingenhoven, who now commanded the unit. The remaining 6 Me 110s had been left with no other choice than to land, as they were running out of fuel, and Hansen had taken a quick decision: land and fire from the ground, creating a defensive perimiter defending the Junkers from the Norwegian machine-guns. According to Hansen:

"*All of us pilots, with the exception of* Lieutnant *Lent and* Gefreiter *Kubisch,*[33] *met together. We had all suffered varying degrees of damage from the Norwegian defenses. Our faces reflected the tension we all felt. Suddenly, I saw several Junkers come in to land. The soldiers quietly disembarked, put on their helmets, and began to lite up cigarettes, ignoring the shots coming from the Norwegian defenders. I told them to stay alert, and that we had to take out the Norwegian positions.*"[34]

Kluge remembers the dramatic landing:

"*On reaching Fornebu, we immediately attempted to land and come to a halt at the end of the runway, but we quickly turned (we had the wind behind us!). We finally managed to stop the plane some 10m from the end of the runway. The soldiers started to leave the aircraft, and we were immediately engaged by the Norwegians. At least one round hit the back of the fuselage, but fortunately nobody was hit. In any case, this was no organized attack. While the troops were getting out of the plane I went back in to make sure no arms or munitions remained inside. I then positioned myself at the aircraft's machine-gun, but did not fire. I have to say that, although we had completed our mission, those were difficult moments....*"

More Junkers followed Kluge's plane in to land; among them was the aircraft piloted by *Unteroffizier* Rosskothen, followed by that of the Austrian *Leutnant* Bruno Maurer. They had flown to Norway together, passing through the fog in the Oslo fjord. None of the radio operators aboard had heard the message to turn back. One of the last Ju 52s to land with this initial group was that of *Hauptmann* Flakowski (who later, following his encounter with the military attaché *Hauptmann* Spiller, assumed command of Fornebu airfield).

The aircraft, many of which had landed under fire or in bad conditions, gathered at the end of the runway. The third plane to arrive began to burn, but its occupants were able to escape without injury; in the fourth, the soldier in charge of the machine gun had been shot in the hand. Another Ju 52 landed with such speed that it was about to collide with Kluge's plane. Kluge recalls that the *Lufthansa* personnel present at the airfield before the attack began were tasked with marking a "T" on the runway, in order to mark the direction of the wind and to provide a reference for the German pilots during the attack. However, it appears that this mission was never accomplished.

Ingenhoven was organizing the occupation of the airfield when, at around 09:33 h, the first aircraft carrying paratroops arrived. These were the three Ju 52s carrying the 19 *Fallschirmjäger* (including 9 NCOs and 5 soldiers[35]) commanded by *Oberleutnant* Wilhelm Götte, together with a medical officer. One of the paratroops was wounded in the leg before landing while flying over the Oslo fjord. Observing that the situation appeared unstable, Götte decided to abandon the jump, instead deciding for a landing directly on the western runway, out of range of the Norwegian machine-guns. The paratroops, together with some infantrymen from II./IR 324 and the pilots of their aircraft, were able to form a group of 30 men. They soon overcame the resistance of the two machine-guns and the searchlight crews, and then took control of the airfield's communications center.

20 minutes after this, some time between 10:05 and 10:17 h, more Ju 52s belonging to Wagner's unit (KGr zbV 103) landed with more men of II./IR 324. They did so on the northwestern edge of the airfield, where the Norwegian machine-guns did not present a serious threat. The Norwegian troops soon ran out of ammunition and were forced to abandon Fornebu not long after 10:00 h. They established a new defensive line at Lysaker, 10 km to the north of Oslo, and waited for reinforcements. During the next three hours German reinforcements consisting of more men of II./IR 324 and *Fallschirmjäger* landed aboard the aircraft of KGr zbV 102 and 107. The infantry relieved the *Fallschirmjäger* alredy occupying Fornebu at approximately 11:00 h.

The Germans had captured two 20mm anti-aircraft batteries, 2 machine-guns, and the searchlights. The paratroops had also taken 6 prisoners during the assault.

The Battle for Oslo

Five minutes after the first Ju 52 landed at Fornebu, the Norwegian *Garden* (Royal Guard) battalion was placed on alert. At 09:26 h the battalion commander sent the only available company (the 2nd) to Fornebu. The 3rd had been demobilised, and was in the process of reorganizing, while the 4th had been sent south that same morning to guard the survivors of the *Blücher*. The 2nd Company was ready in half an hour, but their transport took another half hour to arrive. If they had taken the direct route to Lysaker, where the machine-gun platoon was putting up resistance, they may have been able to make a significant difference to the German arrival at Fornebu. Lysaker was a key point on the road to Oslo from Fornebu. With a small bridge over the river in Norwegian hands, the German advance on Oslo would have encountered serious difficulties. However, the 2nd Company of the *Garden* chose an alternative route, advancing on foot to Lysaker. They came under continual attack by the *Luftwaffe*; losing valuable time, they attempted to coordinate with a company of the 5th Infantry Regiment that had recently arrived from Trandum. They did not reach the bridge until 12:00 h, and were not ready for the assault until after 13:00 h.

As has already been mentioned, following the cancellation of the assault by the *Fallschirmjäger* and the order to turn back, many of the aircraft in the second wave flew back to Ålborg airfield, which had been in German hands since early that morning. Others had had to make emergency landings in the north of Denmark. When the few aircraft that had not heed the order landed and took Fornebu, as has been described, the remaining aircraft involved in the operation headed back to Norway. The rest of the *Junkers 52* belonging to KGr zbV 103, carrying the main body of the 2nd Battalion, 324th Infantry Regiment (II./IR 324), landed between 10:30 and 11:00 hours, and the German forces began to deploy and head towards Oslo. At 10:55 h the first German troops arrived at Lysaker. The Norwegian machine-gunners withdrew and the German advance was unhindered. By 12:30 h they had arrived at the outskirts of Akershus.

Several *Fallschirmjäger* load their weapons containers (*Waffenbehälter*) onto a captured Norwegian truck. The containers were not used, as the paratroops did not jump as planned. Each container is marked with a number so that they could be easily identified by the *Fallschirmjäger*. The truck belonged to the Norwegian 1st Dragoon Regiment quatered in Akershus, but stationed in Fornebu. In the background is a civilian Ju 52 belonging to *Lufthansa*. (Bundesarchiv Koblenz)

The Oslo commander signed the official surrender at 14:00 h, the same time that the main part of 2./FJR1 arrived at Fornebu. What happened to them during the attack?

Following the order to turn back, they arrived in Ålborg at 10:30 h. When they were informed that Fornebu had been occupied by German forces the *Junkers* were refueled, and the *Fallschirmjäger* left their RZ parachutes and collected their weapons. Everything was ready by 13:00 h, and they took off again for Norway, arriving at 15:00 h in Fornebu, together with III./IR 307. According to Metscher:

"*The landing in Fornebu was not at all easy; there were several smoking and crashed Junkers left lying on the runway, which made it difficult to manoeuvre. The landing and later take off had to be done quickly, as there was no possibility of remaining on the airfield....*"

According to Melchior:

"*Without receiving orders, we all hurried to get to the exit of the airfield at the end which borders on a road. The passing cars were stopped and their drivers forced to carry our troops to Oslo. Once in the city we headed for (and occupied) the Town Hall).*"[36]

Fallschirmjäger near the restaurant at Fornebu airfield. Probably from the 2nd Company, 1st Parachute Regiment (2./FJR1). All are wearing the typical uniform of the German airborne forces in 1940: the M 38 jump suit without pockets, the M 38 helmet, and side-lacing jump boots. (Bundesarchiv Koblenz)

Nevertheless, not all the paratroops initially taking part in the operation returned to Norway: the 1./FJR1 and the *Nachrichtenzug* (Battalion Signals Platoon) flew back to Schleswig from Ålborg. A Platoon from the 2./FJR1 did the same. This meant that the 2./FJR1 was missing 4 of its Groups during the "second attack."

In Oslo itself the barracks and military acadamies had been evacuated, but the *Garden* Battalion, the anti-aircraft defenses, and Kjeller airfield, to the east of the city, were included in the official surrender. During that afternoon the situation became almost surreal when the airfield commander considered—quite logically—that his unit had surrendered, when in fact it was behind the Norwegian defensive line being maintained by the 5th Infantry Regiment, located in Nitelva, also east of Oslo. That the surrender agreement was not questioned illustrates perfectly the disorganization and confusion experienced by both the Norwegians and Germans during that foggy morning in April 1940. Per Waaler remebers events as follows:

"Once the German capture of Fornebu was inevitable and the arrival of our reinforcements impossible, we withdrew. We were trying to avoid being surrounded. We were ordered to Lysaker and to the fort at Akershus. I went accompanied by two other soldiers. We took a machine-gun and located ourselves on top of a tanker. A little later we abandoned it in a wood. Once we were on foot we noticed that there was a strong German presence in the area. Almost miraculously we saw two girls travelling in a private car. They stopped when they saw us and got us out of there and took us to Snaroya. From there we began walking along the beach (by now unarmed) to Lysaker. Finally, about 30 of us from Fornebu were able to join up at Akershus. We received orders to go to Maridalen. We were told that there we would find an arms dump and supplies and we could re-equip ourselves."

A view of Fornebu airfield in German hands. The Ju 52 that had transported the *Fallschirmjäger* and infantry can be seen on the runway. (Óscar González)

The airfield now occupied, German troops inspect the Norwegian anti-aircraft defenses located next to the runway. The photograph shows a Norwegian *Colt* machine-gun employed in the anti-aircraft role. (Óscar González)

The Assault on Fornebu – minute by minute

There follows a chronological account of the main events during the assault on Fornebu airfield. All events are according to German time.

01:02 The Oslo air defense command declares a state of maximum alert, *Beredskap 3*.

01:15 The sirens sound for the first time over the city, although no enemy aircraft appear.

01:20 Blackout ordered, although the order was carried out much later.

01:45 The pilots and ground crews of *Jagevingen* are placed on alert. Officers are informed that the forts in the Oslo fjord had fired on unidentified foreign naval vessels. The aircraft are dispersed along the runway.

02:35 All remains calm in Oslo.

03:00 Personnel at Fornebu return to their barracks. They are informed that the fighting in the Oslo fjord was against German naval units that had entered the fjord following an engagement with the Royal Navy.

05:00 Personnel at Fornebu are again put onto alert.

05:10 Oslo air defense command again declares a maximum alert *Beredskap 3*. Aero-engines heard over the airfield.

05:13 Blackout and Air raid alert over Oslo.

05:15 *Wezerzeit* (H Hour) for the Germans.

05:21 *Oscarsborg* fort, in the interior of the Oslo fjord, opens fire on the *Blücher*. The explosions can be heard in Fornebu.

06:00 End of Blackout. The clouds begin to disperse. Above them can be heard the sound of aero-engines. Two *Gladiators* are ordered up (nº 433, piloted by Finn Thorsager, and nº 425, piloted by Arve Braathen), who take off on a reconnaissance mission. Thorsager spots and repeatedly attacks a Dornier (presumably a Do 17 from *Fernaufklärung Gruppe 120*) until the latter escapes into the clouds. Braathen also spots an aircraft, but does not manage to get it in his sights. His radio fails and, after spending a time searching for the enemy, he returns to Fornebu.

06:55 Three *Gladiators* are sent to patrol the Oslo fjord. These aircraft are piloted by Krohn, Schye, and Waaler. They fly to Dröbak and return without spotting any German planes. In one of the aircraft neither the radio nor the machine-guns function correctly.

07:00 Oslo continues to be calm. At around the same time the anti-aircraft guns at Fornebu are ready to fire. There are three emplacements along the most recently constructed runways. There are also two machine-guns used for training at the northern edge of the airfield. However, none of them have any protection close at hand.

07:30 Finn Thorsager lands following his patrol. The unit is informed that 15 aircraft have flown over Malmo heading north at 06:18 h. Their ETA at Oslo is calculated, and it is decided to send up the *Gladiators* to intercept them, as Oslo is considered to be their target.

07:42 Krohn, Schye, and Waaler return to Fornebu.

08:05 Five *Gladiators* set off on the mission decided 35 minutes earlier. These are nº 429, piloted by Tradin; nº 433, by Thorsager; nº 425, by Waaler; nº 423, piloted by Krohn; and lastly, nº 427, piloted by Schye. The planes climb to 1000 meters and then head south, along the western side of the Oslo fjord. After flying over the area where the *Blücher* had been sunk they patrol around Dröbak.

08:30 Air raid alert over Oslo. Two *Gladiators* have broken spark plugs and are not operational until 08:30 h. These are nº 413, piloted by Braathen, and nº 419, piloted by Lütken. The latter also has problems with his radio. At the moment of the German attack *Gladiator* nº 415 is being repaired on the runway.

08:35 The Norwegian *Gladiators* are flying at an altitude of 1,800 m when they spot 8 German Me 110s heading north 600 m below them. The German formation is *Staffel* 1./ZG 76, which has been tasked with supporting the paratroops at Fornebu. Lieutenant Tradin orders the *Gladiators* to break formation and attack. The dog fight begins and more German planes arrive. Two Me 110s and 2 He 111s are shot down; the Norwegians lose *Gladiator* nº 427. When *Gladiators* nº 419 and 425 land to rearm, they are attacked and destroyed on the ground by the Me 110s. Only one is able to take off again (nº 423).

08:15 Time planned for the airborne assault.

09:00 German Me 110s attack Fornebu (destroying the two fighters already mentioned). The attack scatters the unprotected Norwegian machine-gunners.

09:19 The first Ju 52, commanded by *Hauptmann* Wagner, tries to land at Fornebu from the south. Wagner and four other men are killed in the attempt and the aircraft aborts the manoeuvre, flying to Ålborg (Denmark).

09:20 The second Ju 52 lands without problems and heads towards the hills at the western edge of the airfield, where the troops disembark. There, *Leutnant* Helmut Lent,[37] piloting Me 110 "M8 + DH," who has had one of his engines hit by anti-aircraft fire, also lands, leaving the runway and crashing into the fence of a private house near the airfield. He had previously shot down *Gladiator* nº 427, flown by Schye. The remaining Me 110s and more Ju 52s follow him in to land.

09:26 The *Samlestasjon* (communications center) for the Oslo area informs the *Garden* (Royal Guard) that the Germans have landed at Fornebu. The Guard's commander orders the 2nd Company to the airfield.

09:33 Three Ju 52s carrying paratroops from I./FJR1 HQ land at Fornebu.

10:00 The anti-aircraft machine-gun platoon and the Norwegian military personnel withdraw from Fornebu towards Lysaker. At the exit to the airfield they run into the Germans but no shots are fired.

10:05 The commander of the Norwegian Royal Guard receives orders to counterattack the Germans at Fornebu, but not to risk his unit if the enemy resists and holds onto their positions. In this case his mission is to block the road to Oslo.

10:05 The Norwegian searchlight detachment withdraw to the west of the airfield (across a frozen area).

11:30 From now until 12:00 h, the bulk of the German troops arrive at the airfield.

15:00 Eight Ju 52s transporting men of 2./FJR1 arrive at Fornebu. The rest return on the 12th, together with 1./FJR1.

Some Considerations

Up to that moment the *Fallschirmjäger* had been encountering serious operational and organizational difficulties, although they were able to overcome them successfully. Their performance was rather less than satisfactory, and it can be said that the successful taking of Fernebu had more to do with the mistakes made by the Norwegians, which proved fateful

Once in German hands, between 10:30 and 11:00 h the rest of the Ju 52s belonging to KGr zbV 103 landed at Fornebu, carrying the main body of the 2nd Battalion, 324th Infantry Regiment (II./IR 324). Here, aircraft from this wave are about to enter the Oslo fjord. (Óscar González)

given the "avalanche" of German troops and materiel they faced, rather than the actions of the German paratroops (who in reality played little part in the action). The Norwegians had not foreseen an attack of this type, and their strategy was excessively centered around defense (understood traditionaly). If, for example, their automatic weapons had been deployed with more resolve, German difficulties in the south of the country would have been greatly increased.

Isolated decisions—in all cases very risky, almost dramatic; although very typical of the German strategy in combat—resulted in Fornebu falling into German hands, but it was not according to plan, and not even according to the most recently received orders. The airfield at Stavanger/Sola was only captured once reinforcements had arrived (although here the *Fallschirmjäger* were to "perform" well in its capture), and Oslo/Fornebu was only fully under control following the arrival of the 163rd Infantry Division.

The capture of the Danish and Norwegian airfields was key to the sussess of operation *Weserübung*. The *Fallschirmjäger* met stiffer resistance in Norway than in Denmark. The first obstacle to be overcome was the adverse weather conditions; only at the last minute did the sky clear sufficiently for the air transportable operation to begin. However, the bad meteorological conditions were decisive in the development of the airborne mission. The Germans also had many problems in reaching the weapons containers. In Sola, for example, many of the containers remained out of reach, and the paratroops were literally pinned down until they could get to them. This aspect merits further consideration.

This first operation established the difficulty in dropping the weapons in containers. Instead of the paratrooper jumping with his weapons, as the Allies did later, the weapons were dropped in containers, together with the ammunition. This created serious difficulties,

The remains of a Ju 52 on one of the runways at Fornebu, damaged during landing on 9 April. The number of Ju 52s damaged or crashed at the airfield between 9 and 11 April was 16 (10 aircraft on the 10th), resulting in 8 men killed, 4 wounded, and 3 reported missing. (Óscar González)

above all when the containers could not be reached under enemy fire. Locating these containers was essential in order for the *Fallschirmjäger* to be quickly ready for combat. A basic tenet was that until the paratroops recovered their weapons they were basically defenseless. This problem was not solved after the Norwegian campaign. Furthermore, it was never resolved satisfactorily (even though the *Lehr* units rehearsed alternative methods), except for troops transported in gliders. The need for the containers was due to the use of the RZ type parachutes, which did not allow the *Fallschirmjäger* to be dropped with much weight.

In the end, the factor of surprise (wisely exploited by the Germans), and the capacity for decision—audacious as it was without doubt—on the ground, together with Norwegian indecision, were a significant influence on the capture of the first objectives on Norwegian soil.

The Incursion at Elverum

To sum up, and in order to support these reflections, we should comment on the attempt to capture the Norwegian Royal Family and members of the government carried out by around 96 paratroops of 2./FJR1 on the night of 9/10 April. Although Oslo had fallen, the King, Haakon VII, had enough time to escape by train, together with the nation's gold reserves and his government, a little after the invasion had begun. The city of Elverum was the meeting point.

Fallschirmjäger from the 1st Regiment (FJR1) at Fornebu, 9 April. It is very probable that the officer on the left is *Oberleutnant* Wilhelm Götte, who commanded the first group of paratroops to land at the airfield. (Ernst Mössinger)

A sketch of Wilhelm Götte drawn by the celebrated illustrator of the time, Willrich. Götte was born in Omaruru, in German South West Africa, on 11 August 1915. This was the officer who took Fornebu at the head of a handful of paratroops from *Stab.*/FJR1. Götte was one of the first *Fallschirmjäger* to land at 09:33 h on 9 April, when chaos reigned in the German ranks due to the heavy fire from the Norwegian guns. With a small group of around 30 men (from *Stab.*/FJR1, together with troops from II./IR 324 and pilots) he took on the Norwegians, enabling more German aircraft to land. Following Fornebu and the incursion at Elverum, he took part in the fighting at Dordrecht, Holland, on 10 May. He later returned to Narvik, attached to *Gruppe Walther*. Wilhelm Götte died in Crete on 20 May 1941 at the start of the invasion, and his remains are buried at the cemetery in Maleme. (Ramon Boronda)

In the confusion of that day, following several pauses, the aeronautical attaché at the German Embassy, *Hauptmann* Eberhard Spiller,[38] took command of the parachute company, with the main mission of capturing the King. Spiller was in Fornebu when the Germans assaulted the airfield, and the first thing he did, at 11:00 h, was to order *Oberleutnant* Götte and his men to Oslo as the German advance guard, and they went to the embassy to communicate the capture of the airfield. They arrived at mid-day in requisitioned vehicles. The group, together with the embassy's naval attaché, returned to Fornebu at 14:00 h, neutralizing a Norwegian anti-aircraft battery on the way that had been abandoned by its crew.

German Intelligence had information that the Royal Family and the government were in Hamar. The *Stoßgruppe Götte* (Attack Group Götte), reinforced by half a machine-gun platoon, received new orders to head for Hamar and capture the King. Approximately 30 km north of Oslo they encountered Norwegian units that offered hardly any resistance. As a result of this an officer and 22 cavalry troopers were captured. Two Norwegian liaison officers were later added to the group of prisoners. The Germans were aware that there were more Norwegians along the route, so Götte, given the incertitude, decided to return to Oslo. However, on the way back they were in for a surprise; they met up with Spiller and Walther at the head of 2./FJR1 heading for Hamar. This was when Götte realized that Walther had been able to return to Norway (after the first attempt had been aborted by *Oblt.* Drewes' decision to turn back to Germany due to the dense fog).

Eberhard Spiller, aeronautical attaché to the German Embassy in Oslo on 9 April 1940. His activities in the Norwegian capital included espionage and preparations for the German invasion. He was also tasked with providing information on the Norwegian government, and especially the Royal Family. (Guhnfeldt Archive)

What had happened to Walther? He had arrived in Ålborg at 15:00 h. With him was *Hauptmann* Gröschke, commanding 2./FJR1. During the landing one of the Junkers had crashed. Without losing any time, Walther and Gröschke headed for the Oslo Town Hall along with their men and Spiller. There they received instructions to continue to Hamar and capture the Royal Family. However, Walther's orders mentioned nothing about this latter mission (they only indicated the possibility of taking Kjeller airfield, located approximately 17 km northeast of Oslo, once Fornebu was in German hands). Walther had few effectives and not enough men to take the capital (the sinking of the *Blücher* had put paid to any plans for a landing). Spiller and Walther ignored this important detail. Presented with this situation (precipitated action and lack of information on the real situation of German forces), the decision to penetrate the Norwegian lines without having first secured Oslo seems rash. It appears that the order came from the Ambassador, Dr. Bräuer.

At 17:00 h on the 9th Walther, Spiller, and their group (2nd Company, 1st Parachute Regiment), supported by half an infantry company with machine-guns, headed for Hamar on board four requisitioned buses, a truck, and the German military attaché's car (driven by his chauffeur, Lambert Menner). Although preparations for the mission were hurried, they were able to advance 150 km northeast into enemy territory. As we have seen, they

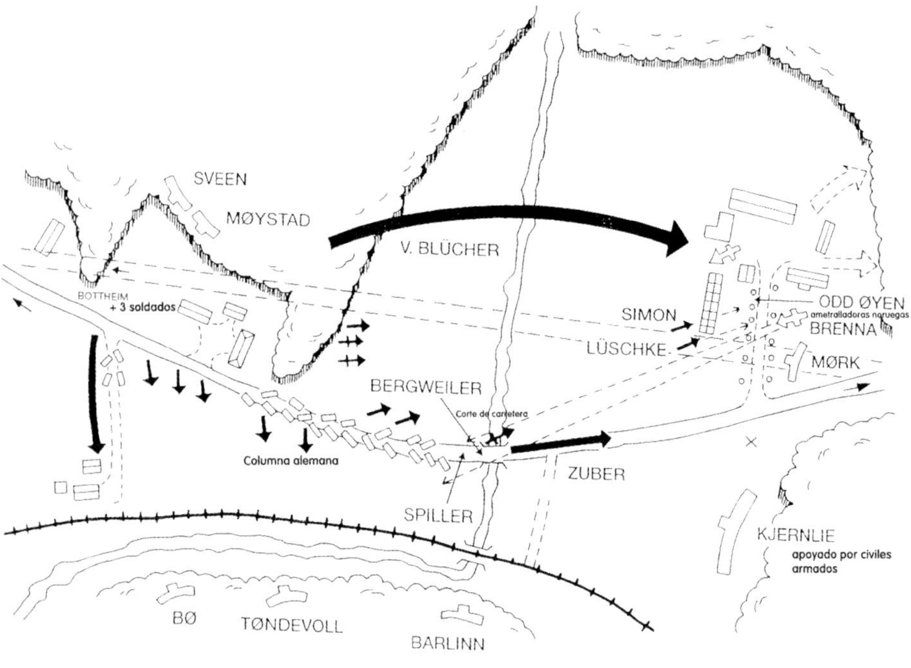

Graphic representation of the deployment of German and Norwegian forces during the fighting at Midtskogen. At 03:00 h on the 10th Walther's men were stopped by a barricade blocking the road at Midtskogen, 4 km from their objective. They were confronted by 63 soldiers, 3 machine-gun sections, and 1 mortar section belonging to the 1st Company of the Norwegian Royal Guard (*Garden*). They had come from Terningmoen, near Elverum, and were commanded by Major Helset, with Captains Rognes and Møystad. The black arrows show German movements. (Andreas Hauge/Óscar González)

Midtskogen Farm today.

met up with Götte and his men on the way, who then joined the group. In total there were 80 paratroops and 120 infantrymen armed with 20 MG 34s. Bruno Melchior[39] was part of the group:

"*Walther and the other officers appeared with a* Hauptmann *at 17:00 h. I remember he was wearing uniform and a leather overcoat. He had only a Shell road map in his hands. He was the air attaché at the Embassy,* Hauptmann *Spiller.*"

The group arrived in Hamar from the south at midnight. Following an exchange of shots with a group of Norwegians who tried to defend a bridge the Germans entered the town. They then found out that the Royal Family had gone to Elverum. A detail of paratroops remained to occupy the public buidings and cut communications, while the main body continued their advance at 00:45 h to their objective. Melchior was one of those who stayed in Hamar:

"*The route was complicated, due to the bends in the road. After one or two problems breaking the resistance in Hamar, my group, El* Gruppe Biehl *(commanded by Sepp Biehl, of the 2nd Platoon under Von Blücher), received the order to occupy the telephone exchange. I was given command of this 'operation' while the rest contiued to Elverum.*

I remember that there were two men and two women in the room where I was located, once the installations had been occupied. We did not let them near the telephones, so they could not cut or use the communications. I tried to make them understand that they would be in no danger if we decided to cut communications. I also tried to explain that we were not against the Norwegians, but rather the British, who were also planning to occupy the country. The women made coffee and the situation remained tense. At 02:00 h one of the women asked me in English if she could go home. At first I refused, thinking she could warn the Norwegian soldiers. She swore that she would not do so and finally I let her go home."

At 03:00 h on the 10th, Walther's men were stopped by a barricade blocking the road at Midtskogen, 4 kilometers from their objective. They were confronted by 63 soldiers, 3 machine-gun sections, and 1 mortar section from the 1st Company of the Norwegian Royal Guard (*Garden*). They had come from Terningmoen, near Elverum, and were commanded by Major Helset, and Captains Rognes and Møystad.[40] However, these men did not form an excellent unit of elite troops, but rather they were an ad hoc unit which had been hurriedly formed from support personnel.

A heavy firefight began (lasting almost an hour), in which Spiller was mortally wounded in the chest by machine-gun fire. Taken to Hamar, he died at 11:30 h the same day. The Germans lost a total of four men killed. Several men were wounded in the ambush, among them *Leutnant* Zuber,[41] leader of the 1st Platoon, 2nd Company, and *Oberjäger* Redlin. All German casualties during the incursion were at Midtskogen.

Although Midtskogen was finally captured, Walther decided to return to Oslo, given the strength of Norwegian resistance. *Leutnant* Graf von Blücher's Platoon formed the rearguard as they withdrew. He later wrote in his report:

"*At around 03:10 h we encountered a barricade blocking the Elverum road. We came under attack from machine-gun and rifle fire from all sides.* Hauptmann *Gröschke gave orders to his Company. The First Platoon deployed along both sides of the road. The Second deployed into the woods to the left.* Hauptmann *Spiller took up position with the 1st Platoon when* Leutnant *Zuber was wounded. Meanwhile,* Oberjäger *Krämer tried to return fire with his machine-gun, sweeping the road and the enemy's positions. Together with Krämer was* Gefreiter *Herbert Bergweiler, 20 years old, who was mortally wounded. We came under heavy fire from the Norwegians.* Oberjäger *Luschke and* Oberjäger *Simon*[42] *tried to silence the enemy machine-guns with grenades.*

To the left of the road, in the direction of Elverum, some 100 m from our positions, was a farm. Blücher's Platoon was given the order to attack it, in order to outflank the enemy. Zuber's group, for their part, continued to press their frontal attack despite the fire from the Norwegian machine-guns and the 80 cm of snow that lay on the ground. At last, the enemy gave in to the pressure of our attack and withdrew towards Elverum. Apart from capturing several soldiers, we also took 5 machine-guns and 200 rifles. Finally, Blücher took charge of securing the road...."

Melchior continues:

"(...) *Very early in the morning, at a quarter to five, my group leader, Biehl, returned to the telephone exchange at Hamar with prisoners. The rest of the* Fallschirmjäger *came with the vehicles a little later. I boarded a bus which appeared to be filled with captured Norwegian weapons.*"

This German advanced guard—always on the move—caused a lot of damage to the Norwegian ability to mobilize troops along the Oslo – Hamar axis (creating chaos and confusion along the route), as well as lowering Norwegian morale. According to Melchior:

"*The Norwegians were taken completely by surprise, as they had not expected to meet Germans operating in this area. Travelling in the bus, as we were taking one of the corners on the narrow road we ran into a dark green Opel* Blitz *truck. Without waiting for orders, we approached the back of the truck and pointed our MP 38 machine pistols at the Norwegian soldiers in the back. As this was a stretch of road with a lot of bends we only saw three Norwegian trucks, but we were able to disarm this unit without firing a shot.* (...) *I took a pair of Norwegian binoculars which had been made in Jena, Germany. On requisitioning their trucks we encountered serious problems due to the fact that our drivers were unfamiliar with the road.*"

This occurred to the south of Hamar. Walther's men captured approximately 500 men and 30 officers,[43] including Colonel Meinick and Captain Sæbøe, chief of staff to General Hvinden Haug, all of them belonging to the 1st Dragoon Regiment. The officers were taken to Oslo (used as a shield to ensure safe conduct in order to avoid barricades on the return trip), while the rest were dispersed by firing shots into the air. In Walther's judgment, they did not pose any threat.[44]

Monument commemorating the fighting at Midtskogen. (Cato Edvardsen)

The column of paratroops aboard the Norwegian trucks, half of which were being driven by men without driving licenses, were halted once more by a situation which was ably managed by Walther. At 11:30 h, around 30 km south of Minnesund, they stopped at a bridge. The Norwegian defenders were well armed and equipped, and able to rapidly reduce the German party. A Norwegian officer, who was aware of the composition of the German force, came out to parly with Walther, informing him that he faced three regiments, and therefore resistance was useless. Walther, surprisingly, drew an "ace up his sleeve" and answered the Norwegian with the ruse that three *Fallschirmjäger* had jumped after him, and these would attack if his column was not allowed to continue unmolested. Faced with this threat, the Norwegians allowed Walther's column of 50 vehicles past unopposed, Norwegian prisoners included. According to Melchior:

"My group was travelling aboard an Opel Blitz, *and we were the spearhead of Walther's column. We had mounted a machine-gun on top of the cabin of the truck. (...) We arrived at a bridge 30 km south of Minnesund and observed the situation through binoculars. The bridge and its surroundings were occupied with Norwegian soldiers. Two men approached us from the bridge. When they reached the middle of the bridge a shot rang out from our side and the Norwegian on the left fell. A medic quickly retrieved him and took him to the rearguard. Meanwhile,* Hauptmann *Walther and some other officers came over to where we were. A Norwegian also came over in order to parly. I heard how the latter was completely aware of our composition and the route we had taken. 'You are only 100 men. We outnumber you and have artillery support. It makes no sense to fight, you must surrender,' he said in perfect German. It was then that Walther responded: 'Tell your commander we jumped with three regiments.* Leutnant *Graf Blücher commands the 1st on your left flank, and* Leutnant *Zuber the 3rd on your right flank. They will attack in 15 minutes if you do not let us continue.' (...) The Norwegian returned, telling us that we were free to pass. The Norwegian soldiers had left their weapons on both sides of the road and remained standing, flanking it. We had our weapons at the ready and looked on in curiosity at the scene. Our column passed over the bridge without incident and we continued on our way to Oslo."*

Walther arrived in Oslo at 17:00 h. He reported to the commander of German forces in the capital and also the commander of 163 ID, *Generalmajor* Engelbrecht, who was informed of the audacious mission Walther had undertaken.

Walther returned with a booty of 3 85 mm guns, 7 heavy machine-guns, 21 light machine-guns, 600 rifles, and 220,000 rounds of ammunition, as well as the captured vehicles. The *Fallschirmjäger* of the 2nd Company were finally able to sleep in Oslo City Hall after 48 hours awake and constant tension.

Norway was not prepared for war, and this is made patently obvious by the "raid on Elverum"; further proof of the strange atmosphere surrounding the first German actions undertaken in the country. Various Norwegian units, well positioned along the route, could have "eliminated" the German company with little problem, but in spite of this they were able to return to Oslo. There is another significant fact regarding the Norwegian attitude: a farmer went to hand over his requisitioned horse to the mobilisation center in Terningmoen, near Midtskogen. As he neared the fighting, a Norwegian soldier recommended that he move away immediately. "*Can't you hear the shooting?*" insisted the soldier, to which the farmer replied "*You mean they are firing with live ammunition?*"

The 2nd Parachute Company (2./FJR1) was employed in small-scale actions during the days that followed. On the morning of the 11th, together with two companies of infantry, they deployed to the area north and east of Oslo. They left at 07:30 h heading for Lillestrøm-Fedsund. They were stopped at a bridge that had been previously blown up by the Norwegians. *Leutnant* Zuber, commanding the platoon in the vanguard, directed the attack against this focus of resistance. The rest of the Company continued on its way, avoiding the fighting, and headed north, crossing the river Vorma at an intact bridge at Swansfossen. Some 10 km north of Eindsvoll, the new platoon forming the advance guard—composed of two groups—under command of *Leutnant* Graf von Blücher[45] attacked another point of resistance. They came under machine-gun fire from armed civilians. These were killed. Meanwhile, other units from the Company took up positions four kilometers from the road. The infantry attached to Walther did not take part in these actions, as the buses carrying them had broken down on the way. The 2nd Company returned to Oslo that same day (11th) with one man severely wounded and 20 Norwegian prisoners, including two civilians. They had also captured a heavy machine-gun, 3,000 rounds of ammunition, and 10 rifles.

On 12 April, 11 NCOs and soldiers of the Company, under *Leutnant* Zuber, received new orders to support an infantry battalion deploying in the area of Spydeberg. It was supposed that there was a Norwegian division in this area. Zuber's mission was to go to the aid of an infantry platoon pinned down by Norwegian fire. The paratroops were able to reach the objective, but during the return they came under machine-gun and artillery fire, which resulted in a *Oberjäger* and a *Gefreiter* being seriously wounded. The latter, called Karl Rudat, died while being carried to safety. *Leutnant* Zuber and his men arrived back in Oslo at 16:00 h.

Lastly, on 13 April, 2./FJR1 received a new mission. They were to deploy to the southwest of Oslo, in the area of Drammen, Titunsberg, and Porsgrunn, some 40 km away. Their objective was to clear the area of Norwegian resistance and destroy a transmitter. The two 85 mm guns captured on the incursion to Elverum were to be used on this mission; 25 artillerymen would accompany them to crew the guns. On the way to Drammen, due to the inexperience of the drivers, a truck was involved in an accident which resulted in two *Fallschirmjäger* being seriously injured, while another 5 were slightly hurt. Once moving again they were attacked by five Norwegians, who later surrendered. Finally, they reached Porsgrunn and destroyed the transmitter. In spite of the condition of the roads, the mountainous route, and the inexperience of the drivers, the Company returned to Oslo on 14 April at 01:00 h.

---

20 Guhnfeldt, C.: *Fornebu 9. April*. Oslo, Wings Forlag A/S, 1990.

21 http://surfcity.kund.dalnet.se/norway_krohn.htm

At dawn on 9 April 1940, the *Jagevingen* at Fornebu had 7 of its 10 *Gladiators* ready for action. The unit had 10 pilots available, three of whom were still undergoing training. The *Gladiators* were 413, 419, 421, 425, 427, 429, and 433. The 7 operational pilots were Lt Rolf Torbjørn Tradin, Lt Drag Krohn, Lt Arve Braathen, Sub Lt Finn Thorsager, Sgt Per Waaler, Sgt Kristian Fredrik Schye, and Oskar Albert Lütken. The Norwegian Air Force had a total of 74 aircraft on 9 April 1940.

22 The crews were as follows (pilot/observer):

Oblt. Werner Hansen/*Uffz*. Walther Gross; *Ltn*. Helmut Lent/*Gefreiter* Walther Kubitsch; *Ltn*. Erhard Kort/ *Obergefreiter* Heinrich Bockheimer; *Uffz*. Helmut Mütschele/*Obergefreiter* Karl Ludwig Lorey; *Ltn*. Gerhard

Böhmel/ *Gefreiter* Enno Gruschwitz; *Oberfeldwebel* Gerhard Herzog/ *Feldwebel* Paul Wellenkötter; *Ltn.* Hans Ulrich Kettling/ *Obergefreiter* Friedrich Wilhelm Volk; and *Feldwebel* Johann Schönherr/*Uffz.* Horst Hoffmann.
23 According to the document *Befehl der Gruppe XXI (BA-MA RH 24-21/17)*: "*After the drop, I./FJR1 protected the later landing of* '1.Lufttransportstaffel' *and all the troops who landed after, in such a way that an exit to the west towards Oslo was secured.The commander of I./FJR1 is the only one responsible for the taking of Fornebu (...). So that the landing proceeds rapidly, it is also necessary to take the airfield at Kjeller (17 Km northeast of Oslo). I I./FJR1 is tasked with this mission (without doubt companies), which will head for the objective overland, once Fornebu is secured.*"
The Army Air Service (*Hærens Flyvåpen*) had 20 *Tiger Moth* and 16 *Fokker* aircraft at the airfield at Kjeller.
24 According to Wilhelm Metscher, "*The operation will begin with the radio transmission of the following order: 'Wesertag [D Day], high tide 9 metres. Weserzeit [H Hour], 5:30 h.'*" The planes carrying the *Fallschirmjäger* would take off at 5:40 h.
25 Walther decided to travel in the formation's lead aircraft, and not with the Battalion HQ (*Stab*). It was a decision he was to regret.
26 15 Ju 52s transporting the 1st Company. Regarding the plane carrying *Feldwebel* Brand, Renisch (1990), p. 11, incurs a contradiction in his account, stating "*flying over the Skagerrak, Leutnant Mössinger lost the aircraft flying on his left* [II. Zug]," but later, a photo caption states "*the lost aircraft belonged to I. Zug.*" Guhnfeldt (1990), p.141, does not indicate the platoon it belonged to, simply that they were paratroops of the 1st Company. Golla (2006), p 101, although not completely, follows Renisch's version; that is, that the aircraft carried *Fallschirmjäger* of *II. Zug*. In this text, the version held to is that of a man who took part in the action, *Feldwebel* Alexander Uhlig, leader of the 4th Platoon, who states that "*Feldwebel Brand was 2ic to Leutnant Becker, who commanded I. Zug.*"
Apart from Brand *Obergefreiter* Wilhelm Etzel, *Gefreite*r Gerhard Senkel, *Obj.* Stamer, *Jäger* Günther Fritz, *Jäger* Günther Drews, *Jäger* Heinz Peter, *Jg.* Haidle, *Jg.* Hamels, *Jg.* Josef Rommel, *Jg.* Schiefelbein, and *Jg.* Güse were also killed (although the latter is not officially confirmed in the "*Volksbund Deutsche Kriegsgräberfürsorge e.V.*").
27 According to Mössinger: "*I suddenly saw a British aircraft appear between the clouds, which then flew alongside us. It was 150 m from us. The British fighter then disappeared amongst the clouds. I am not an expert on aircraft, but when I later described it, I found out it was a* Bristol Blenheim. *As a result of its attack we lost the aircraft that flew on the left* (sic) *in my* Kette."
28 Guhnfeldt, C (1990), pp. 141-142, states that only one aircraft was lost, as opposed to Metscher. His detailed information is corroborated by Golla, K (2006), p. 101. Nevertheless, other secondary sources, such as http://surfcity.kund.dalnet.se/norway_tradin.htm, support the thesis that the aircraft was brought down by Norwegian fighters, and that it was transporting paratroops of the 2nd Company. The first is quite probable, but the second is impossible. Uhlig, who participated in the operation, underlined the falsehood of that theory: "*The 2nd Company did not lose an aircraft.*"
29 The argument began in the Ju 52 when Drewes gave the order to turn back. According to Mössinger, the *Fallschirmjäger* in the aircraft told him that the two were so heated that they almost came to blows. Walther wanted to take Fornebu.
30 Melchior, B.: *Oslo Einsatz 1940*, DDF, 4/1997, pp. 11-13.
31 All the times referenced in the text are based on German standard time.
32 As has already been mentioned, nearly all the *Fallschirmjäger* transport aircraft turned back: those carrying Walther and part of his *Stab*, and those of the 2nd Company, landed at the recently captured airfield of Ålborg. The Battalion Signals Platoon and the 1st Company landed in Schleswig.
33 They landed in the garden belonging to the Theodorsen family. Cut off from the rest of the pilots, they were surrounded by Norwegian soldiers. They negotiated a kind of cease fire, a "gentlemen's agreement." Germans and Norwegians conversed without putting down their weapons. One of the Norwegians was pilot Oscar Albert Lütken, who had studied in Germany.
34 Guhnfeldt (1990), p. 166.
35 Belonging to the Battalion HQ (*Stab*). As has already been commented, one of the Ju 52s that landed initially was the one assigned to the Signals Platoon, carrying several *Fallschirmjäger*.
36 Melchior, B.: *Oslo Einsatz 1940*, DDF, 4/1997.
37 Helmut Lent was born on 13 June 1918 in Pyrehne, in the region of Landsberg, which formed part of Warthe/ Neumark. He joined the *Luftwaffe* on 1 August 1936. After participating in operations over Norway (he escorted Ju 87 *Stukas* at Narvik), he was transferred to the *Nachtjagd* (night fighter) unit. On 5 October 1944 one of the engines on his Ju 88 G-6 (W.Nr. 751081) "D5 + AA" failed as he was attempting to land at Paderborn, and he collided with an electric cable. He survived, but the rest of his crew were killed. Lent died from his wounds a few days later, in hospital in Paderborn. He was posthmously promoted to the rank of *Oberst*.
Helmut Lent was credited with 110 victories; of these, 103 were at night. His total included 59 four-engined bombers and a Mosquito. He received the *Ritterkreuz* on 20 August 1941. The Oak Leaves "*Eichenlaub*" were

awarded on 6 June 1942; the Swords "*Schwertern*" on 2 August 1943; and the Diamonds "*Brillanten*" on 31 July 1944. He flew with the following units: ZG 76, NJG 1, NJG 2, and NJG 3.

38 Eberhard Spiller was born on 7 May 1905 in Thorn, in Pomerania. The son of a soldier, he joined the army in 1925, and the air force from 1932, where he reached the rank of *Hauptmann*. He married Ursula Syring in Berlin in 1935. Spiller taught tactics at the *Luftkriegsschule* in Gatow in 1937. Between the summer of 1938 and 4 September 1939 he served in the German Embassy in London. When war broke out he went to Rotterdam and then the Hague.

He was sent to the German Embassy in Oslo as aeronautical attaché in 1939 (the ambassador was Dr. Curt Bräuer). His mission was espionage and the preparation for the German invasion. In February 1940 he travelled to Berlin to receive specific instructions. He was to report on the Norwegian airfields, as well as its air force and defense installations. He also had to gather information on the Norwegian government and, more specifically, the Royal Family. To this effect he organized grand receptions, the most important with 200 guests. On 8 April he received instructions to be at Fornebu at 05:15 h to aid the airborne landing.

According to the account of pilot Per Waaler, in February 1940 there was already the feeling that the Germans were planning something against Norway. He and his fellow pilots were indignant when they were ordered to allow Spiller to inspect the installations at Fornebu. "*As a pilot, he was immediately able to spot defenses and our weak points*," remembers Waaler in an interview with the author. According to him, even before the invasion it was common to hear aircraft flying overhead photographing the airfield. "*Many times we received reports from Kjeller airfield that several planes had violated our air space. We could never intercept them because our communication system was slow and the warnings came over the phone minutes,at times hours, late.*"

39 For Melchior's complete narrative, see: Melchior, B.: *Oslo Einsatz 1940*, DDF, 4/1997, pp. 11-13.

40 Møystad became leader of *Rikshird*—the Norwegian version of the Nazi SA—following his country's surrender.

41 *Leutnant* Hans-Georg Zuber was leading the 1st Platoon of the 2nd Parachute Company. He recovered from the wounds he received at Elverum and jumped in Crete in 1941, and later fought in North Africa, Russia, and Monte Cassino, where he was again seriously wounded. He survived the war and joined the *Bundeswehr*, reaching the rank of *General*. He died in 1995.

42 It would appear that both died on the Leningrad front in 1941. *Oberfeldwebel* Alfons Johann Simon was killed attacking Russian positions in Wyborgskaja on 13 November 1941. (Cf. Hauge, A.: *Kampen på Midtskogen*, 1995, p. 57 and Broder (2007), p. 131)

43 Ernst Mößinger mentions 900 men. Bruno Melchior lowers the figure to 400-500 troops.

44 Other Norwegian soldiers were less fortunate, such as Captain Øivind Øi. When the raid on Hamar began he was captured and shot by four paratroops (*Oberleutnant* Götte, *Oberjäger* Willi Müller, *Oberjäger* Alfred Fellmann, and *Oberjäger* Jan van de Sand, all from the Battalion *Stab*). They headed for Oslo in a taxi to gather information on the confused situation in the capital. When he tried to unholster his pistol he was killed by a burst from a MP 38.

45 Wolfgang Henner Peter Lebrecht Graf von Blücher was born on 31 January 1917 in Altengottern, near Mühlhausen. After serving in an anti-tank battalion he volunteered for airborne training. This was at the end of 1939. He was posted to 3./FJR1, based in Stendal. He was awarded the Iron Cross 2nd Class for his part in the Oslo/Elverum.

On 10 May 1940 he jumped with his platoon (the 3rd Platoon 2./FJR1) at Tweede Tol, near Dordrecht (Holland), participating in the intense fighting for control of the city. On 24 May *Leutnant* von Blücher was awarded the EKI and the *Ritterkreuz* for this action. He returned to Norway at the beginning of June and jumped at Narvik. Blücher took part in the assault on Crete in 1941, again leading a Platoon of 2./FJR1. He fought in the area around Heraclion (Candía) airfield, capturing a hill. He was killed in action on 21 May 1941. His two brothers, Lebrecht, 19, and Hans-Joachim, 17, were also killed on Crete.

Fallschirmjäger of the 2nd Company forming up following their landing at Fornebu at approximately 14:00 h on 9 April. The airfield had by then been secured, and these troops were preparing for their first mission on the ground: the capture of the Norwegian Royal Family. (Óscar González)

5

Dombås

"Carry out a drop at Dombås, cut the railway line and telephone communications, and block the road, with the objective of impeding the supply of the Norwegian forces and the British advance."

This was the order given to the 1st Company (1./FJR 1),[46] commanded by *Oberleutnant* Herbert Schmidt. The date chosen for the operation was 14 April, and the paratroops were to take off from Fornebu. The unit had been in the reserve for the attack on the Oslo airfield and was not needed in the assault, given the speed and success of the operation.[47] The action at Dombås was not foreseen in the initial plans for operation *Weserübung*. The decision to take the objective through a rapid action using all the parachute troops available in Norway came from Hitler himself.

The landing by British troops in Namsos, located 220 km north of Trondheim, which took place on 13 April, was the cause of the decision to carry out an operation to impede their advance, creating an obstacle at Dombås, 250 km northwest of Oslo. It was also decided to bomb the British ships with German aircraft operating from Sola, in Stavanger. Finally, German motorized units would attack from Lillehammer in an attempt to link up with the airborne force.

Schmidt's unit arrived in Oslo aboard 15 Ju 52s at 19:00 h on 13 April. The day before they had received the order to fly to Stendal from Schleswig, where they had gone when they had received the order to abort the operation at Fornebu. The 1st Company was augmented with other units: a platoon from the 2nd Company (the *III. Zug* of *Feldwebel* Bobrowski) and the Battalion signals platoon. They landed in Stendal on 12 April at 13:00 h. That same day, at 15:30 h, they received the order from *X. Fliegerkorps* to go immediately to Oslo.

Curiously enough, and there is no clear reason why in the various sources consulted, only the 1st Company was given orders to proceed to Oslo, even though the 3rd and 4th Companies—also under the command of *X. Fliegerkorps*—were quartered in Stendal from 11 April. At this point no Allied landing had taken place in Norway.

Two other *Luftwaffe* units were to take part in the mission together with the paratroops of 1./FJR 1: *II./ Kampfgeschwader zbV 1* , which was to provide the paratroops with information on the possible drop zones, as well as transporting them to the objective and resupplying them. The other unit was the *3./Stuka 1*, tasked with destroying the Åndalsnes-Dombås railway line, especially to the northeast.[48] The paratroops were given the mission of ensuring the destruction of the rail communications and blocking the road (*Riksvei 50*) between Oslo and Trondheim. This would cut Norway in two.

The Preparations for the Mission

The 1st Company was billited at the Stabekk school, not far from Fornebu, awaiting orders. At the airfield the weather was bad on 14 April, which caused some officers to criticise the order to take off. Specifically, the *Stukas* refused to fly as support to the Ju 52s. All of this occuring just one hour before the *Fallschirmjäger* were due to take off. Presented with this situation, Göring gave the order for immediate reports on the meteorological conditions at Dombås. This was done, but it did not assure Schmidt, who only had a chance to see a map of the area minutes before take off. The platoon leader was only able to get a glimpse of the conditions in which his men were to jump. *Oberleutnant* Wilhelm Metscher, of *II./ Kampfgeschwader z.b.V 1*, was also to participate in the mission. He remembers:

"*We transported the 1st Company to Oslo/Fornebu on 13 April. I remember seeing the wrecks of several Ju 52s as we landed, many of them burned. Nevertheless, the airfield was operative, and even had some Me 110s available to protect it. After landing we were billited in a school not far from Fornebu. We sat at the desks and ate while we waited. The transport group's commander, Karl Drewes, got hold of a car in order to travel to Oslo to receive precise orders. I went with him and was surprised on arriving at the command post to see men in Norwegian uniform speaking perfect German. These were infantrymen who had survived the sinking of the* Blücher *and had lost all their equipment. They had been issued dry Norwegian uniforms.*

At mid-day on 14 April the order arrived from the chief of staff of Heeresgruppe Norwegen, *located in an Oslo hotel, for the commander of the transport group, Drewes, and the commander of the* Fallschirmjäger, *Schmidt. When Drewes and Schmidt asked for information on enemy forces in the area they were told the situation was unknown; there were no maps of the objective, and not even the drop zone was known with exactitude. Of course, there was no information on weather conditions over the objective. Nothing at all! And all this was discussed over the phone....*

Once we had returned to the school we were able to obtain a school map that showed our objective: Dombås. We moved out to the aircraft. There was no going back...."

The discussion had taken place with *Oberst iG* Knauss, a *Luftwaffe* officer attached to the Staff of *General* von Falkenhorst, head of *Gruppe XXI*. Hitler's order was being passed on from one man to another like a hot potato. Knauss, halfway between impotence and ignorance—who lacked the experience to conduct a parachute drop—arrived at the conclusion that a reconnaissance flight would be required first in order to clarify the weather conditions over the objective. It was decided that Schmidt would go on the flight.

However, at 16:00 h the *Luftwaffe* commander in Norway, *General* Kitzinger, intervened. He sent his chief of staff to Fornebu, *Generalmajor* Wilhelm Süssmann, with the order to activate and facilitate the mission. He was looking for his "moment of glory," having recently joined Kitzinger's Staff, and pointed out that given an order from the *Führer* neither the weather nor the enemy had an opinion in matters. Therefore, the mission was to be executed immediately.

He got his way with the paratroops, but there was nothing he could do to pressure the "veteran" *Oblt*. Dilley, commander of the *Stukas*. Dilley flatly refused to fly in the fury of the rain and snow. However, what could a young paratroop officer like Schmidt do in the face of the pressure from Süssmann and the threat of a court martial?

Therefore, at 17:00 h 4 officers and 176 other ranks of the *Fallschirmjäger* took off aboard 15 Junkers 52/3m. Each aircraft carried 12 paratroops, as well as 4 weapons containers. "Heavy" armament consisted of 18 MG 34s, plus another four mounted on tripods.

The formation flew in 5 *Kette*, five flights of three planes. The force was distributed as follows: *Oberleutnant* Herbert Schmidt, Company commander (12 men); Commander of 2nd Platoon, *Leutnant* Ernst Mössinger (36 men); *Leutnant* Fritz Becker (Schmidt's 2ic), commander 1st Platoon[49] (36 men); *Feldwebel* Bobrowski leading 3rd Platoon (36 men); *Feldwebel* Alexander Uhlig with 4th Platoon[50] (22 men)[51]; and finally, commanding the Battalion's (I./FJR1) Signals Platoon (36 men) was *Oberleutnant* Gerhold[52].

The Stabekk school, on the outskirts of Oslo. It was here that the 1st Company were awaiting orders. (Óscar González)

The take off was not made during good weather, which resulted in the first *Kette* leaving 15 minutes before the second. The rest took off at intervals of 3 minutes. The order was as follows: *Kompanie Trupp/IV. Zug–Nachrichten Zug–III. Zug–II. Zug–I.Zug*. In any case, the last planes could not take off before 17:45 h. According to Metscher:

"*I was flying the aircraft leading the formation.* Oberstleutnant *Drewes sat on my right as co-pilot;* Unteroffizier *Schoz was radio operator, and Erich Feldmann was flight engineer and 'jump master' for the paratroops (including* Oblt. *Schmidt). We tried to fly in close formation so we would not lose sight of each other in the adverse weather conditions. There was no other option.*"

As the formation was flying over Hamar the Norwegian forces opened fire. Some of the aircraft were flying low, and one was hit by anti-aircraft fire over Lillehammer and was forced to make a crash landing near a farm in an area known as Lysgårdsjordet. All the occupants survived, but they had to open fire on Norwegian troops approaching the plane. In the ensuing fire fight one of the paratroops was killed: the "jump master," who was shot in the head, and three others, including the pilot, were wounded. The Germans were forced to surrender.[53] Thirteen Germans were taken prisoner. This aircraft had been carrying the MG 34s of *Olt*. Gerhold's Signals Platoon.

The German aircraft were forced to fly at low altitude (200 m, and at times as low as 60/80 m) following the rail line from Oslo into the Gudsbrandstal valley towards Dombås. It was no easy task to pilot the Junkers in strong winds and at low altitude, surrounded by thick, snow-covered forests. Only five of the fifteen crews flew at higher altitude by instruments.

Dombås Station, photographed before the war. The occupation of this important communications hub would impede the supply of Norwegian troops, as well as the advance of British troops landing at Namsos on 13 April. (Óscar González)

Commemorative postcard of Herbert Schmidt by Willrich, the celebrated illustrator of the time. (Óscar González)

The Junkers were over the objective at 19:30 h. However, the run of bad luck was to continue. The plane carrying *Feldwebel* Gonchorowski, second in command to Mössinger, was hit and crashed into Mount Gråberget.

The remaining aircraft had to make the drop as quickly as possible, as they were running low on fuel. This meant that the Company was dropped at 6 different places, which also meant that none of the Platoons were able to muster all their effectives once they were on the ground.[54] Metscher continues:

"*When we reached the objective we began to come under fire. I could hear the shots impacting the fuselage. My flight engineer later reported 169 bullet holes. I think he was exaggerating, but there were at least 50 or 60... Fortunately we were able to drop the* Fallschirmjäger *(although in a very disordered way) despite the hail of bullets. We attempted to leave the drop zone as soon as possible, but still did not feel safe. We tried to gain altitude above the clouds. Finally we reached a safe height of 2500/3000 m.*"

Schmidt and his HQ jumped 8 km south of Dombås next to a river and the road that joined the town with Dovre. Becker and his men landed in the mountainous terrain around Hjellsetra, northeast of Dombås. Mössinger's Platoon jumped at Li farm, 3 km south of Dombas, in the main valley. Bobrowski's Platoon landed in the mountainous outskirts of Dombås. Uhlig and his men were in Lora, far to the west, near the river Laagen, and lastly, Gerhold Platoon at Kjörem-Nonshö/Hareggen, a mountainous area southwest of Dombås. All jumped after 20:00 h except Schmidt (19:45 h) and Uhlig (4th Platoon, at 20:00 h).

Above left: Alexander Uhlig, born in Lepizig on 9 Februaury 1919. He volunteered for the first German parachute unit in the autumn of 1937, which would be the seed of the later "*Fallschirmjäger Regiment 1*" formed in 1938. As a member of this unit Uhlig participated in the occupation of the Sudetenland in October 1938. Alexander Uhlig was awarded the Knight's Cross (*Ritterkreuz*) on the 29 October 1944 while he was a *Oberfeldwebel* commanding the 16./FJR 6 in Normandy. (Alexander Uhlig) Above right: *Feldwebel* Gerhard Broder with his son in 1944. Broder was born in 1919, and joined the Army as a paratrooper in 1938. He jumped at Dombås with the 2nd Platoon. He also fought in Crete, Russia, and Monte Cassino. He can be seen here wearing the following decorations: Ribbons of the EKII and the 1941-1942 Eastern Campaign Medal, EKI, *Luftwaffe* Ground Combat badge, silver wound badge, and the parachute insignia (*Assmann model*). (Óscar González)

Below: Panoramic view of Dombås. (Óscar González)

The Norwegian Defenses

The Norwegian unit charged with the defense of Dombås was the 11th Infantry Regiment (11 IR), commanded by *Oberst* David Thue.[55] The men had been mobilized since the first day of the invasion (9 April), and had concentrated at Setnesmoen camp, near the coast of Åndalsnes. They were well trained in the use of the Colt machine-gun. 696 soldiers and 55 officers of the 2nd Battalion, commanded by *kaptein* Naviesaker, were sent to Dombås, according to plans. They traveled by train, arriving on 11 April.

Ivar Sæther, a Norwegian soldier who fought at Dombås. (Mølmen Archive)

On 14 April at 04:00 h the Battalion was deployed as follows: *kaptein* Navelsaker with Battalion HQ and the 6th Company, commanded by *kaptein* Kavli, were at the hotel in Dombås (301 men); *kaptein* Sandnes' 5th Company was in Steinbakken (149 men); the 7th Company, under *løytnant* Rypdal, in Dombvang (approx 145 men); and *løytnant* Berstad's 8th Company were at the town telegraph office, as well as occupying another three buildings (159 men).

On 14 April, at 18:25 h, a message was received from the village of Otta, in the lower valley, reporting German planes heading northwest up the valley, towards Dombås. All the machine-guns in the defensive positions were at action stations within 5 minutes. The troops were expecting to be bombed, and were surprised to see parachutes descending from the first planes. There were also civilian defenders amongst the soldiers (equipped with the issue *Krag-Jörgensen* rifle).

Norwegian troops, well equipped for winter warfare, head for Dombås. (Mølmen Archive)

The Drop at Dombås

Becker (First Platoon)

26 men of this platoon (another 10/12 did not join them, probably landing in Trondheim) jumped at Fokstua, near the train station and the Hjellsetra farm, in the Dovre valley, 8 km northeast of Dombås. This drop was critical due to the very low altitude at which it was made and the strong winds. As a result one soldier was killed when he landed on power lines and another 6 were injured, some of whom were dragged along the ground, unable to cut the cords of their chutes. The injured men were placed in a nearby cabin. Many of the containers could not be found.

Becker was disorientated and without maps, but he managed to find Fokstua station and the railway track going to Trondheim. During 15 April he approached to within 2 km of Dombås, advancing 7 km aboard 3 wagons (with an MG 34 mounted in the first). The 19 paratroops of his command were unkowingly heading straight for the positions of 11 IR. According to Mössinger it was a naive action. One paratrooper died when he was hit by a Norwegian sniper, and the rest were captured along with their weapons; it was the first time the Norwegian troops encountered an MP 38 machine pistol.

Panoramic view of Dombås and the Dovre Valley. (Óscar González)

Above: *Fallschirmjäger* from 1st Platoon captured at Dombås railway station. It is obvious that they were not equipped for the snowy conditions: Their M 38 jump suits were useless compared to the winter camouflage of the Norwegian troops. The Norwegians were armed with the *Krag-Jørgensen* 6.5 mm rifle and *Colt* pistol, produced under licence by *Kongsberg våpenfabrikk*. (Kristian Hosar) Below: View of Dombås from Fokstua, 1st Platoon (Becker) drop zone. The photograph was taken during the war, sometime after the Norwegian surrender. (Óscar González).

Uhlig (Fourth Platoon, machine-guns)

The 22 men of the Platoon jumped at Hosetmoen, 1.5 km southeast of the Lora station and less than 30 km west of Dombås, next to the railway line to Åndalsnes. Some civilians witnessed their landing and immediately telephoned the 11 IR in Dombås. A detail was sent to Lora to capture them. It was getting dark when the Norwegian troops took the road to Åndalsnes. Meanwhile, Uhlig was heading from Hosetmoen to Flittibua, with the intention of finding the road to Dombås.

Above: Lora, west of Dombås. The position was occupied during the late afternoon of 14 April 1940 by the men of 4th Platoon, commanded by *Feldwebel* Alexander Uhlig. To the right of the road (out of the photograph) is Flittibua. The arrow behind the cabin marks the spot where the Germans set up a machine-gun position. Günther Backhaus was mortally wounded in the fighting. (Alexander Uhlig) Below: Lora, rail track. The arrow indicates the place where Uhlig's men (4th Platoon) cut the telephone line on the afternoon of 14 April. (Alexander Uhlig)

Temporary grave at Dombås of *Fallschirmjäger* Günther Backhaus (21/10/1913–14/04/1940). He was assigned as the n° 2 in a machine-gun team in Uhlig's 4th Platoon. He died from his wounds during the Platoon's long march through the snow. The building in the background was a church that was still under construction in April 1940. According to local inhabitants, two other makeshift graves (*Leutnant* Erich Schiffrer and his observer, Schneider, crew members from a shot-down Ju 52) can be found next to the school. (Óscar González)

The Norwegians soon found them, coming under machine-gun fire from the *Fallschirmjäger*. The troops took cover. Two officers, armed only with Colt M 1914 pistols, attempted to observe the German positions, but they too were forced to take cover from the German machine-guns. Paratrooper Günther Backhaus, 27 years old, was killed in the exchange of shots.[56]

Uhlig came to the conclusion that it would be impossible to advance along the road. The Germans had to advance 13 km along the banks of the river Lågen in order to approach Dombås. In the early hours of the morning of 16 April Uhlig and his men found themselves in Flitti, next to the river. It had been a hard march, lasting 6 hours over difficult ground, mostly covered in snow, and carrying the heavy machine-guns. However, the Norwegians had been controlling all their movements, and finally Uhlig had no option but to surrender at mid-day on the 16th at a place called Hov, south of Lesja and 12 km east of Lora. Uhlig narrates his experience in Dombås thus:

"We had to make our drop around 250 km from Oslo (350 km by road), in a mountainous area and with a lot of snow on the ground. We were not equipped with suitable camouflaged uniforms for the terrain. The Norwegian superiority was patent. However, in spite of these factors against us, each platoon in the Company was determined to do its duty as best it could. By 16 April we had run out of ammunition and had to surrender."

Uhlig's 4th Platoon spent the night of 15/16 April in a cabin such as this. (Alexander Uhlig)

Gerhold (Signals Platoon)

The Platoon had lost some of its effectives and all of its machine-guns (the Platoon's 6th Group) in the aircraft brought down over Lillehammer. The other two planes in the Platoon's *Kette* dropped the remaining 24 men and their equipment in the mountainous area 13 km southwest of Dombås, next to a point 1,579 m high on Mount Fauttjøn, in the area of Kjøremnonshøe. The area was covered in snow and the men did not have skis, only a bicycle they were able to requisition.[57]

They made contact with a group from the 1st Platoon, but all of them were lost and tired, so Gerhold ordered them to dig holes in the snow in which to pass the night.

On the morning of the 15th they descended the valley, marching north, where they encountered a column of Norwegian trucks some 6 km from the road to Åndalsnes. They managed to approach the Dalom farm, south of Bølia, 9 km west of Dombås, but were discovered and came under machine-gun fire. The Platoon, with only 4 rifles between them, surrendered on 15 April. The farm had been surrounded by Norwegian troops equipped for winter warfare.

Schmidt (Company HQ - *Stab*), Mössinger (2nd Platoon), Bobrowski (3rd Platoon)

Schmidt and his group (12 men) flew following the rail line until they were dropped near the Dombås-Dovre road, in the Hagevoll/Bjørkhoel area,[58] about 6 km south of Dombås. As soon as they landed Schmidt fired a red flare to indicate his position. The group soon ran into problems, as they were unable to find their weapons containers.

Schmidt's group had not been long on the ground when his men stopped and captured a taxi. As soon as the occupants were out of the vehicle (the taxi driver and a woman), several *Fallschirmjäger* got in and headed for Dombås. Schmidt halted as he neared each bend in the road, and this prudent action was to save the paratroopers from disaster. At one of the stops he observed two Norwegian trucks heading towards them. A 6.5mm *Madsen* machine-gun was mounted on the roof of one of the trucks, which immediately opened fire on the taxi. The Germans returned fire, forcing the Norwegians to withdraw, but Schmidt had been hit twice in the abdomen. *Oberjäger* Jung was also seriously wounded, and later died, while another *Oberjäger* was taken prisoner. No more than half an hour had passed since the drop, and Schmidt found himself wounded and without his Company.

Mössinger had jumped only 3 km south of Dombås, in the vicinity of Li farm, at a place called Hjellådalen (2/3 km from Lie). Mössinger heard the shooting between the Norwegians and Schmidt's men, and with the main body of his group—around 24 men—joined them to the east at Øien. Mössinger[59] describes the events surrounding his drop:

Above and next page: The *Fallschirmjäger* jumped at Dombås at approximately 1900h. The photograph shows part of Mössinger's group jumping 3 km south of the town, near Li farm, Hjellådalen (2/3 km from Lie). (*Dovre Kommune*, courtesy of Arne Gunnar)

"We made a flight of about 260 km, most of which was done at low altitude, along the Grudbran valley. As we flew over Hamar we drew heavy anti-aircraft fire. Of the 15 Ju 52s, 2 were brought down by the Norwegian batteries and the remaining thirteen planes dispersed, which ment that the drop was dispersed. We formed a total of 6 isolated groups (Kampfgruppen). *This prevented us following the initial plan, which was based on all of us being dropped in a compact group south of Dombås.*

We had lost part of our Platoon (Gonchorowski's 5th Group[60]) when their Ju 52 was brought down over Dombås. The two remaining planes dropped their Fallschirmjäger *around 19:20 h. Of these, one was killed upon landing."*

Schmidt, wounded as he was,[61] did not cede command to the next officer in rank, *Leutnant* Mössinger, but decided to form a defensive position at the farm in Hagevoll-Bjørkhoel, about 4.5 km southeast of Dombås. All of this occured during the early hours of 15 April. Nevertheless, it was the latter who was to direct German movements from then on.

As had happened with Mössinger's Platoon, Bobrowski had also lost one of his Groups. He and a reduced number of his Platoon (29 *Fallschirmjäger*) jumped 3 km from Engjekollan, on Mount Hejllhø, landing at a point 1,173 m high, around 3/4 km east of Dombås.

However, 10 minutes before part of his unit (1 *Feldwebel* and 6 men) had mistakenly jumped over the town, south of the station. *Feldwebel* Sagasser, the Platoon 2ic, and *Gefreiter* Kurt Wietzig were killed either as they descended, or in the brief hand to hand fighting that follwed. Another two paratroops were wounded and the rest taken prisoner.

Bobrowski managed to approach to within 400 m of Dombås, reaching the road between the town and Dovre. There he was engaged by Norwegian troops, 4 km to the south of the town, and two *Fallschirmjäger* were killed (an *Oberjäger* and a private). Finally, he was able to link up with a patrol from the 2nd Platoon, returning from sabotaging the rail line north of Dombås. Brobowski and his men—28 in total—joined Mössinger/Schmidt on 15 April.

A German soldier poses next to the remains of Mössinger's 5th group's aircraft (that of *Feldwebel* Gonchorowski). This Ju 52 was hit by machine-gun fire from the Norwegian positions around Dombås, resulting in the death of the pilot and observer. Twelve *Fallschirmjäger* managed to jump 1.5 km southeast of the town, but all except three men were wounded by the machine-gun fire. The plane crashed into Mount Gråberget, along with the weapons container. The survivors, armed only with their pistols, surrendered the following day (15 April). (Óscar González)

A Norwegian family poses next to the remains of the Ju 52 shot down over Dombås. This photograph was taken after the German occupation of the town. (Øivind Solvik)

The Net Tightens

There remained a force totalling 2 officers and 61 other ranks (4 groups in a platoon), deployed in an area 30 x 15 km. Nevertheless, they were able to cut the railway line northeast of the position occupied by Mössinger, the telephone lines, and the road (during the 15th and early hours of the 16th).[62] They used sand to write messages in the snow for the *Luftwaffe* active in the area: "*Ammunition and food!We are resisting!*" Finally, they established another, smaller defensive position 1 km to the southeast, on a hill near the road and Hagevoll, at a place called Rausandhaugen. They also captured a number of Norwegian troops in several engagements.

The Norwegians hardly had sufficient forces to quickly crush the perimeter established by Schmidt, as almost all their resources were being employed in the south.

At 07:00 h on 15 April, around 70 men of 11 IR attacked from the east, without knowing the exact disposition of the enemy. The *Fallschirmjäger* reacted quickly and opened fire, repelling the attack and killing two Norwegian soldiers. A German aircraft flying overhead also intervened, killing another Norwegian.

However, the day was to be marked by an incident. A column of 24 Norwegian soldiers, aboard two trucks, escorting several fleeing ministers, was making its way along the Dombås road. By coincidence they ran into the paratroops. There were several cars behind the lead truck, and in them traveled the ministers (one of them was Anders Rasmus Frihagen, minister of commerce) and an English diplomat; in another was a businessman

The Ju 52 piloted by Wilhelm Metscher. He had to make an emergency landing at Hønefoss on the return flight to Oslo-Fornebu. According to Metscher, "*bearing in mind that the aircraft had been hit, it was a masterly landing; nobody was hurt. We were 60 km north of Oslo, but we were able to contact Fornebu by telephone from a neighboring farm. After spending a frozen night in the cabin, a rescue group came for us in the early morning.*" Metscher wrote on the photograph, which had been taken by the Norwegians: "*Mein Tante Ju*" (Mi Tía Ju, as it was referred to by the German pilots). (Wilhelm Metscher)

Hagevold (or Hagevoll) farm, next to the Dombås-Dovre road, the first of the *Fallschirmjäger* defensive positions. The photograph was taken in April 1941. (Ernst Mössinger)

called Gittersen. The rear of the column was occupied by the other truck. These vehicles were intercepted by the *Fallschirmjäger*, who opened fire on them. Gittersen and 3 of the Norwegian soldiers were killed. The survivors rapidly abandoned the vehicles. When the *Fallschirmjäger* inspected the vehicles they found one of them contained 2,000,000 Norwegian Crowns. However, it was not money, but rather food and medical assistance that the paratroops urgently needed. Schmidt describes the event:

"*At mid-day a liaison arrived at the command post and reported:* 'Herr Oberleutnant, *we have found a large grey parcel full of money.' The* Hauptfeldwebel *quickly confirmed the news. An enemy car had tried unsuccessfully to traverse the road during the night and had been stopped by our men. On closer inspection it was found to be carrying money, which was duly counted. We could hardly carry it because of the weight; we had approximately 2 million Crowns in our hands. We were suddenly aware of our newfound wealth; we were rich men. We all began thinking about how we would transfer the booty to Oslo. The news of the treasure spread like wildfire through our position, from trench to trench. Everybody was enthusiastic because we had relieved the enemy of his money.*"[63]

Present day view of Hagevold, looking towards Dovre. (Øivind Solvik)

The Norwegian command decided to maintain the pressure from the east and ordered more troops to the area, as it became vital to reopen the road and railway link. Control of the road was crucial and necessary for the escape of the King, Haakon VII.

Reinforcements came from a company of the 5th Infantry Regiment (*Östoppland*), commanded by 41-year-old *kaptein* Eiliv Austlid. No sooner had the attack begun than Austlid and six of his men[64] died under a hail of bullets from the German positions. Austlid died at 13:00 h, shot through the heart attempting to take out a German machine-gun nest. During this attack the *Fallschirmjäger* captured 32 of Austlid's men (4 of whom were wounded), as well as capturing 3 Colt machine-guns and ammunition. With the failure of the counter-attack, another company from the 5th Infanttry Regiment under *kaptein* Bottheim[65] approached from the south of the Dovre valley to Dombås. By mid-day on 16 April they were in position to attack.

Another unit, the 5th Company from 11 IR, under *kaptein* Sandnes, made an attack from the west at 06:00 h the same day. They tried to approach by train, but a stretch of the line had been blown up by the paratroops, who tried all means to insure the Norwegian pincer movement failed. As they could not approach by train the 5th Company returned to Dombås. Immediately, 70 soldiers boarded five trucks and headed southeast, in the direction of the Dovre valley. A woman informed them that the Germans had spent the night at the nearby Ulekleiv farm. The Norwegians decided to continue on foot. When they were within 350 m of Hagevoll they came under fire from the German positions on the hill. Two Norwegians were killed and the rest decided to return to Dombås. The German positions had been located but they were resisting.

The fighting continued. Pressure brought to bear on the Germans mounted and was aggravated by the heavy snow that began falling. This also hindered the use of the

Expeditionary Corps.

Sargeant of the I. *Fallschirmjäger*.

Norwegian air force lietenant.

Color map showing German airborne operations in Norway. (Illustration: Iñaki Merino)

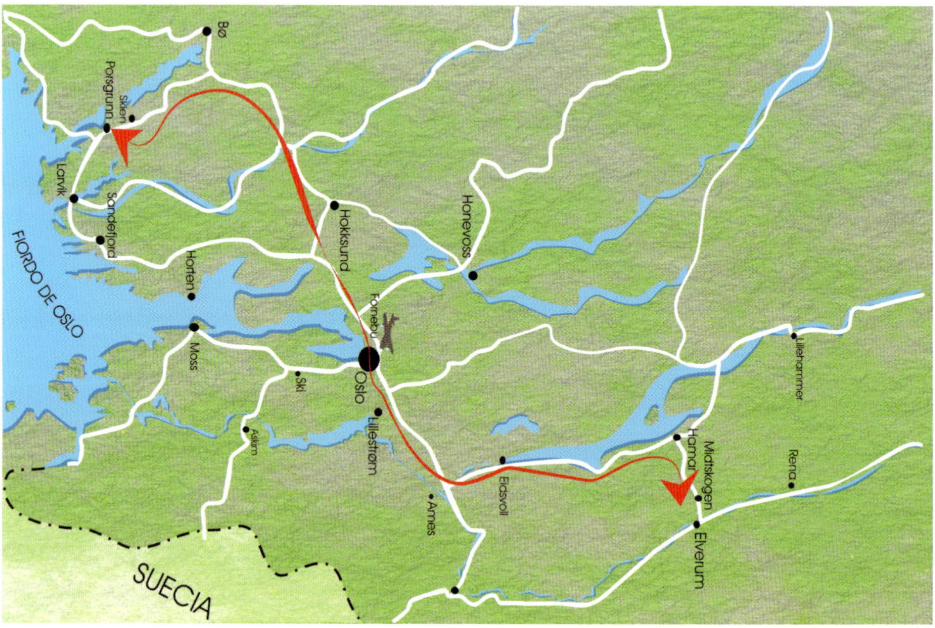

Color map showing the route taken by the paratroops from Oslo to Elverum. (Illustration: Iñaki Merino)

View of Narvik in 1940. ("Narvik im Bild")

Above: View of the Rombaken fjord, at Straumen, in 1940. ("Narvik im Bild") Below: View of Narvik in July 2006. The photograph was taken from the Ankenes Heights, looking north, on spot height 295. On 28 May 1940, Poles and Germans fought over control of these Heights, which were vital for holding Narvik. On that day elements of the company commanded by *Oberleutnant* Rieger (*Gebirgsjäger* dropped at Bjørnfjell) counter-attacked, and in bitter hand to hand fighting partially occupied the position. However, it was in vain, as they were soon forced to retire. Rieger was wounded and taken prisoner, and Warrant officer Bollenberger was killed. (Simon Orchard)

Drop zone and initial positions held by the *Fallschirmjäger* at Dombås. (Illustration: Iñaki Merino)

FOKSTUA
DOMBÅS
HAGEVOLL
LINDSØ
DOVRE

Paratrooper's M-38 helmet. (Bernardo Castañón Collection).

Narvik Shield awarded to *Fallschirmjäger* Albert Valjeur for his participation in the Norwegian campaign. (Óscar González).

Luftwaffe parachute insignia with the mark of G.H. Osang, a Dresden jeweller. (Óscar González)

Epaulet of an *Oberfeldwebel* of *Gebirgsjäger* Regiment 137, the mountain unit that received parachute training. (Óscar González)

Badges belonging to Gerhard Broder, who jumped at Dombås, Narvik, and Crete, demonstrated by the Narvik Shield and the Crete cuff title. His parachute insignia is the "Assmann" model. (Gerhard Broker)

Private's "*Fallschirmjäger* Regiment 1" cuff title. One of the earliest insignia in regards to the paratrooper uniform. It was instituted in 1939, and it was only authorized to be worn on the right sleeve of the four-pocket jacket. (Óscar González)

Paratrooper helmet M-38, MP-40 rifle—evolution of the MP-38 used in Norway—and the P-38 pistol and its holster. (Bernardo Castañón Collection, Jaime Chasco, and Elías Ruiz)

Bjørnfell today.

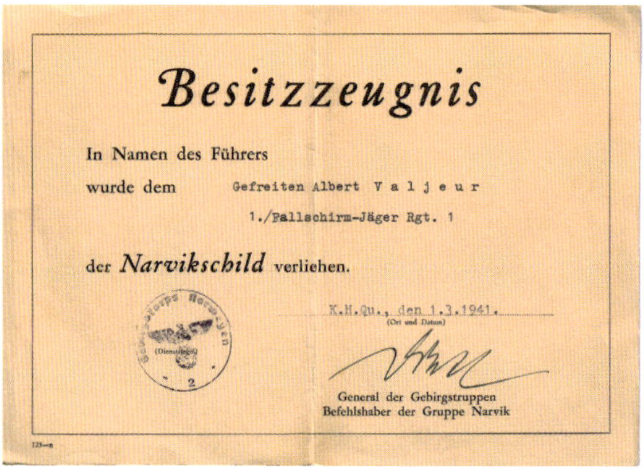

Besitzzeugnis

In Namen des Führers

wurde dem Gefreiten Albert Valjeur

1./Fallschirm-Jäger Rgt. 1

der ***Narvikschild*** verliehen.

K.H.Qu., den 1.3.1941.
(Ort und Datum)

General der Gebirgstruppen
Befehlshaber der Gruppe Narvik

Document conferring the Narvik Shield on *Fallschirmjäger* Albert Valjeur, signed by Dietl. (Óscar González)

Wilhelm Gott, leader of the paratroopers who took a leading role in the capture of Fornebu airfield.

Illustration of Herbert Schmidt, leader of the German paratroopers in Dombås.

Norwegian mortars. Captain Sandnes gave the order to send more reinforcements. Captain Kavli's 6th Company was tasked with reinforcing the position.

Without doubt the day had worn out the Germans in Dombås. Their situation gave little room for hope.

During the night of 15 April the Norwegian net had begun to tighten. The patrols sent out by Mössinger from Hagevoll confirmed what they all feared: they were surrounded, and Norwegian reinforcements were arriving (1 platoon) from Åndalsnes. Three patrols were sent out during the early hours of the 16th, each consisting of two privates and an *Oberjäger*. None returned.[66] Later it was confirmed that one of the men had been killed and the rest taken prisoner. A Norwegian soldier had also been killed in the action.

The skirmishes continued all day, with more Germans taken prisoner.

6th Company, 11 IR, occupied the western flank while the 5th made new attacks, the last with the mortars. The pressure on the German paratroops was increasing, and they finally decided to raise the white flag. It was 17:00 h, and they needed to gain time at all cost.

Feldwebel Bobrowski, on the left, leader of 3rd Platoon (from the 2nd Company), and *Leutnant* Mössinger, leader of the 2nd Platoon, visiting Dombås in April 1941, a year after the attack. Here they pose next to Johan Jörgensson Hagevold, then 72 years old, owner of the Hagevold (Hagevoll) farm where the *Fallschirmjäger* made their first stand. Mössinger is wearing the parachute insignia of the "*Heer*" ("*Fallschirmschützenabzeichen des Heeres*"), showing that he had undergone the FIB (Infantry Paarachute Battalion) course. A member of Schmidt's group, he was the only one with this insignia. (Ernst Mössinger)

A prisoner took a message to the Norwegian lines. The man in question was Captain Austlid's driver, captured the day before. The message was as follows: the Germans held 40 prisioners and threatened to shoot them if the Norwegians did not cease firing. Captain Sandnes decided to use the same strategy against Schmidt. He sent a German prisoner (presumibly *Feldwebel* Alexander Uhlig, leader of the 4th Platoon) to inform Schmidt that they had over 100 prisoners who would meet the same fate should the Germans carry out their threat.

The Germans were left with no other option than to flee in order to avoid being surrounded. At 22:30 h on 16 April, 56 *Fallschirmjäger*, together with 35 Norwegian prisoners, broke out through the left flank, moving southeast in Norwegian vehicles under cover of darkness. However, they ran into Captain Bottheim's Company and there was another intense fire fight.

The fact was that the Norwegian defense minister had issued an order the previous night insisting that the "*Dombås road must be reopened in two hours.*" The route was of vital importance; the King, Haakon VII, and his government were in Otta, on their way to Åndalsnes, with the intention of reaching the north of the country.[67] There was the serious risk that they would be captured. Bottheim's unit were not sure where the Germans were. The Norwegians advanced along the road, dispersing to avoid the risk of being surprised. They ran into the Germans when they neared Landheim. The paratroops opened fire, wounding several Norwegians. Now Schmidt's position was known. What was worse was that the Germans had captured four of the Company's officers. Schmidt and his *Fallschirmjäger*, together with their prisoners, were able to dig in near Tofte, not far from the Lindsø hill. They had held their first defensive position from 11:00 h on the 15th to 22:30 h on the 16th.

Mössinger remembers events:

"*During the night of the 16/17 April the Norwegians located our position and we were forced to march. We were approximately 47/48 paratroops, plus 3 seriously and 6 lightly wounded men. We also had about 35 prisoners with us. We drove south, carrying the wounded in the requisitioned cars. However, after 700 m we found the road blocked at Arnekleiv, some 6.5 km southeast of Dombås. They formed a line, blocking our path from the railway line to the river. We tried to fight our way through. We finally broke through, but at the cost of 2 men killed and another 4 wounded. The Norwegians also took casualties. We took around 20 prisoners as well as capturing several machine-guns.*

We were all exhausted, and after continuing another 2 km along the road we made a brief stop near a place called Sørigard. Meanwhile, Bobrowski and I made an exploration of the area and located another defensive position. This was a high point near the hamlet of Lindsø, 2 km to the east. From there we could control both the railway line and the road, and it also made a good spot for the Ju 52s to find and resupply us."

Their situation was desparate, and Schmidt was deteriorating from his wound, being carried on a door by his men. They could only hope for a miracle. The Germans set up a defensive position. However, Captain Sandnes was controlling all their movements.

Ernst Mössinger (left) and Bobrowski on the Ronn bridge, near Dombås, during the visit made in April 1941. (Ernst Mössinger)

Mössinger continues:

"*Without the enemy being able to stop us (the praise for this must go to Brobowski, who was masterly at deceiving the Norwegians), we approached Lindsø before mid-day on 17 April. Of our group of 63 paratroops, 4 were dead and 13 were wounded or had disappeared.*[68] *All those wounded who were fit to fight made a tremendous effort to reach the defensive position on the hill. The 50 or so Norwegian prisoners helped us with the more seriously wounded men. At this point I should mention the action of* Jäger *Pähler, who alone, armed only with a pistol, took 11 prisoners.*

We set to work and were able to cut the road. With our remaining explosives we blew up the railway line. The defensive perimeter (between 200 to 300 m diameter) was protected by 7 machine-guns, which gave us considerable firepower. Nevertheless, our ammunition was scarce. One of our Fallschirmjäger *died in the fighting with the Norwegian vanguard, while another and a Norweggian prisoner were wounded.*

Some of the inhabitants of Lindsø abandoned the hamlet. Others stayed put, and these sought protection from the fighting alongside the wounded in the stone-walled stable."

On 18 April the *Fallschirmjäger* received ammunition and food dropped by a Ju 52. Regarding the first: "*it was dropped without a parachute, and this resulted in 90% being rendered unusable,*" according to Mössinger. The paratroops were able to communicate with the aircraft.[69] Schmidt became more pessimistic as the day wore on. In the afternoon the pressure was racheted up as grenades exploded all around. There was a brief ceasefire at 17:00 h when both sides were able to recover their dead and attend to the wounded. During

Temporary graves belonging to *Fallschirmjäger* fallen in action. The infantry in the photograph arrived after the town had fallen into German hands on 1 May 1940. The epitaph reads "*Fallen in Dovre for the* Führer *and the Fatherland.*" (Óscar González)

this pause Sandnes communicated to Schmidt that if he did not surrender, the fighting would continue without any consideration for the prisoners and hostages.[70]

Surrender and Captivity

On 19 April the Norwegians decided to take the initiative. From the west the 11 IR had brought forward their mortars. From the east the Norwegians had a field gun and numerous effectives. They opened fire with mortars and the battery of 75mm guns.

Lieutenant Karsten Sveen,[71] an officer in Bottheim's Company, was sent to parly with Schmidt. He was chosen because of his almost fluent German. Sveen made a makeshift white flag and began walking unarmed towards the German positions. He was blindfolded and brought before Schmidt. Sveen asked him to surrender, but Schmidt would not give way, arguing that "*a German officer never surrenders*." Schmidt declined the offer and pointed out he held prisoners and civilian hostages (51 military personnel, including *Major* Kjøs, and 12 civilians). The Norwegian insisted that they too held 90 paratroops prisoner, and that surrender was the most reasonable solution: "*if I do not return in 20 minutes*—he continued—*the final assault will begin; the number of those who die will depend on you*." Schmidt suggested that one of his men speak to the Norwegian officer in command, Captain Sandnes, to negotiate. Sveen agreed, and he returned to his lines with the paratrooper, who was to speak by phone to the *kaptein*.

The bombardment continued, and a grenade exploded in the door of the building housing Schmidt, wounding a *Fallschirmjäger* in the head. This was enough to sink the morale of the unit. Even so Schmidt refused to surrender, exhorting his men to keep going and carry out their "*duty to fight for the* Führer." Then another grenade exploded, wounding another paratrooper. Two Germans fell this way, while three others were gravely wounded (one later dying).

Kaptein Sandnes gave Schmidt's envoy no choice: "*either surrender or we attack. If you choose the first, fire three shots*." The paratrooper returned with the message.

The fighting in Lindsø had ended, and the German paratroops are led into captivity surrounded by civilians and Norwegian soldiers as they pass by the Klokkarhaugen farm. (Dovre Kommune, courtesy of Arne Gunnar)

Just at that moment another Ju 52 flew over the area to drop more ammunition and supplies, but Schmidt transmitted the message "*Wir ergeben uns* (we are surrendering)."[72] Ten minutes had passed since the ultimatum, and it was impossible to gain more time. Three red flares went up over the German position to indicate the surrender. At 14:00 h some 40 to 45 Germans stopped resisting.[73]

Mössinger recalls the details of the surrender as follows:

"*During the fighting at our final position at Lindsø 6* Fallschirmjäger *were killed and another 5 wounded. Finally Bobrowski and myself, together with the four Group chiefs, decided to surrender, and Schmidt gave his consent; he had been against this course of action, believing reinforements would come from the south.* Jäger *Ungeheuer and* Jäger *Broder, who were crewing the last remaining machine-gun, had run out of ammunition.*

We were taken to Dovre and put in a cinema. They gave us our first hot meal in 5 days. The Norwegian civilians also assisted with feeding us. Our first night as prisoners of war passed quietly. The next day we were taken to Dombås, and there we were 'shown' to some high ranking British officers. We were exhausted, and felt like animals being exhibited to the public at some zoo. We underwent our first interrogation at the hands of British and Norwegian officers. However, the Norwegian behavior to our wounded was exemplary, keeping their promise made in the surrender agreement; that is, we were not handed over to the British. They took them immediately to hospital.

We were moved from one provisional camp to another. The dreams of sleeping in a bed were unrealized, and we had to accustom ourselves to the fish soup served daily."

Albert Valjeur was one of the *Fallschirmjäger* in Mössinger's Platoon. His testimony adequately describes the reality of the battle:

"Our mission was to stop the British advance to Oslo, while at the same time facilitating the passage of our own troops into northern Norway. The latter became a reality on 6 May, when German troops occupied Dombås. For us Fallschirmjäger, *they came as our saviors, liberating us after three weeks in captivity (...)*

My first jump into enemy territory was a far cry from what I had first imagined. Norway is a mountainous country, and offers few opportunities for parachute drops. Before boarding the Ju 52s, the recce aircraft reported that the objective was covered by a dense fog which made the drop impossible. However, a little later the order arrived from the Oberkommandant*: 'the drop must take place immediately.'*

The unit, composed of 180 Fallschirmjäger *aboard 15 Ju 52s, took off in 5* Kette, *each of three planes. We climbed to 3,000 m and headed towards Dombås. Before arriving at the objective, the commander of the group gave the order to descend below the clouds and fog in order to get a better view of the drop zone. This caused the Norwegian anti-aircraft*

Hotel in Dombås. The Germans were brought here from Dovre and interviewed by British officers ("*as if we were savages,*" in the opinion of Ernst Mössinger). However, they were not handed over to the British. (Óscar González)

The *Fallschirmjäger*, once prisoners, were taken from Dombås to Kristiansund, where they were held in the school. This photograph, taken by Albert Valjeur, shows a Norwegian soldier standing guard. The fact that the Germans were allowed to keep their cameras demonstrates the relaxed attitude of the Norwegians. (Óscar González)

Albert Valjeur in a photograph taken in 1941 after Crete. Born in 1920, he volunteered for the *Fallschirmjäger* in November 1939. Dombås was his baptism of fire, jumping with the 2nd Platoon under Mössinger. He also took part in the fighting at Narvik. In 1941 he jumped at Crete, with the mission of destroying the Gournes radar station near Heraklion. In his own words he lived through an inferno when he landed directly on British positions (Wolfgang von Blücher, 17, the youngest of the three brothers killed in Crete, was in his platoon). He also fought at Leningrad, Schlüsselburg, Orel, and Monte Cassino, where he was severely wounded in the neck. Following a year in rehabillitation, he returned to the front with the rank of *Feldwebel*, ending the war as an American prisoner. (Óscar González)

batteries to open fire. We suffered numerous hits and a fire, but fortunately none of us were hurt. However, the second aircraft in our Kette *caught fire and crashed into a rock face.*[74] *Our pilot and the other Ju 52 managed to gain altitude and avoid the AA. Once this was accomplished we were given the signal to jump. We jumped in a heavy snow storm onto ground covered with the same. Our weapons containers, which were dropped with us, sank into the thick snow and we were unable to recover them.*

We headed for the valley and found a small wood. We dragged ourselves over the snow in order to reach it. Once done we were more protected and under cover, and we could rest a little. But the Norwegians, equipped with skis, had located our position and moved towards us.

The following morning we decided to approach the valley, and that was when we came under fire. We suffered our first casualties, and we could only defend ourselves with machine-pistols, pistols, and hand grenades: short range weapons. The rest of our weapons were lost in the snow.

The Norwegians now knew our position and had us in their sights, but out of range of our own weapons. We took many casualties.

We had to conserve ammunition and remain silent during long hours. We were unable to lower our guard that day. Two days had passed since the jump and the cold was unbearable. We had to move to stop ourselves from freezing. However, the shooting continued and the casualties mounted. We could hardly attend to our injured comrades. We resisted another

According to Alexander Uhlig, "*3 or 4 days after arriving in Kristiansund* [28 April], *a unit of Ju 87* Stukas *attacked the town. It was clear that our forces did not know where we were. We found ourselves in a difficult situation, but we were lucky, as the wooded buildings around us were destroyed, the school was undamaged.*" (Óscar González)

two days like that. Our ammunition ran out and so did our other supplies. We were unable to bury the dead or tend the wounded. We had no choice but to surrender.

The Norwegians took us prisoner. Remember, they were troops well equipped for the snow, with skis. I also remember that they collected up our dead and tended to our wounded. In the valley, during these first moments as prisoners of war, we were correctly treated by the Norwegians. They took us to the town of Dovre. We were gathered together at a large building, where they attended to us without too many considerations. We had to sleep on the floor, but in our damp uniforms it was impossible to get to sleep.

We were taken to an island aboard a fishing boat. We remained there for three weeks until we were liberated by our troops on the 6 May.

It was during this short time that I came to realize that the war was not some infantile game of 'good guys versus bad guys.'"

Uhlig remembers in detail what happened during the days of captivity that followed:

"A provisional camp in Åndalsnes was the gathering point for the prisoners of 1./FJR1. While we were being taken there Oberjäger *Hartwig and* Gefreiter *Koslowski escaped, but were soon recaptured by the British, who were retreating rapidly towards Åndalsnes, then taken to Great Britain and then on to Canada. We were reunited 7 years later in Camp n° 23, back in Britain.*

We were taken to Kristiansund aboard small fishing boats (131 men in total) on the night of 20 April. This was a picturesque town located between three islands on Norway's west coast, 60 km north of Åndalsnes. Our new prison camp was a school located in the center of town. Conditions were 'primitive.' We were guarded agressively. Our guards would shoot towards the windows if we dared to peer out.

The "prison" school at Kristiansund today. (Alexander Uhlig)

The men were transferred from Kristiansund to the island of Averøy on 29 April. The "*Bruhagen*" school became their new prison. They were liberated by a machine-gun detachment of RGG ("*Luftwaffe Feld Regiment General Göring*") on 5 May. This photograph was taken moments after their liberation. (Óscar González)

We were joined by other prisoners, one of whom was a civilian, a German businessman who had nothing to do with the war. The others were the seaplane crew from the cruiser Hipper, *a* Leutnant *of the* Luftwaffe, *pilot of an Arado 96, and an* Oberleutnant *observer from the* Kriegsmarine. *They had been shot down while attacking a Royal Navy vessel, captured by Norwegian Navy personnel, and accomodated in a hotel during their first days of captivity.*

Three or four days after landing on Kristiansund,[75] *the town was attacked by a squadron of Ju 87* Stukas. *It was immediately clear that our people were unaware of our presence there. We were in a difficult situation, but as the wooden buildings surrounding us were damaged or destroyed the school building remained intact. The town was attacked again on 29 April. This time the school was hit, and we were forced to abandon it before it burned to the ground. We were escorted to the port, crossing the town in flames as we did so. We were forced to wait for our boats in the middle of the bombing. Each of us remained silent, knowing this could be our last moment. Our guards were not in a better position, something that did not worry me, as they had been shooting at unarmed prisoners during the last few days. I only felt sorry for a pretty young Norwegian girl, daughter of the officer in command of our guard detail. During each air attack she became stricken with fear. Unfortunately I was unable to console her, but she did at least distract me from the deplorable situation in which I found myself.*

Left: The same view of the "*Bruhagen*" school 60 years later. (Alexander Uhlig) Right: The "*Bruhagen*" school 60 years later. (Alexander Uhlig)

Finally, we were taken to the island of Averøy. The Bruhagen *school was to be our new place of internment, but with the same miserable treatment. On the morning of the following day, 30 April, a shot broke the calm. A guard had fired at one of the closed windows of the school, killing our comrade* Gefreiter *Gerhard Schallok from the Signals Platoon (5th Platoon). Our morale was affected due to this cowardly murder.*

On 5 May we awoke to a lovely Spring day. Suddenly, something drew my attention. Was it the familiar sound of a BMW motorcycle, or was I really dreaming? What happened next was like a scene from a movie: our school had been surrounded by several motorcycles with sidecars. Next, the machine-gunners trained their weapons on the school while the riders took cover. The action only lasted seconds: there was no order and no shots. Silence reigned for a few moments, and then our guards came out with their hands up. With great precision we had been liberated by a machine-gun detachment from the RGG (Luftwaffe Feld Regiment General Göring).

After this we could not enjoy a long awaited vacation in Germany. Just 9 days later I jumped again with my unit (we were the first) at Narvik."

Including the man killed on the island, German losses in the operation were 15/18 *Fallschirmjäger* killed in action,[76] 10 seriously wounded, and 20 with various lighter wounds. The Norwegians lost 19 men killed and another 20 wounded.

Following the Norwegian surrender in the south the *Fallschirmjäger* were liberated from the camp. They were given a week's leave in Oslo.

Averøy, 5 May 1940. Members of "*Luftwaffe Feld Regiment General Göring*" who liberated the *Fallschirmjäger*. (Óscar González)

Some Considerations

The easy victories won by the *Fallschirmjäger* in Denmark, Oslo, and Stavanger encouraged Hitler to use them as a vanguard in the improvised operation at Dombås. The *Führer* had placed great hope in the first airborne operation of the *Fallschirmjäger*, so that as a result of the success on 9 April he had no doubts in using the elite of his armed forces again.

We have already seen that the operations carried out by the German paratroops in *Weserübung* revealed themselves to be anything but "easy" victories. At the Norwegian airfields the situation could be resolved because the German's military preparation was considerably superior to their opponents, who never had the initiative. This factor, and to a large part luck, avoided disaster.

But the action at Dombås was a total failure. Responsibility for this does not lie with the 4 officers and 174 other ranks who took part. Only two people, together with Göring, must take the blame. One of them was *Generalmajor* Wilhelm Süssmann, the *Luftwaffe* liaison officer assigned to the Staff of General Falkenhorst. His was the tactical responsibility that the operation went ahead without any other considerations, despite the unfavorable weather conditions.[77] The other was the Company commander, *Oberleutnant* Schmidt, who supported the attack without reservations from the beginning. He had been waiting for his "moment" ever since his failed participation at Fornebu on the 9th. Later, his naive optimism would cost dearly. The warnings from both the transport and *Stuka* pilots that the conditions were not right for success went unheeded. Sufficient preparations had not been mede to ensure the success of the operation. Planning had been nonexistent; the orders were issued to the *Fallschirmjäger* and the pilots over the telephone from the OKW in Berlin at noon on that same day (14 April)!

Oberleutnant Herbert Schmidt recovering from his wounds in hospital in Berlin on 31 May 1940. Born in 1912, he was a member of FJR1 from 1938 to 1940. In March 1940 he was given command of the 1st Company. His men considered him enthusiastic and active, although Mössinger and other survivors of Dombås were very critical of his "*rash and naive attitude*." After being captured, and seriously wounded, he was taken to Ålesund hospital, finally being liberated at the beginning of May. He was awarded the *Ritterkreuz* on 29 May 1940. He died on 15 June 1944 in an ambush in Talvern-Nénèze (Brittany) carried out by the French Resistance. A 12-man-patrol from the 4th Company, 1st Battalion of the FTP led by Bénoni Lamour fired at a car carrying General Bernard Ramcke and officers from his staff (2. FJD), among whom was Schmidt. He published the book "*Die Fallschirmjäger von Dombas*" in 1941. ("Die Fallschirmjäger von Dombas")

The operation was inadaquately prepared, with insufficient air reconnaissance, mistakes made during the drop, and lack of contact between the Groups, which inevitably became split up and isolated. An operation of that type basically required more time to prepare. The risk of being far from friendly lines, in unknown terrain, requires a thorough knowledge of the ground. This would have mitigated the weakness of the paratroops immediately following the landing.

The later official German propaganda did not present the truth about the operation, nor highlight those responsible for the disaster. As can be expected, their information did not correspond with the loss of a company of *Fallschirmjäger*, with 15 dead and 30 wounded soldiers. Nor did it mention the fact that of the 15 planes that transported them to the objective only 7 managed to return to their German bases.

From the beginning the fighting at Dombås was unequal, because the paratroops had to fight in conditions for which they were not prepared, without adequate uniforms, unable to reach their weapons containers, scattered in isolated groups

A German soldier poses next to the sign in Dombås station after the Norwegian surrender. (Óscar González)

Post-war photo of Dombås station.

Above: Front page of the magazine "Der Landser" dedicated to the mission at Dombås. (Óscar González) Below: The Tålleras bridge, 15 km south of Dombås. The bridge was blown up on the night of 30 April, in a last desperate attempt by the Norwegians to halt the German advance. However, the destruction of the bridge did not prevent the Germans from occupying the town on 1 May. (Óscar González)

over an area of 30 x 15 km, at an altitude of almost 1,600 m, without radio contact and possessing just one 1:100.000 scale map (Schmidt's). The Company had already lost a third of its men in the first 24 hours, among them 2 officers and 2 *Feldwebel* platoon leaders. Finally, in a dead end situation and desparate, they were forced to surrender to much better equipped Norwegian units.

The words of Ernst Mössinger are very critical towards the preparation of the mission, "*the dream of a quick victory by the* Fallschirmjäger *at Dombås was born from the propaganda directed by Göring*." In reality only a handful of paratroops (two Groups from Mössinger's Platoon and two from Bobrowski's) were able to act south of Dombås, blowing up the railway line and blocking the road.

The Norwegians, for their part, better prepared for the snowy conditions as they were, did not demonstrate enough decision and paid for their tactical mistakes (the death of Captain Austlid, for example).

Following their liberation, the *Fallschirmjäger* did not receive the logical and awaited home leave in Germany, instead being sent to make another combat jump at Narvik to support the besieged *General* Dietl. In Mössinger's judgement:

"*The all-powerful* Reichsmarschall *Göring and the loyal* General *Student could not allow us a swift return to Germany, because our testimonies would have revealed the version of the paratroop victory at Dombås to be nothing more than an official lie.*"

View of the Tålleras bridge. German engineers are attempting to repair the damage. (Óscar González)

Dombås station, which was bombed by the Germans. (Óscar González)

The Norwegian Karsten Sveen (left) and the German Ernst Mössinger in 2002, next to the monument erected in Lindsø in memory of the fallen. (Kristian Hosar)

46 The "new company" was formed at the beginning of 1940, because after the 1st and 5th were disbanded to form *Sturmabteilung Koch*, the 1st Battalion of FJR1 was short of a company. The Battalion had been formed on 1 April 1938 and designated the 4th Battalion *General Göring Regiment*. It originally had 5 companies.
In 1940, personnel for the new 1st Company were taken from the other three companies in the 1st Battalion, the exception being *Leutnant* Mössinger's Platoon, which came from the 2nd Battalion (based in Braunschweig).
47 Neverthelss, the unit sustained casualties before going into action at Dombås: a Ju 52 carrying paratroops of 1./FJR1 (1st Platoon), commanded by *Leutnant* Fritz Becker, was shot down on 9 April over the Skagerrak sea, on their way to Fornebu. The Ju 52 was that of *Feldwebel* Theo Karl Brand, previously mentioned.
48 Cf. *Abschrift. Verbindungsstab der Luftwaffe bei Gruppe XXI. Oslo 14.4.1940*. According to this order, 2 *Fallschirmjäger* companies were proposed. In reality, only one took part in the attack. This order came from the recently created *Heeresgruppe XXI*, based in Oslo. The participation of the other company, the 2nd (2./FJR1), was canceled due to the state of exhaustion of Walther's *Fallschirmjäger* following Elverum and Oslo. This company was not at 100% fit for duty at 01:00 h on 14 April.
49 The loss of the Group from the 1st Platoon (9 April) was made up with 12 paratroops from the 2nd Company.
50 This platoon of 22 men (not 26, as was normal) shared their *Kette* with the company HQ. The platoon leader, *Feldwebel* Uhlig, two liaisons, a medic, two machine-gun crews, and two anti-tank rifle teams (*Panzer Büchsen*) flew in two Ju 52s. They were also theoretically equipped with a 50 mm mortar, but this was missing at Dombås.
51 Alexander Uhlig was born in Lepizig on 9 February 1919. After finishing high school in 1937 he joined the *Reicharbeitsdienst*, completing the two years military service required before further study. In the autumn of 1937 he volunteered for the first German parachute unit ("*one day an officer arrived wearing an Iron Cross 1st Class and a diving eagle insignia, which we had not seen until then. He jumped up on a podium and through a megaphone announced that he needed 500 men to form a parachute battalion. Later I learned that this man was Major Bruno Bräuer.*"). This unit was to be the seed of *Fallschirmjäger Regiment 1*, formed in 1938. As a member of this unit Uhlig took part in the occupation of the Sudetenland in October 1938. Alexander Uhlig was awarded the Knight's Cross (*Ritterkreuz*) on 29 October 1944 as a *Oberfeldwebel* commanding 16./FJR 6. During the Normandy landing, Uhlig's men defeated an entire American battalion, taking 230 prisoners, including the battalion CO and 11 other officers.
52 The composition of Schmidt's force varies according to the sources quoted. It was "around 170" (*etwa 170*) according to the *Abschrift. Verbindungsstab der Luftwaffe bei Gruppe XXI*; 183 according to Albert Valjeur; 4/181 (4 officers, 181 men) acording to Bjørn Dalen; **4/174** states Alexander Uhlig; 4/180, 4/179, and **4/176**, according to Mössinger. Mossinger's figure is taken as a "starting point," following the criteria of Karl-Heinz Golla (2006), p. 109. They flew in 5 *Ketten*, which is 15 Ju 52s. Each plane carried 12 *Fallschirmjäger*. As has already been stated, to the 144 men of the company must be added 36 more from the battalion signals platoon, so that "on

paper," 4 officers and 176 other ranks formed the unit. However, Alexander Uhlig states that the 4th Platoon (which he himself commanded) had only 22 men. This would give a btotal of 178 *Fallschirmjäger*.
53 Around 25 Norwegian soldiers commanded by *løytnant* Trygve Dalsegg confronted the paratroops. The wounded Germans (among them *Oberjäger* Schröter) were taken to hospital, and were liberated a few days later by troops of the 196 ID, which occupied Lillehammer on 24 April. The rest of the prisoners were sent to Britain.
54 Regarding the 15 planes carrying the company, two were shot down. Only 5 were able to return to Fornebu; 2 reached the Trondheim-Jonsvannet airfield, which was in German hands. Three landed in Sweden: the first on the frozen Lake Vänern, near Mariestad. Its crew were unharmed and interned; the plane was returned to Germany on 2 September 1940. The second crashed near Uddevala, south of Gøteborg. It was hit by *Bofors* anti-aircraft guns as it flew over Swedish infantry positions. There were no survivors. The third landed in Silverbo, next to Grebbestad (north Gøteborg). This aircraft was also returned to Germany on 2 September. Lastly, 3 aircraft were damaged by Norwegian anti-aircraft fire and had to make emergency landings (in Kongsvinger, Ringebu, and Hønefoss), resulting in irreparable damage.
The aircraft that landed in Hønefoss was that of *Oberstleutnant* Drewes, *Gruppenkommandeur* of the elite unit transporting the paratroops, the *II./ Kampfgeschwader z.b.V 1*. Together with his adjutant, *Oberleutnant* Wilhelm Metscher, they piloted the Ju 52 carrying Schmidt. The intense enemy fire damaged the port engine. They began the return to Oslo when it was getting dark. After three and a half hours in the air, and with serious problems to reach Fornebu (apart from the engine, the radio had also failed), they made an emergency landing to the north of Oslo, near the Nedder Lysse farm. In his own words, "*Bearing in mind the aircraft was damaged, it was a masterly landing; nobody was injured. We were 60 km north of Oslo, but we were able to contact Fornebu by phone from the farm. After spending the night freezing in the aircraft's cabin, a rescue group came for us first thing in the morning.*"
Although these details are supported by the research of the Norwegians Mølmen (1996) and Solvik (2006), we must make room for other opinions on the "return" of the Ju 52s to Fornebu, such as that of Alexander Uhlig and Wilhelm Metscher, who state that the number of aircraft that returned to Fornebu was 7 (1 landed in Sweden, 3 in Trondheim, 2 were shot down, and another 2 were torced to make emergency landings on their return to Oslo).
55 Also known as *Mørebataljon*. Cf. Hauge, A.: *Kampene i Norge 1940 (Bind 1)*, Sandefjord, Krigshistorisk Forlag A.S., 1978, pp. 251-263.
56 Günther Backaus (21/10/1913 – 14/04/1940) was an *Oberjäger*, and was under arrest in Stendal on 11 April. He volunteered for Dombås to restore his honor. Uhlig accepted him because he was a man short. Backaus had been demoted to *Jäger* (private), which meant he could not enter combat with his unit (he did not fly to Norway on 9 April). He was assigned to serve a machine-gun in Uhlig's platoon. He died from his wounds, as he was unable to cope with the long march made by the platoon. He is buried in Trondheim.
57 One of the *Fallschirmjäger*, Hubert Hopf, jumped too soon and was lost. He spent some time sheltering in a cabin completely disorientated. He was able to cover his uniform with civilian clothes and enter Dombås. There he took refuge again in a basement, where he was discovered on 29 April. He was sent to England and later Canada, returning to Germany in 1947.
58 Also called Hagevoll or, depending on the local dialect, Hågåvoll. In the text both Hagevold and Hagevoll are used.
59 All of Ernst Mössinger's account was obtained either by letter or personal interview.
60 The plane was hit by machine-gun fire from Norwegian positions in Dombås. The pilot, *Leutnant* Erich Schiffrer (Austrian), and the observer, Schneider, were killed. Twelve *Fallschirmjäger* (1 *Feldwebel* and 11 men) managed to jump 1.5 km southeast of the town. Nine of the paratroops were wounded before jumping due to the machine-gun fire; others were shot while they were jumping. According to Alexander Uhlig (based on the report made by Gonschorowski after the event), a member of the crew, the machine-gunner *Flieger* Roth, was able to jump free and survived [surprisingly Mølmen (1996), p. 155, states he died in the jump, although this was not confirmed in the "*Volksbund Deutsche Kriegsgräberfürsorge e.V.*"]. The plane crashed into Mount Gråberget with the weapons container on board. The survivors, armed only with pistols, surrendered on 15 April.
61 He was attended, as were the rest of the wounded, by *Sanitäts-Oberjäger* Werner Rachold. No medical officer jumped with the unit.
62 Damage which the Norwegians did not repair until 29 April. There is no doubt the Germans accomplished an important part of their mission.
63 Schmidt (1941), pp. 85, 86. Although the money was "*later recovered, by the Norwegians*" [Gericke (1941), p. 73].
64 Magnus Bredesen, Per Olafsen Illevold, Asbjør Aasen, Olaf Nyfløtt, and Olaf Korssjøen were killed, along with Austlid and his adjutant, Lorenz Christoffer Brun.
65 Curiously, originally from Bottheim, some 9 km west of Dombås.
66 They headed northwest from Dombås, arriving at Sønstebø, Jorn, and Soleglad. One of them was commanded by *Oberjäger* Kochanowski. Although his men accomplished their mission to cut the railway line, they were taken

prisoner by Norwegian ski troops. The Norwegians could move across the snow with relative ease, and soon located the Germans following the explosions on the railway line.

67 In fact Austlid's unit, which fell in combat at Hagevoll, was one of the groups escorting the Royal Family. Together with members of the government, they had stopped their train journey in Otta, 40 km from *Dombås*, on the night of 14 April. The group continued to Dovre by car. It was there that two ministers, one of whom was Trygve Lie (who after the war became the first UN Secretary General), ordered Austlid to make an attack. The ministers judged that various survivors from a downed German plane had cut the road. (Cf. *Kaptein som døde to ganger,* in *Aftenposten,* 25 February 2001.) That the *Fallschirmjäger* were close to capture the king is confirmed by the following fact: after the war the Norwegian and German press published articles relating that the column in which the King was travelling was attacked by *Fallschirmjäger* between Dovre and Dombås. The King had to jump from his vehicle and take cover off the road; he later returned on foot, together with his companions, to a safer area. Although in a confused way, what is being described are events happening to the Norwegian column on 15 April.

68 According to Gerhard Broder, member of the 3rd Platoon, 2nd Company, commanded by Bobrowski, the number of wounded was 12, 2 of them seriously.

69 Nevertheless, the first resupply mission was carried out on 15 April. *Leutnant* Zuber of 2./FJR1 received the direct order from Walther at 07:00 h. The Ju 52 was from *Kampfgruppe Major von Jena* and flew from Oslo. In spite of the atmospheric conditions and coming under intense Norwegian anti-aircraft fire, they were able to locate the main body of Schmidt's men 1 km south of Dombås ("*the command post was marked with a swastika*"). The plane could not make radio contact with the men on the ground because its radio and antenna were damaged, as well as its starboard engine. It was a miracle that the plane managed to return to Oslo. According to Zuber's report, there were approximately "*40 impacts in the fuselage.*"

On 17 April Walther ordered new supply and reconnaissance missions. This time *Feldwebel* Herbert Lüsing of *Stab I.*/FJR1, aided by *Obergefreiter* Bokermann, were charged with executing the mission. They travelled aboard a Ju 52 (NGDY) of 1./*Kampfgruppe* 104 piloted by *Uffz*. Wiedemann on the 18th; the radio operator was *Uffz*. Fleckner and the 3rd member of the crew was *Uffz*. Hauser. Bad weather made things difficult, and added to this was the Norwegian anti-aircraft fire. After several minutes of searching, and just when they had decided to return to base, they located the German flag on some stables, 10 km southeast of Dombås. They first attempted to establish radio contact on frequency 4455 (3850) Khz. They dropped the *Fallschirmjäger* under intense fire "*overcoats, 6,000 rounds, food and medical supplies*." After gaining height they tried again to establish radio contact, this time with success. Schmidt reported that "*48 men continue to resist*" and asked "*Where is the infantry?*" In response, Lüsing asked if there was an area where the infantry could land. Schmidt responded in the negative. Before returning to Oslo, Lüsing insisted that they remained tuned to the same frequency, as he would return the next day. Schmidt did not answer. The plane landed in Oslo at 16:00 h.

Without denying the value of Lüsing's report, it is still not completely clear how (not even Ernst Mössinger gives a convincing answer to this question) the air crews communicated with Schmidt's *Fallschirmjäger*. During the invasion of Norway, the operations in Holland, or even the assault on Crete (talking of 1940 and 1941), there was no way of establishing radio contact between the *Fallschirmjäger* and the radio sets used by the *Luftwaffe*. Communication between the ground and air was not really an option. How was it possible at Dombås? Perhaps with captured Norwegian equipment?

70 The possibility of an exchange was considered: that of handing over Schmidt and a Captain plus 40 Norwegian soldiers on the condition that the former would be taken to hospital and treated. Schmidt refused.

71 Karsten Sveen (31/08/1914 – 24/12/2003) is one of the numerous Norwegians who, after first fighting against the Germans, later joined the ranks of the *Waffen SS* (*Den Norske Legion*). Before Dombås, he took part in the fighting around Midtskogen on 10 April, foiling Spiller's attempt to capture the government and the Royal Family. When his unit surrendered to the Germans he became a prisoner of war until he was liberated on 2 June. He enlisted for service with the Norwegian *SS* in 1941, serving as a platoon leader at the acadamy in Elverum. From there he went on to the "Norwegian Legion," commanding the 2nd Company. He was sent to the *SS-Junkerschule "Braunschweig"* to be trained as a company commander. He later trained French volunteers and was director of the *SS* acadamy in Kongsvinger until 1944. He was awarded the EKII and the black wound badge. He attained the rank of *Legion-Obersturmführer*. After the war he was tried and sent to prison, later finding work as an insurance agent. In the last years of his life he kept in contact with Ernst Mössinger, promoting the memory and paying homage to all those who fell at Dombås.

72 It was the same aircraft as the previous day. *Feldwebel* Lüsing carried "*9.000 rounds of ammunition, flares, and rations*" for the *Fallschirmjäger*. The plane took off from Oslo at 09:30 h. His plan was to fly at low altitude (20 m) on arriving at Dombås, with all the supplies being dropped without parachute. The Norwegian anti-aircraft fire was as intense as the day before. While they were descending as planned (280-300 m) they received a message from Schmidt: "*Return immediately; we are surrendering!*" The answer from the Ju 52 was "*Hang on: the infantry and tanks are advancing at all speed.*" Schmidt's response was clear: "*Go back. We have surrendered.*"

The farewell from both parties was brief: "*We will see you again back home.*" Before signing off Lüsing asked how many enemy troops there were (Norwegian or British), but did not receive an answer. Lüsing continued with his report: "*I can see two soldiers at the stable, but I cannot distinguish if they are German or Norwegian. I spent about 20 minutes flying around in circles trying to contact them, without success. Neither could I clearly define the movements of the enemy troops. As we were coming increasingly under enemy machine-gun fire we decided to return to base and not to drop the supplies (...). We landed in Oslo with bullet holes in the fuselage and the fuel tank.*"
Herbert Lüsing (born 8 December 1913), veteran of the Condor Legion, died in the assault on the island of Crete on 20 May 1941 at the rank of *Oberfeldwebel*.
73 Mössinger puts it at around four in the afternoon, but this does not seem to be that reliable. The "*Abschrift. Verbindungsstab del Luftwaffe bei Gruppe XXI*" concluded in its report that the surrender took place at 15:00 h. However, in Lüsing's report, after witnessing the surrender, stated that "*We landed in Oslo at 12:50 h.*" Using Golla (2006) as the principle guide on this issue, it can be established that the surrender was probably completed at approximately 14:00 h.
74 Valjeur makes reference to the Ju 52 from the Platoon's 5th Group, led by *Feldwebel* Gonchorowski.
75 This occurred on 28 April.
76 According to several reports 6 fell at Hagevold, 3 at Lindsø, and another 3 at Ulekleiv. According to Mössinger 5 were from his platoon. Ten are buried in the military cemetary in Havstein, Trondheim. Among the dead were: *Jäger* Ernst Winterhagen, *Unteroffizier* Heinrich Zufall, *Obergefreiter* Michael Menter, *Gefreiter* Josef Schluga, *Gefreiter* Johann Kreuselberg (all of them from the "extra" platoon from the 2nd Company, under Bobrowski), *Jäger* Hermann Kuffner, *Jäger* Rudolf Fell, and *Oberjäger* Johannes Bremser [as well as *Leutnant* Paul Sagasser, *Gefreiter* Kurt Wietzig (also from the 2nd Company), *Gefreiter* Gerhard Karl Schallock, and *Oberjäger* Günther Backhaus].
77 When the operation failed he was about to be tried. Only Göring's direct intervention saved him. He died on 20 May 1941, at 6 in the morning, as he was heading for Crete aboard a DFS 230 glider. The Ju 52 towing the glider had to make a sudden manoeuvre to avoid colliding with a Heinkel He 111. This caused the cable connected to the glider to break, and as a result the glider crashed on the island of Aegina, killing all on board.

6

Narvik

Following their liberation the paratroops were taken to Oslo, first in boats, then aboard trucks, and finally by train, arriving on 9 May. Slowly they recovered form their captivity, being billited in pensions, hotels, and official buildings adapted for their use. Albert Valjeur remembers:

"*During the trip all of us were radiant with joy. The sea in the capital was spectacular, and we all stripped off and ran naked to have a dip. Finally we could bathe ourselves adequately. When we arrived in Oslo we were given new uniforms. We were billited in a school and had decent meals. However, we did not have beds to sleep in, having to use the floor, as the beds were needed in the hospitals for the wounded.*"

Uhlig recalls: "*we also received our salary for the four weeks we were in captivity.*"

On 11 May the ceremony was held for the award of the Iron Cross 2nd Class (EK II) for all the paratroops who had participated in the operation at Dombås. "*A day after we arrived in Oslo we were gathered together in the playground at the* Stabekk *school, and after a few words from General Falkenhorst, we were decorated with the EK II,*" continues Valjeur.

General Falkenhorst was not the only high ranking officer present, as Generals Förster and Kitzinger were also there, the latter being the commander in chief of the *Luftwaffe* in Norway and the "suicide" mission at Dombås. In the opinion of many paratroops—among them Ernst Mössinger—the awards were an attempt at repairing the "mistake" made in initiating the operation at all cost.

However, Kitzinger did not just have medals for the *Fallschirmjäger*; he also came with an order for the 1st Company to jump again at Narvik. The three Generals therefore communicated these new instructions to the Company's platoon commanders on 10 May. Alexander Uhlig, leader of the 4th Platoon, was present at the meeting:

"*After praising our actions at Dombås they informed us of General Dietl's situation. He urgently needed reinforcements. A seaborne landing was impossible because the British*

Opposite: 11 May, the ceremony for the award of the Iron Cross 2nd Class (EK II) for all those who took part in the operation at Dombås. Albert Valjeur remembers, "*the day after our arrival, we were gathered in the playground of the 'Stabekk' school and after a few words from General Falkenhorst, we were decorated with the EK II.*" (Óscar González)

controlled the port on the coast. Neither was an airfield available. Only the Fallschirmjäger *could help the* Gebirgsjäger *in Narvik. All the paratroop units were being used in the invasion of Holland, so we were the only ones available.*

They asked us if we wished to help our comrades in Narvik. We responded that we would do it if we were given the arms and aircraft to do the job. The three weeks in captivity had not diminished either our morale or idealism. We therefore volunteered for Narvik."

The "Narvik Problem"

In order to analyse the participation of the *Fallschirmjäger* in Narvik, it is necessary to return to the beginning of the invasion of Norway. Narvik was the objective of the Mountain troops (*Gebirgsjäger*) under General Dietl. The initial plan did not contemplate the use of the paratroops at Narvik. However, events developed unexpectedly, placing Dietl's troops in a series of predicaments.

It can be stated without too much hesitation that this was to be the first case of something which would become habitual by the end of the war (and generally from the conquest of Crete): the use of the *Fallschirmjäger* as infantry to support and reinforce troops in tight spots. In fact, to use the term of veteran German paratrooper Richard Kloes, as a *fire brigade*.

Generaloberst Eduard Dietl in Oslo, awarded the Knight's Cross in July 1940, following the Norwegian surrender. Born in 1890 in Bavaria, he was an officer who was very close to Hitler and National Socialism, with great experience in mountain warfare. After his resistance in Narvik he was decorated and elevated to the status of hero by the Nazi propaganda machine, directed by Goebbels, who described him as "*... the authentic peoples' General.*" From commanding a division at Narvik he was next placed in command of an army corps for the invasion of Russia, covering the left "arctic" flank and the capture of Murmansk, the main port for the Allied supply convoys. He failed to take the city. He was killed in an air accident in the summer of 1944. (Óscar González)

On 9 April the troops of the 3rd Mountain Division (3.GJD), commanded by *Generalleutnant* Eduard Dietl, were transported aboard 10 destroyers of Naval Group 1, under *Kommodore* Friedrich Bonte, and landed in Narvik and quickly occupied the city. However, the naval battles around Narvik between the 10 and 13 April were to have dramatic consequences for the German troops: the Royal Navy put paid to the 10 German destroyers with relatively light British losses.

Events developed as follows. Five Royal Navy destroyers entered the port of Narvik on 10 April, taking advantage in a breach in the *Kriegsmarine's* defense; a battle then developed based completely on the element of surprise. The audacious action saw the German destroyers *Anton Schmidt* and *Wilhelm Heidkamp* sunk in quick succession, with another three seriously damaged. *Kommodore* Bonte was killed in action when his ship, the *Wilhelm Heidkamp* (Z 21), was sunk. The British lost two destroyers in the action, including the flag ship captained by Warburton-Lee, commander of the British forces. The remaining German destroyers were lost on the 13th. *Fragattenkapitän* Erich Bey, commanding the 4th Flotilla, who had taken command following Bonte's death, carried out a defensive manoeuvre in which three Royal Navy ships were damaged. Once their ammunition was exhausted Bey ordered his surving ships to run themselves in the Rombaken fjord.[78]

In Narvik, Dietl's troops were left isolated more than 1,000 km from their own forces, and what is more, with declining morale. During that period the German forces in the rest of the country were not great in number, and were still engaging the Norwegians. At sea British superiority was overwhelming. However, the Allies did not take advantage of the situation.

Post card of *Gebirgsjäger* with MG. (Óscar González)

Edelweiss badge of the *Gebirgsjäger*. (Óscar González)

In spite of the naval disaster, German ground troops in Narvik had had the necessary time to reorganize. On the 9th there were only three battalions of mountain troops: one in Narvik and two in the Bjerkvik/Elvergårdsmoen area, totalling 2,000 men.[79] Further to this, some 2,600 sailors from the lost German flotilla had joined Dietl (they were to earn themselves the nickname *Gebirgsmarinen*, or "Alpine-Sailors"). Between 9 April and 6 June around 4,715 were under Deitl's command.

General Dietl had concentrated in clearing the railway line by way of a surprise attack on the Bjørnfjell station (carried out on 16 April by 1./GJR 139, commanded by von Schlebrügge); they shattered the defense of the Norwegian garrison, who had fled from Narvik on the 9th. Nine Norwegian officers and 60 other ranks were taken prisoner. As a result of this operation the Germans were able to control the railway line from the Swedish frontier. From 1 May the Germans established their General Headquarters at Spionkop, a 500 m hill near the station in a desolate landscape of lakes and rocky crags.[80]

The Norwegians deployed troops north of Dietl's position from Kirkenes. These were well trained troops accustomed to the snow and cold weather. The Germans used two of their mountain battalions to halt the attack. The Germans had good defensive positions from which they could control wide swathes of ground with machine-guns. However, the Royal Navy's control of the fjords was something they could do little about (2 cruisers and 5 destroyers commanded by Captain L. H. K. Hamilton aboard *HMS Aurora*). This forced the Germans to use a long line of communication between Bjørnfjell and Bjerkvik, crossing the mountains to the north of Lake Hartvik. The Allied plan contemplated a frontal attack from the northeast against Lapphaug, the highest point on the road between Fossbakken and Gratangen, the latter being at the level of the fjord. Another movement from the south, involving a battalion, had the objective of cutting the German retreat.

In the Narvik area the Allies began their attack on 27 April, with 9,000 men (3 French Alpine Battalions, 2 Foreign Legion battalions, among whose ranks there were Poles, Spaniards, and Italians, 4 Polish battalions—the *Podhale* Brigade—and 3,000 Norwegians), who were to link up with the 10,000 Norwegians under General Ruge. In the first fortnight of May the Alies tightened the noose around Narvik with the support of the Royal Navy and Airforce, retaking some of the villages around the city but without penetrating the city itself, which was well defended by the Germans, who had received reinforcements. The advance on Narvik was on three fronts, trying to capture Ankenes and Øjord, and cutting the railway in Hundalen, just 10 km from the Swedish frontier.

The gravity of the situation was such that Hitler authorized Dietl to withdraw into neutral Sweden. Deitl rejected this proposal, stating that he would resist. This he did, as well as controlling the railway and keeping the Norwegians at bay or defeating them.

Meanwhile, on 10 May the Germans had begun their offensive in the West (*Fall Gelb*), invading the Low Countries and threatening France with the same. The British considered it better to withdraw from Norway, leaving it to its fate; the French proved more indecisive, believing that to withdraw would help the Germans, raise their morale, convert the Allied withdrawl into a disaster, and leave a negative impression on Britain's and France's Allies. This was the opinion of the French General Béthouart, and it was one which partially prevailed; it would be necessary to strike a blow against the Germans and make a well prepared, orderly withdrawl.

The *Gebirgsjäger* continued to resist Allied pressure, but the reverse suffered by the Allies in France accelerated events.

The Allies decided to begin a slow withdrawl in the second half of May. On 24 May, to the irritation of the Norwegians, they began retiring their troops in other areas of the country, leaving Narvik, where they were still fighting, till last.

On 27 May 24,000 French, Norwegian, and Polish troops attacked at different points at the same time, breaking the German resistance (who in order to avoid being trapped withdrew from the city), and on the afternoon of the 28th occupied Narvik, leaving everything ready for the evacuation of Norway. In a way the occupation of the city was to facilitate this. On 31 May the Allies abandoned Bodø, to the south of Vestfjorden. On 8 June they evacuated Harstad, and on the 9th, Narvik, just before German reinforcements travelling overland arrived in the city. The last Norwegian troops surrendered on 12 June, although the Norwegian Army had officially capitulated on the 10th.

What follows is a detailed analysis of events.

Dietl's Strategy: Defense at all cost

Given the adverse situation, Dietl made maximum use of the human and materiel resources at his disposal. The crews of the German ships lost at Narvik used uniforms and equipment confiscated from the Norwegians. Nevertheless, the lack of adequate equipment (warm clothing, sunglasses, and material for fighting in the snow) was a handicap for the Germans, unlike their Norwegian adversaries. Some German units, for example, only ate hot food three times in five weeks.

The railway line was cut once the bridges at Norddals had been passed, but Dietl wanted to control them at all costs.

The situation was as follows: two battalions were deployed north of the Rombaken fjord (I./ y III./GJR 139) under command of *Oberst* Alois Windisch[81] in an attempt to confront the Norwegian threat. The *Gruppe Windisch* held the line north of the front Oalgge–Pass–Elvenes–Labergdalen. The II./GJR 139, led by *Major* Arthur Haussels, were converted into *Gruppe Haussels*, which included the German sailors, employed mainly in defense of the railway line. Located in Narvik, their mission was to hold the city and secure the southern shore of the Rombaken fjord. They would later be reinforced by I./GJR 139, taken from Windisch's command.

The first Norwegian attack took place east of Elvenes on the 24 April. The 3./GJR 139 resisted the attack of a Norwegian battalion from the north. The Germans had to withdraw to the west. *Major* Stautner, under the orders of I./GJR 139, organized a counter-attack during the morning of the 25th, causing numerous casualties among the 1st Battalion of the Norwegian 12th Infantry Regiment, as well as capturing 144 prisoners.

During the days that followed, Narvik and the railway line continued under fire from the cruisers and destroyers of the Royal Navy. Everything indicated a large scale attack was coming. Dietl ordered that Narvik be held as long as possible. The 6./GJR 139 was to protect the left flank, deploying to the Ankenes area. There they held until the end of May, being supported and relieved by the 8./GJR 139, facing two Polish battalions and taking enormous casualties.

The attacks on the northern flank, defended by Grupe Windisch, continued unceasingly. It was feared that the Norwegian troops of General Fleischer (especially the *Alta* battalion, perfectly equipped for the conditions and advancing tenaciously since 28 April) would overwhelm the German lines from the east, next to the Swedish frontier. Therefore the weak reserves, comprising Von Schlebrügge's 1./GJR 139, moved from Bjørnfjell to support Windisch.

On 7 May superior Allied forces forced Windisch to retreat to the Bukkedalen–Laeigastind–Roasme line. The 6th and 7th Norwegian brigades, along with the French Alpine troops, overwhelmed the Germans.

Gruppe XXI, which commanded Dietl's troops, judged the situation to be "critical" on 5 May. It seemed that the Allied attack was being directed at the railway line to the Swedish frontier. The aim of the occupation of Narvik was to isolate it from the rail link. Windisch's left flank was blocked holding the Norwegians, and his right was threatened.[82] The situation became so desperate that Dietl was advised to withdraw, after having held as long as possible, and even cross into neutral Sweden. The heights and positions south of Narvik could not be held for much longer, as the German forces were exhausted and constantly engaging the Allies.

It was in this difficult context that support from the *Luftwaffe* was initiated. The *Luftwaffe* was limited by the fact that Trondheim was at the maximum range of its aircraft, and Narvik was still further north. Only small groups could attack the Allied ships stationed in Harstad and in the fjord to the west. These actions were of limited help; furthermore, they were conditioned by the weather and the range of the aircraft. Regarding the last consideration, three types were employed: Do 24 and Do 26 seaplanes; Ju 90s, which were versatile and apt for the supply conditions in Narvik; and the Ju 52s, fitted with extra fuel tanks (which meant that they could only transport 10 paratroops). Weather conditions, for example, were the reason only two of the six seaplanes (Do 26s) sent were able to land in Narvik on 8 May. The rest did so on the 11th, which meant that two companies of *Gebirgsjäger* could be resupplied.

The Beginning of the *Fallschirmjäger* Participation in Narvik

On 11 May the paratroops received the weapons, parachutes, and equipment necessary for the coming mission. On 14 May the first Groups and Platoons boarded the Ju 52s. Nobody seemed concerned that half of the men had just spent three weeks in captivity in several different prison camps due to the *Luftwaffe* bombing. The Company had only received 35 replacements from Germany from the *Fallschirmjäger Ergänzung Bataillon* (*FschErgBtl*), a unit established for support and covering losses. Kurt Barank was one of the replacements. He remembers his first meeting with the "Dombås veterans":

"*My first impression of these men was that they had not been sufficiently rested before starting a new mission. Their thoughts were in Germany.*"[83]

Left: *Fallschirmjäger* landing at Bjørnfjell station. (Óscar González) Right: A paratrooper about to land at Bjørnfjell. In Alexander Uhlig's own words, "*We were the first paratroops to jump north of the Arctic Circle. The drop zone was so small that only three men could jump on each pass of the Ju 52.*" ("Narvik im Bild")

Three rifle platoons, a signals platoon (*Nachrichten Zug*), and a machine-gun platoon (formed into 5 Groups, or *Truppen*) were the available force. This is what had been decided by the *Luftwaffe* High Command (OKL, or *Oberkommando der Luftwaffe*).[84]

Albert Valjeur recalls:

"*On the 12th we received the order: fly from Trondheim to Narvik. In Oslo we were reinforced by a platoon of young paratroops recently arrived from Germany. Our mission was to aid the* Gebirgsjäger. *The British had landed in Narvik, and we had lost part of the vital rail link carrying mineral ore from Sweden, and Germany needed it.*"

That same 12 May they flew to Trondheim in *Lufthansa* planes. Once there, they flew in Ju 52s that had arrived from Germany, specially prepared with extra fuel tanks to enable them to make the round trip Trondheim–Narvik–Trondheim. It was a quiet flight, and during the 400 km trip they did not encounter any enemy fighters. But they could not fly on the 13th, as had been planned. The weather forced the flight to be delayed. The *Fallschirmjäger* had the day free in Trondheim. According to Uhlig, "*I visited the city and the cathedral. I still had enough money to spend in cafés and restaurants, so we spent a good while in Café Müller.*"

Left: *Leutnant* Becker harangues his men as they gather at the main building of Bjørnfjell station on 14 May 1940. The photo is a clear example of the variety of uniforms worn by the "Narvik" paratroops; the M 38 jump suit without pockets, and the peculiar M 36 with double vertical zip (man on the right). Also the M 38 paratroop helmet with double emblems. ("Narvik im Bild") Right: A paratrooper about to land at Bjørnfjell. In the words of Alexander Uhlig, "we were the first paratroopers to jump north of the Arctic Circle. The area was so small that we could only jump 3 paratroopers on each pass of the Ju 52." (Óscar González)

Photo of a group of *Fallschirmjäger* who jumped at Bjørnfjell station on 14 May around 11:00 h. There were 66 *Fallschirmjäger* in total, 3 officers and 63 men under *Leutnant* Becker, leader of the 1st Platoon at Dombås. Two groups from 1st Platoon jumped, the Company HQ (*Kompanietrupp*) and the 4th Platoon of *Feldwebel* Alex Uhlig, the "*Schwere Zug*" with machine-guns. (Óscar González)

In the outskirts of Narvik they were awaited anxiously on the 12th, but Dietl was informed of the delay. A hypothetical drop zone had been considered—Lake Hartvik, northwest of the German positions—but this was discounted, as Allied pressure was very strong in this area.

Finally, on **14 May**, the first members of 1./FJR1 left for Narvik aboard 6 Ju 52s. The drop was made at 400 m to the north of Bjørnfjell at about 11:00 h. From the station, near the Swedish frontier, Dietl directed the German troops in their resistance to the Allied pressure. There were 66 *Fallschirmjäger* in total (3 officers and 63 other ranks) commanded by *Leutnant* Becker, leader of the 1st Platoon in Dombås. Two groups from the 1st Platoon jumped, the Company HQ (*Kompanietrupp*), *Feldwebel* Alex Uhlig's 4th Platoon, and the *Schwere Zug* with machine-guns (9 MGs, 4 lMGs, and 5 SMGs). Uhlig recalls:

"*We were the first paratroops to jump north of the Arctic circle. The drop zone was so small that only 3 paratroops could jump on each pass of the Ju 52. I hit my head on a rock as I landed and lost conciousness. 3 days later I had recovered and marched to the front with my unit.*"

This first contingent of *Fallschirmjäger* headed north of Bjørnfjell on the 14th to the area of the Kuberget massif, located in the northwestern angle of the northern sector. This formed the right flank of *Gruppe Windisch*.[85] They arrived at the train station at 23:30 h, which was located in the middle of the massif, between spot heights 790 and 860. They lacked the most basic equipment to fight in the arctic conditions (overcoats, rucksacks). On top of this, they hardly had time to rest at the station; they had had to leave most of their warm clothing at Bjørnfjell and rush to spot height 820, reaching it at 01:00 h on the 15th, to urgently reinforce the 1./GJR 139 under *Major* Hans von Schlebrügge, the "pearl" of the units forming *Gruppe Windisch*. Exhausted and frozen, they discovered that a Norwegian attack had just been repulsed. Their first moments in the new positions were the hardest. They had spent several hours covering the 3 km, in single file and in dense fog.

A Ju 52 supply plane dropping its cargo over Bjørnfjell. ("Narvik im Bild")

Oberjäger Sepp Steinhardt, member of Mössinger's platoon, who jumped on 16 May at Bjørnfjell. Along with the *Fliegerbluse* and paratrooper trousers he is wearing mountain boots. He wears the EKII ribbon, awarded after Dombås. (Óscar González)

The area in question was between Lake Jern and spot height 620, the latter north of Lake Holm. The troops occupied positions at different altitudes, such as spot height 794, where they set up two machine-guns, and the foothills of spot heights 1,067 and 620.

On **16th May** at 02:30 h, the other 22 men of the Signals Platoon were dropped (*Nachrichtenzug*) under command of *Olt* Gerhold. This group—the same as Mössinger's—had gone to Bjørnfjell on the 15th, but had had to turn back due to the heavy anti-aircraft fire from the British ships at Narvik. On the 16th, flying along the Swedish frontier (and coming under Swedish anti-aircraft fire), they were able to reach their objective. Gerhard Broder remembers the dramatic trip:

"We flew to Bjørnfjell on the 15th. Our group of three aircraft (Kette) *flew at 2,000 m. After an hour in the air the pilots, with extraordinary ability, descended and gained speed. The British*

anti-aircraft guns opened fire, especially those on a ship located in the fjord we were flying over. The pilots reacted and contiued along the designated route. However, unfortunately, one of our aircraft was shot down over Narvik. It was Feldwebel *Hinrichsen and his men. Before joining the paratroops he had been an artilleryman. This was his first action. It appeared that the plane was shot down by a British fighter and was forced over Swedish territory. Six paratroops were able to jump. (...) The rest of my unit had to return to Trondheim, as it was impossible to jump due to the bad weather.*"

Gerhold's unit was tasked by Dietl with all the communications in his command post. Gerhold and his men carried out their duties efficiently. Proof of this is that, because of the communications it was possible to reduce the wastage in mortar rounds by 5%. This was dropped in overloaded containers on the German positions. Gerhold was able to contact Oslo, and the loads were modified.

This same day the *Fallschirmjäger* deployed at Kuberget tried desperately to defend spot height 1,067. The Norwegians, equipped with skis and snow camouflage, harrassed the *Fallschirmjäger* positions with machine-gun fire and mortars, but in vain.

On the rest of the front the situation was critical. The Allies were threatening Øjord, on the north shore of the Rombaken fjord. Windisch defended Narvik as best he could. In the south, the 6./GJR 139 withstood the pressure from the Poles. There was an attempt to organize a counter-attack by this company together with the 7th, but it was stopped with heavy German losses.

Furthermore, the connection with the *Luftwaffe* remained erratic.

As has already been mentioned, Mössinger's Platoon also jumped on the 15th (1 officer and 74 men), equipped with 12 machine-guns, in two waves—one in the morning and the other at night—also at the Bjørnfjell train station. Broder continues his narration of events:

"*Just before we jumped we could see sailors in their blue uniforms looking up at us. There were black rocks pointing dangerously out of the snow. In fact, I found myself heading towards one. I guided myself away as best I could and landed some three meters from it. I finally found myself in Narvik....*"

Well armed *Fallschirmjäger* under Becker form up next to Bjørnfjell station. Almost all wear the regulation airborne helmet (the M 38), although a few have the M 35 with *Luftwaffe* insignia. ("Narvik im Bild")

Paratroops, mountain troops, sailors, and Norwegian prisoners (background) gather next to Bjørnfjell station. Albert Valjcur recalls, "*At last we were able to jump at Bjørnfjell.* Gebirgsjäger, *sailors, and Norwegian prisoners gathered at the train station. We could rest a few hours before beginning the march to our assigned positions.*" (Óscar González)

Several men, among them *Fallschirmjäger*, observe the effects of Allied bombing at Bjørnfjell. (Óscar González)

Left: Once at Bjørnfjell station, the *Fallschirmjäger* gather and check their weapons. Most are wearing the pocketless M 38 jump suit. ("Narvik im Bild") Right: Immediately after the drop at Bjørnfjell a *Feldwebel* chats with a recently landed paratrooper. Although not certain, the NCO, according to Albert Valjeur's account, is probably from Mössinger's Platoon. ("Narvik im Bild")

Valjeur also remebers the jump:

"*As we flew over the Beis fjord we came under anti-aircraft fire from the British ships. Finally we reached Bjørnfjell and jumped.* Gebirgsjäger*, sailors, and Norwegian prisoners congregated at the train station. We were able to rest a couple of hours before continuing on our way to the positions assigned to us in the Kuberget area (spot heights 820 and 860).*"

The paratroops, minus four men who had been injured (Mössinger was also injured, although not seriously, when he hit a rock), occupied positions in the area near Lake Jern and Kuberget during the first hours of the following day. Any reinforcements were welcomed by von Schlebrügge. He was also supported by the 3./GJR 138 under Ploder, who held spot height 620, 9 km to the north of Bjørnfjell. Albert Valjeur continues:

Left: Bjørnfjell station, located 514 m above sea level, as it is today. Right: Bjørnfjell from the Swedish frontier.

Above: Remains of a German paratrooper helmet found in Bjørnfjell in 2004. (Simon Orchard) Below: Remains of German mortar found near Bjørnfjell in 2004. (Simon Orchard)

"Weather conditions made defense of the front line extremely difficult. To this can be added supply problems (supplies were brought in by the Ju 52s) and with our equipment: our rubber-soled jump boots were inadequate for the frozen rocky terrain; many men had to use clothing confiscated from the Norwegians, because they lacked the appropriate cold weather clothing...

We fought shoulder to shoulder with each other, paratroops, mountaineers, and sailors. Nevertheless, we could not hold on to our inicial position for very long. We were forced to withdraw, although the slogan continued to be 'resist to the last round.'"

It was impossible to carry out reliefs, and any evacuation implied serious problems, so that everyone was taken with panic at the thought of being wounded, given that it was impossinle to be transported to the first aid post.[86] Paratrooper Gerhard Broder describes in detail the conditions in his position:

"*I asked one of the* Gebirgsjäger *the distance to the nearest first aid post, and he replied '8 hours.' I realized that in the case of serious injury my chances of survival would be null.*"

The trend during these days was Norwegian attacks followed by German counter-attacks, losing some positions and holding onto others. On the 16th, at 11:00 h, the Norwegians attacked the positions of von Schlebrügge's group on spot height 794, approximately 1.5 km from Kuberget. Von Schlebrügge had two machine-gun sections and a group from the 1st *Fallschirmjäger* Company. They were able to hold their positions during the next 12 hours. Nevertheless, in the end they were forced to retire in the face of a Norwegian attack with ski troops supported by artillery and mortars.

Mössinger's men relieved the exhausted units of 1./GJR 139 under von Schlebrügge, who had lost 13 killed, 25 wounded, 27 missing, and 7 reported sick (probably frostbite) after several days resisting on the frozen Kuberget massif. The *Fallschirmjäger* took advantage of the equipment left behind by the *Gebirgsjäger* in order to fight off the cold and snow. There was, however, something they could not protect themselves against: the well directed fire of the Norwegian artillery and their well camouflaged snipers. On the 17th *Jäger* Franz Lajdych was hit by a shot in the stomach; he was followed on the 20th by *Gefreiter* Zimmermann and *Jäger* Eckert, also killed by sniper fire. Gerhard Broder was a comrade of Zimmermann:

"*Friedrich Zimmermann was in the habit of hanging his helmet on a pole and using it to distract the enemy while he observed their positions. Unfortunately, he was spotted by a sniper and shot in the head. He was killed instantly. He was buried in our positions on the Kuberget. In fact, it was done by a friend of his, Ruth. Zimmermann was a reservist; he was married and had a son. At least he did not suffer a painful death. He would never be judged for events which took place during our stay in Oslo, drinking in the Casino-Bar.*"

Among the wounded were *Oberjäger* Elsner, and again (although without serious consequences) Mössinger, from grenade splinters on the 20th, which injured his eyes and face.

Remains of a German container used for dropping ammunition, weapons, and supplies. Found near Bjørnfjell in 2004. (Simon Orchard)

Present day view of Bjørnfjell. (Martin Oscarsson)

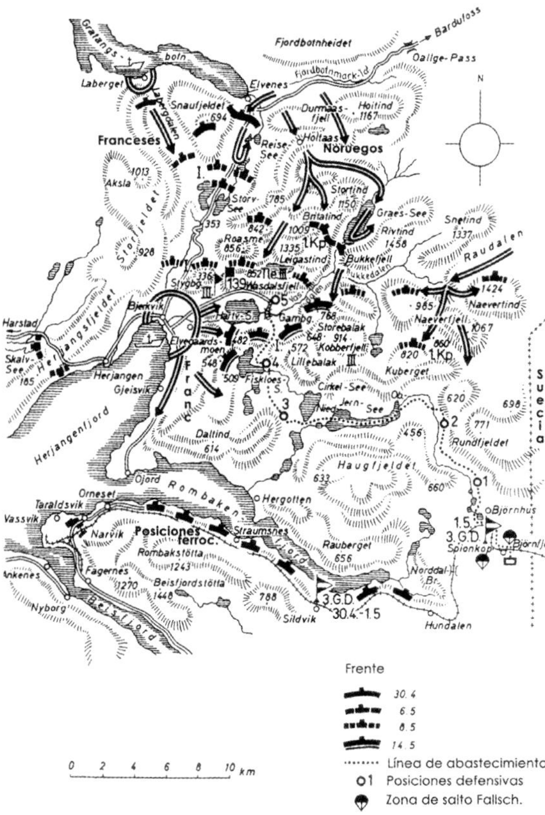

Map showing positions at Narvik. (Alex Buchner/Óscar González)

Fallschirmjäger in their positions on the Kuberget massif, north of Bjørnfjell. They lack the most basic equipment (overcoat, rucksack) to operate in a mountain environment. They were hurriedly deployed to spot height 820, arriving on 15 April, in order to urgently reinforce I./GJR 139, commanded by *Major* Hans von Schlebrügge, the "jewel" of the units forming *Gruppe Windisch*. (Óscar González)

The *Fallschirmjäger* took advantage of the personnel equipment left by the *Gebirgsjäger* to fight off the cold and snow. However, there was something from which they could not protect themselves: the well directed Norwegian artillery fire and the well camouflaged snipers. (Óscar González)

During the days that followed, *Gebirgsjäger* and *Fallschirmjäger* attempted to contain the Norwegians, who were trying to reach the Swedish frontier. Windisch had to face two battalions of French alpine troops, half a dozen Norwegian battalions, two battalions of the French Foreign Legion, and a battalion of Poles. Haussels was confronted by the British *24th Guards Brigade*, along with alpine troops of the 12th Battalion and Polish troops of the *Podhale* Brigade.[87]

On **21 May** the Allies landed troops in Troeldal, on the northern shore of the Rombaken fjord, advancing to the northeast and threatening Lillebalak, at spot height 572, and Kobberfjell (spot height 914). Faced with the seriousness of the situation, Dietl decided to withdraw 3 km along the whole northern front. A new defensive line was established between the mouth of the river Storelven to the northeast, passing along the southern shore of Lake Jern, the Holmelven valley, and spot height 620, and finishing north of Lake Holm to the Swedish frontier.

With this new front the units of 1./FJR1 found themselves on the right flank (always supporting the most solid unit in this sector, Von Schlebrügge's 1./GJR 139) next to the river Holmelven, on the northern summit of the Rundfjeldet, at spot height 726 which, unlike Kuberget (then in Norwegian hands), provided an excellent field of fire for the machine-guns. On their right flank, towards the Swedish frontier, they were supported by 3./GJR 138, commanded by Warrant Officer Raabe, composed of 15 mountaineers and 36 sailors. Gerhard Broder remembers that day:

"*The platoon moved to the new position. Our uniforms gave us away and the enemy spotted us without problem. The Norwegians attacked our flanks; they knew the ground and moved quickly. They fired, but fortunately for us their aim was high and their bullets whistled over our heads. The first of our men to reach the summit opened fire on them. I managed to get into position and open up with my MG 34. The barrel became hot immediately. A comrade brought me ammunition and we all did our best to defend our position in the snow.*"

Paratrooper Kurt Barank continues:

"*Once withdrawn, Lt. Becker posted me to the company HQ.* HFw. *Scholer,* Gefreiter *Zentgraf and I received orders to place ourselves in the observation post 1 km from the company command post.* Oberjäger *Scholz covered us with machine-gun and mortar fire just in case. There, in a tent behind a rock, we kept in radio contact with the command post.*

The Norwegians must have seen our movements, because once we were in our observation post they fired mortars with such precision that they mortally wounded Zentgraf, who died a few days later on 29 May."

The fronts stabilized between 17 and 27 May, leading to both sides increasing their patrols, although from 22 May the attacks by the French 14th Battalion on Windisch's positions intensified.

The "*Gebirgsjäger* of the *Luftwaffe*"

Coupled with this action by the *Fallschirmjäger* there was also the landing of 600 *Gebirgsjäger* aboard DFS 230 gliders,[88] commanded by *Gruppe XXI* of the *Luftwaffe*. Recently having made their debut at Eben Emael and the bridges over the Albert canal, landing them created problems due to the broken terrain and the snow (also, at this point in the war it was practically impossible to find sufficient numbers of the craft). On 20 May a small landing strip had been prepared. Even so, on the 23rd it was reported that the gliders would be delayed (until the 28th), mainly because of problems with the landing area (10% casualties had been estimated).[89]

The Germans would not desist, and again attempted to resupply their forces in Narvik. Basically, they continued to bring in artillery pieces for their troops. Twenty-one Ju 52s towing DFS 230 gliders from the 17./KGr zbV 5 flew from Hildesheim to Ålborg, Denmark, on 27 May. On 1 June the aircraft and gliders flew to Trondheim, 650 km from Narvik (except 6 that left from Oslo/Fornebu, where they had arrived on 31 May).

Once there, the plan was for the pilots to be issued civilian clothes and documentation (that of merchant sailors), so that they could cross the Swedish frontier without problems once their mission had been accomplished. The personnel in the German Embassy in Stockholm would do the rest to get them back to Germany.

Paratrooper of GJR 137. (Eric Queen)

Due to the adverse weather conditions and the withdrawl of the Allied troops on 4 June the mission was aborted (they were expected in Narvik on the 4th). The Ju 52s and DFS 230s returned to Hildelsheim on 15 June

Several pilots who had taken part in the missions at Fort Eben Emael and the Albert Canal, in Belgium, had been assigned to the operation. It must be remembered that there were not so many pilots with the right training available. This was the case of Ludwig Egner and Wilhelm Fulda, who piloted DFS 230 gliders on the 10 May as part of *Sturmgruppe Stahl* in the capture of Veldwezelt bridge, or Otto Bräutigam, Erwin Kraft, and Heiner Lange, members of *Gruppe Granit* that landed on Eben Emael.

However, a mission that was carried out was the parachute drop of troops from GJR 136 and 137, who had been sent to the parachute school at Wittstock/Dosse to do an accelerated 7-10 day course. Approximately 220/225 of them belonged to GJR 137. They jumped at Tromsø and Narvik to reinforce Dietl's command. Although their airborne training had been brief, they all received the *Luftwaffe's* parachute insignia. On 9 May GJR 137 received the order for volunteers to form this unit of airborne *Gebirgsjäger* (unmarried men who were not only sons) under the command of *Oblt* Rieger. Following training, which included three jumps—one from 250 m (although the men of 6./GJR 136 only made two jumps)—and packing parachutes, they flew from Værnes airfield near Trondheim, from where they flew to Bjørnfjell to make the combat jump aboard Ju 52s fitted with long range fuel tanks. Because of the extra fuel only 10 men could be carried instead of the usual 12.[90]

The difficulty in getting support troops to the area greatly influenced the German decision to drop the *Gebirgsjäger*. The first *Gebirgsjäger* began arriving in the Narvik area during the first few days of May. But the problems involved in transporting these units were serious. The case of the two companies from GJR 138 will serve as an example:

Paratrooper of GJR 137. (Eric Queen)

Gebirgsjäger of GJR 137 preparing to jump under the intense gaze of a *Luftwaffe* instructor (veteran of the Spanish Civil War) and an officer from their unit. The photograph was taken during the brief period of training undergone at Wittstock at the end of May 1940. It provides an excellent example of the varied equipment worn by the mountain troops at Bjørnfjell: M 38 helmets with double emblem (first man on the left), with the national colors erased (third from left), with the eagle erased (second from right); M 37 paratroop helmet (second from left), M 37 with elasticated band (third from right); and M 36 paratroop helmet (fourth from right). Three of the jump suits are the obsolete M 36 model (second, third, and fifth from left), while the rest are wearing the M 38. The first man on the left is wearing trousers with side pockets with three buttons. Note the "*Bergmutze*" (mountain cap), typical of the *Gebirgsjäger*, on the parachute pack (presumably the RZ 16, as is being worn by the first man on the right) between the two men in the center. (Óscar González)

Hauptmann Hermann Rieger, in a drawing made after Narvik. Rieger commanded a group of *Gebirgsjäger* volunteers, together with *Oblt* Eric Schwaiger, who were trained to jump at Bjørnfjell. Among their insignias it is possible to distinguish the *Luftwaffe* parachute badge and the Narvik Shield. (Bart Jansen)

On 8 May the order was received that the 3rd Company (3./GJR 138) would fly from Trondheim to Narvik. Two aircraft reached the objective (transporting, amongst others, the Company commander, *Oblt*. Ploder), but one plane was hit and had to make a forced landing, losing 17 men. The rest of the unit (50 men) returned to Trondheim. On the 10th, *Leutnant* Adler, with the rest of the company, tried to fly to Narvik again. The mission was partially successful, but only one plane (carrying Adler) was able to land. Another attempt was made. The transport planes came under fire from the British warships as they flew over Narvik. This, together with the bad weather, forced them to return to Trondheim without completing their mission.

The 2./GJR 138, who were also due to fly to Narvik, tried to get there by seaplane on 14 May. The group was composed of *Leutnant* Korber together with four soldiers from the 2nd Company and eight *Luftwaffe* signallers. Soon after take off they were forced to return with a failed engine. On 18 May (the 6th attempt) Korber landed in Narvik with 15 men from 2./GJR 138. Luck was also with the rest of the 3rd Company (*Leutnant* Raabe), who were able to land on the 20th. The men of the 2nd Company who had so far failed to reach Narvik tried on the 21st but without success, again due to weather conditions. On 22 May the main body of 2./GJR 138 finally arrived in Narvik. Around 38 men of 2./GJR 138, commanded by *Oblt* Renner, flew in on *Do Wals* seaplanes.

Given the difficulties, the plan to air-transport the rest of I./GJR 138 was abandoned. The only possibility was to drop the mountain units by parachute.

On 23 May at 22:45 h 1 officer and 65 men of GJR 137, under *Oblt* Erich Schwaiger,[91] were dropped by parachute. Only two men were slightly injured during the drop. Some of the Ju 52s had to fly through Swedish air space and came under anti-aircraft fire. The same day—according to the diary of 2.GJD—another 7 aircraft were expected with *Fallschirmjäger*.[92]

During the days that followed more *Gebirgsjäger* arrived by parachute (always at Bjørnfjell). From 23 to 25 May approximately 220/225 volunteers from I/GJR 137 (and

Recently arrived *Gebirgsjäger* about to leave for their assigned positions. The paratrooper M 38 helmet is visible amongst their equipment. The seated man is sitting on a weapons container, while next to him is a parachute in its transport bag. ("Narvik im Bild")

III./GJR 137), commanded by *Oblt* Rieger and *Oblt* Schwaiger, were dropped, the latter armed with a heavy machine-gun and a mortar.

On the 24th, 55 *Gebirgsjäger* jumped at 22:00 h. They were travelling aboard 5 Ju 52 /3ms of KGr zbV 108, escorted by 5 Bf 110 of I./ZG 76.[93]

At 10:00 h on the 25th another 54 men of Rieger's company were dropped without incident, as well as men from Schwaiger's group. Lastly, that day at around 19:00 h, the rest of Rieger's company were dropped, with some 44 men brought from Trondheim aboard 4 Ju 52s. Everything indicates that one of the officers was *Leutnant* Ernst Graf von Strachwitz.[94]

Reinforcements continued to arrive aboard seaplanes (such as the two that brought 14 *Gebirgsjäger* from 6./GJR 138, landing on the 24th, and 44 men commanded by *Oblt* Renner of 2./GJR 138, who arrived at 19:00 h) or by train through neutral Sweden (diguised as civilian personnel or medics[95]).

The air-transported units of GJR 137 had to integrate themselves into *Gruppe Narvik*, under the command of *Major* Haussels. Rieger's company had the task

Several *Gebirgsjäger* recently arrived at Bjørnfjell on 24 May 1940. M 38 helmet, M 36 jump suit with double zip, and Army *Bergmutze* are all signs that these men are from the small group of mountain troops who jumped at Narvik. Roman Schelch, the man wearing the cap on the left, was killed in action on 28 May; next to him are corporals Doregger and Gattinger,. (Óscar González)

An unseren unvergeßlichen
Sohn und Bruder
Josef Rieger
Oberfeldwebel in einem Geb.-Jäg.-Regt. an der Eismeerfront, Träger des EK I. und II. Kl., Fallschirm-, Infanterie-Sturm- und Verwundetenabzeichen, Narvikschild u. dgl.
welcher am 28. Jänner 1943, um 11.15 Uhr durch einen Kopfschuß den Heldentod fand.
Er stand im 29. Lebensjahre und wurde am Heldenfriedhofe Parkina (Nordfinnland) beerdigt.

Er ruhe in Frieden!

Der Führer ruft, es geht zur Schlacht.
Lebt wohl, ihr Lieben mein!
Habt keine Furcht, der Himmel wacht;
Vertraut auf Gott allein!
Brach auch mein Aug', ward kalt die Hand,
O weinet, klaget nicht!
Starb ja den Tod für's Vaterland,
Den Opfertod der Pflicht.

Er war uns lieb im Leben,
Gedenken wir seiner auch im Tode.

Death notice of a mountain trooper who jumped at Bjørnfjell. He was later killed in the eastern sector. (Archivo Eric Queen)

of reinforcing the northern shore of the Beis fjord, south of Narvik, at Fagernes, where they arrived on the 27th. Schwaiger's unit was transported by train to the sector west of Hundalen on the 24th, later moving to the area between tunnels nº 3 and nº 4 on the railway line, the defense of which was vital to German interests. They deployed to the east of the "Freytag Company," composed of sailors, next to Djupvik. They were there to prevent a hypothetical Allied landing in the northern area of the Rombaken fjord.

In the Ankenes area, west of Narvik, where the 8./GJR 139 had deployed in support and relief of 6./GJR 139, the possibility of an attack towards the Ankenes fjord was considered with the collaboration of the recently arrived *Fallschirmjäger*. Haussels commanded about 3,000 men, more than half of whom were sailors.

2./GJR 138, composed of 82 men (landed in seaplanes), were placed at the disposal of *Gruppe Windisch*.

Men were still being brought in on seaplanes on 28 May: soldiers from 2./GJR 138 and 6./GJR 138, together with anti-tank guns (*Pak*). Two seaplanes moored in the Rombaken fjord were destroyed by British *Hurricanes*. The occupants were captured.

One of the 225 volunteers from GJR 137 who jumped at Bjørnfjell between 23 and 25 May. All were awarded the *Luftwaffe* parachute insignia. The Narvik Shield can be seen among the decorations. (Eric Queen)

(Simon Orchard)

Walther's *Fallschirmjäger* Confront the Allied Troops

Following the rapid conclusion of the campaign in Holland and Belgium the *Fallschirmjäger* of FJR1 were available for deployment in Norway.

I./FJR1 was to be the unit chosen by Student for Norway. A "new" 1st Company was formed, commanded by *Olt* Fischer, with reinforcements drawn from *FschErgBtl*. An 8 cm mortar platoon and a 4th Company were also added to the Battalion, so that by 24 May 25 officers and 735 other ranks were available.[96]

I./FJR1 left their base in Stendal by train and then aircraft for Trondheim (to later jump at Bjørnfjell). The unit followed three routes to Trondheim: *Marschgruppe A* took a train to Ålborg, and then continued by air; and *Marschgruppe B* by train to Frederikshaven, then ship to Larvik, and from there by plane to Trondheim. Both units left Germany on 24 May. *Marschgruppe C* departed on 25 May at 05:00 h, transported by aircraft to Oslo and from there to Trondheim. The unit charged with transporting the paratroops was *Kampfgeschwader zbV 106* from *Luftflotte 5*, flying Ju 90s and Ju 52s. As became habitual in the Norwegian campaign, weather conditions hindered operations, so that only on 30 May (six days after their departure) did the units meet up in Trondheim. A Ju 52 (WNr. 6108) was lost in transit over Rena, south of Østerdalen. With the crew was a German civil servant and nine men of 4./FJR1, together with their officer, *Olt* Heinrich Eckleben.[97]

79 men—two platoons of 4./FJR1 commanded by *Leutnant* Keuchel, and at least one platoon of 2./FJR1 led by *Hauptmann* Erich Waltherr—jumped on **26 May**.[98] Another 10 Ju 52s carried in mountain troops the same day.

Hauptmann Erich Walther (in the center wearing a scarf) at Narvik surrounded by a varied group of men: *Fallschirmjäger*, *Kriegsmarine*, and *Gebirgsjäger*. (Bundesarchiv Koblenz)

During the flight, the plane carrying the commander of the 2nd Parachute Company, *Olt* Tyczka, was intercepted by *Gladiators* of 263 Squadron at Bord, next to Sulitjelma, 75 km to the east of Bodø. The plane caught fire, but the ten paratroops were able to jump. Two were wounded, and together with Tyczka were captured by Norwegian troops. The remaining 7 men managed to reach German lines. Their comrades were later liberated.[99]

The intervention by Walther's paratroops on the eve of the Allied landing at Narvik was crucial. They helped enormously in sustaining the southern sector, defending the railway line.

The Allied Strategy and Attack at Narvik

The intention of the Allies, as well as the Norwegian forces present in the north of the country, was to capture Narvik. These plans came into effect with the landing of the British *24th (Guards) Brigade* from 14 to 18 April in the small port of Harstad, on the island of Hinnoya, 50 km northwest of Narvik.

The intention of the Fleet commander, the Earl of Cork and Orrery, who was given overall command on 20 April, was to send these troops to Narvik and deliver a knockout blow. This was not supported in the beginning by the commander of the ground forces, *Major-General* Mackesy,[100] who favoured a pincer movement from the north and south. Another of the Admiral's plans was frustrated, which was to land a battalion in the city following an intense naval bombardment by the British ships, which included *HMS*

The remains of the battle: French *Hotchkiss H 39 tank*, now next to the Narvik war museum. (Óscar González)

Warspite. However, to bombard the city in this way was deemed to be ineffective. What could be done, supported with the artillery, was to use Norwegian troops of the 6th Division to take Gratangen, located at the end of the fjord of the same name some 30 km north of Narvik. Nevertheless, a German counter-attack on 24 April caused one of the Norwegian battalions to collapse, and the Germans were able to recapture Gratangen.

With the inclusion of French forces on the 27th and 28th commanded by *General de Brigade* Émile Béthouart,[101] and following the failure of the original plan, *Lord Admiral* Cork and *Major-General* Mackesy formulated a new plan. The Allies had a numerical advantage of three to one over the Germans, and absolute control of the sea. This allowed them "relative comfort" in choosing an alternative plan.

Regarding the French deployment, the *Chasseurs Alpins* had 6 battalions and specialist companies in Norway as part of their "French Scandinavian Expeditionary Corps" (CEFE). This had originally been formed to intervene in Finland against the Soviet invasion, but in the end it was deployed in Norway under General Audet. Only part of the force initially envisaged was landed. The CEFE was composed as follows:

- Headquarters (General Audet).
- *1e Division Légère de Chasseurs* (General Béthouart), with six infantry battalions.
- *5e Demi-Brigade* (Semibrigada) *de Chasseurs Alpins* (*Comandante* Brunelli), with the 13th, 53rd, and 67th Battalions.
- *27e Demi-Brigade de Chasseurs Alpins* (Lieutenant Colonel Valentini), with the 6th, 12th, and 14th Battalions.
- 6th Anti-tank Company and the 13th *Chasseurs Alpins Battalion*.
- 31st Ski Company with a section of "*d'éclaireurs skieurs*."
- *13e Demi-Brigade de la Légion Étrangère* (Colonel Magrin-Verneret), with two infantry battalions, composed of 55 officers, 210 NCOs, and 1.984 legionnares.[102] These joined the main body of the French contingent on 6 May.
- *Brigade Autonome de Chasseurs de Podhale*[103] (General Bohusz- Szyszko), with four infantry battalions, which joined the rest on 9 May.
- 342nd and 343rd Independent Tank Companies, with 15 *Hotchkiss H39* armed with SA18 37 mm cannons and 15 Renault FT-17s. Not all the tanks were battle-ready.
- 2nd Independent Colonial Artillery Group, equipped with *Mle1897* 75mm pieces.
- Two 25 mm Anti-aircraft Batteries.
- Transport, Signals, Medical, Logistics, and Engineer units.

12 battalions of infantry in total, including four Polish, supported by artillery, tanks, anti-aircraft, and anti-tank units, plus specialist service platoons, which were landed in Bjerkvik, Namsos, and Narvik.

As a result of the new plan, three battalions of French Alpine troops, reinforced with artillery and three tanks, landed in Sjövengan on 28 April, 20 km north of Gratangen. Later a battalion headed for Labergdal, towards the south, was attacked from the German positions on 1 May (initial contact with the enemy).

In the south, the landing took place at the beginning of May. The *South Wales Borderers* of the *24th (Guards) Brigade*, reinforced with artillery and the *27e Demi-Brigade de Chasseurs Alpins*, which was not in the northern sector, approached Håkvik on the 9th, along the peninsula located between two fjords: the Skjomen and the Beis. The Battalion contented itself with occupying the town, so that things were made easy for the Germans when they came to counter-attack with 6./GJR 139, deploying in the area of the Beis fjord and taking Ankenes, a few kilometers northeast of Håkvik, and reoccupying the heights to the south of the town. The two Allied battalions occupied defensive positions. They were then joined by the Poles of the *Podhale* Brigade, leaving a total of three Allied battalions deployed on the southern front available to take up the offensive from 14 May.

The offensive began on the 12th on the northern flank at Bjerkvik. The *13e Demi-Brigade of the Légion Étrangère*, together with 5 tanks and 12 field guns, attacked under cover from the British ships. Their left flank had been secured by Norwegian troops approaching from the mountains. These men were acclimatised and equipped for the arctic conditions. Another three battalions of French alpine troops protected the Legionnaire's landing from the north and south. The landing took place on 12 and 13 May on the north and northeast shores of the Herjangen fjord, engaging the sailors of *Marine Btl Kothe* and 13./GJR 139. In a matter of hours, the first French battalion took Bjerkvik and the second took Medby. The following day, a patrol destroyed two German planes based on Lake Hartvik. With Bjerkvik and Elevgaarden occupied the Allies deployed along the coast as far as Øjord on the 13 May, at the entrance to the Rombaken fjord, just opposite Narvik. Their objective was in sight.

Windisch's men took up new positions to face the French along the Mebyfjell line (southeast of Elevgaarden), Lake Fiskloes, Lillebalak (spot height 572), Kobberfjell (914 m), and Kuberget (820 m). The withdrawl meant that the Germans lost most of their heavy weapons and provisions. This "evasion" strategy allowed the *27e Demi-Brigade de*

The graves of *Gebirgsjäger* killed at Narvik. The presence of the paratroop helmet shows that these were from the group dropped at Bjørnfjell. It is possible to identify the grave of *Gefreiter* Fritz Wild, born 7 December 1916 in Kapfenberg, Austria, and killed on 28 May 1940. (Óscar González)

Chasseurs Alpins to head south from Gratangen and link up with the *13e Demi-Brigade* in Bjerkvik.

The Allied offensive was accompanied by changes in command and the order of battle. This undoubtedñy hindered coordination (and the possibility of success) of the Allied forces. Mackesy was relieved of his command and was replaced by Claude Auchinleck, who took up his post as the commander in chief of Allied air and ground forces on 13 May. The force was known by the British as the *North-Western Expeditionary Force*. *General de Brigade* Béthouart took command of the ground forces deployed to the north of Narvik.

The only Allied "opportunity" was to be found in this small city in the north of Norway, as they had had to abandon the rest of the country to the Germans. They could no longer rely on any further significant Norwegian resistance. Because of this fact several companies of British troops were sent to cut the road from Trondheim to the north, between

Christliches Andenken
im Gebete an den
Gefreiten (Fallschirmjäger)
Martin Mayer
Zacherlsohn von Klebing
welcher am 28. Mai 1940 bei
Narwik gefallen ist.
R. I. P.

In der Fülle bester Jahre
Eiltest Du dem Grabe zu,
Ohne Schmerzen, ohne Klage
Schläfst in der Ferne Du
Nun in süßer Ruh.

Baur & Söhne, Freilassing

Death notice of *Fallschirmjäger* Martin Mayer, killed at Ankenes on 28 May 1940. The Allies made two attacks that day. The first was along the Narvik peninsula, at Ankenes. Polish troops, under General Bohusz-Szyszko, fought men of II./GJR 139, supported by paratroops. The Germans were unable to hold the position and were forced to withdraw into the interior. The second Allied attack took place north of Narvik. (Eric Queen)

Mo i Rana and Bodø. These units were supported by elements of the *24th (Guards) Brigade* from Harstad. No sooner had Auchinlek taken up his post than he decided to use all of the *24th (Guards) Brigade* and other smaller support units to take the port of Bodø, as well as cutting the road. The transfer of these units from Narvik to Bodø[104] meant that it was impossible to employ any other British units in the offensive of 12/13 May. Tromsø was also an Allied "stronghold," as the King and Norwegian government had been established in nearby Maalsevdal.

Finally, on the night of **27/28 May,** the Allies launched two attacks. The first was along the southern area of the Narvik peninsula at Ankenes. Polish troops under General Bohusz-Szyszko engaged II./GJR 139, who were unable to hold their positions and retreated into the interior. The second attack came north of Narvik. French and Norwegian troops carried out an amphibious assault with the objective of recapturing Narvik itself, which was accomplished. The Legion's 13a *Demi-Brigade*, commanded by General Béthouart, and the Norwegian 6th Division occupied the city (in what was to be the first Allied victory of the war). The 2nd Battalion took the city's hills, pushing towards the railway line. The 1st Battalion had secured the city by that night. The Germans lost 10 artillery pieces and 150 machine-guns, and were forced to give ground in the face of the Allied advance. Béthouart officially declared the fall of Narvik at 22:00 h. The city had been captured, but only to facilitate the Allied withdrawl from Norway.

Several *Fallschirmjäger* together with a member of the *Kriegsmarine* (on the right) at Kuberget. The sailor is wearing a mixture of German (M 38 helmet) and Norwegian clothing and equipment, including the jacket. When the Germans occupied the Elvegårdsmoen barracks at the beginning of the invasion they captured a large number of Norwegian uniforms destined for reservists. The sailors fighting at Narvik were given the nickname "*Gebirgs-Marine*." (Óscar González)

Day by Day Account of the Fighting in Narvik: Defense of the Railway Line and Resistance in the Snow

On **28 May** there was frantic activity on the German side. At 00:10 h (in daylight given the latitude) more *Fallschirmjäger* landed. No drops had been made since the 26th due to the bad weather and lack of transport aircraft. Walther now had 46 more paratroops.

The planes carrying the paratroops were again intercepted by *Gladiators*, this time over Saltdal, southeast of Bodø. One plane was hit and caught fire. Only 5 of the 10 paratroops aboard were able to jump; the rest were killed along with the crew. Another Ju 52 carrying the HQ of 3./FJR1, with their commander *Leutnant* Schmelz, was also hit. The pilot was forced to return to Trondheim, where he had to make an emergency landing near Mo. The crew and all the *Fallschirmjäger* on board were unharmed, and reached the German lines occupied by the 2nd Mountain Division (2.GJD)[105] two days later.

A platoon of 4./FJR1, led by *Leutnant* Keuchel, which had jumped with Walther on the 26th, was placed on alert on the 27th and sent to the southern sector, from Sildvik to the Beis fjord. Their mission was to reinforce the threatened positions of the 3./*Marine Regiment*, commanded by *Oblt* Clemens. They also covered the withdrawl of those units redeploying from Ankenes from positons along the stream at Lakselven. However, these initial orders were altered by *Major* Haussels, commander of II./GJR 139 and the troops in the Narvik sector. He ordered Keuchel's *Fallschirmjäger* to occupy positions near Kvanta, 2 km further to the northeast, along the stream at Mölnelven.

Fallschirmjäger at Kuberget. (Óscar González)

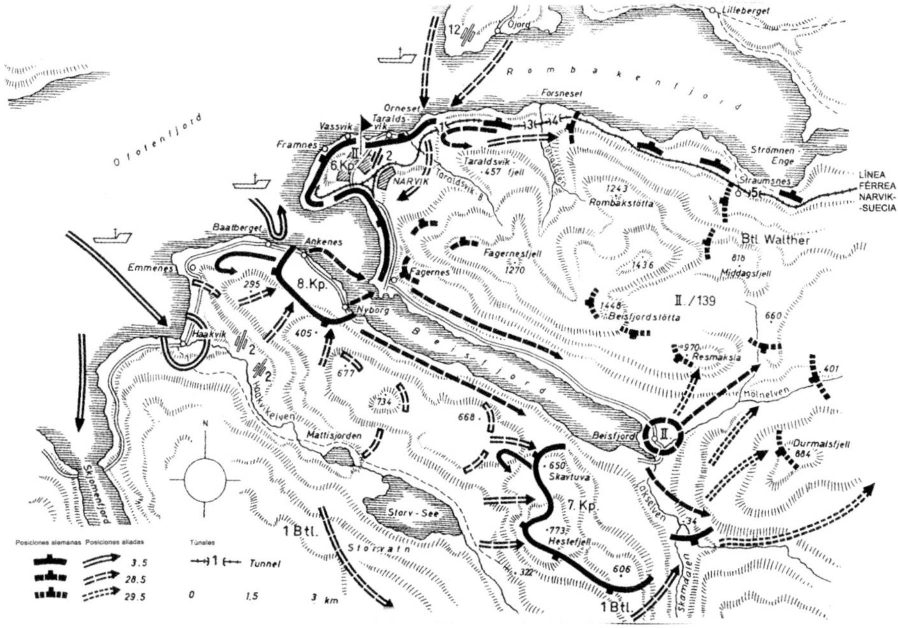

Map showing German and Allied positions in the sector south of Narvik and the railway line. (Alex Buchner/Óscar González)

The Allies were able to penetrate from Narvik to railway tunnel nº 3, defended by Holtorf's battalion of sailors. They had had no problems occupying the area west of Narvik as far as Ankenes. In this area the Poles fought a bitter battle to dislodge the Germans from the mountains of the peninsula. Rieger's company, which had parachuted in, held and then counter-attacked, retaking a few summits only to lose them again almost immediately.

At the same time the Allied air force bombed and strafed the German positions located at Sildvik and Hundalen. The pressure was unbearable, and communication between *Major* Haussels' units became more and more difficult. Haussels' mission was to hold, together with von Freytag-Loringhoven (commanding at least 80 sailors), along a front from the Rombaken fjord to the Beis fjord, across the Rombakstötta heights (1,243 m), Fagernesfjell (1,270 m), Middagsfjell (818 m), and Beisfjordstötta (1,448 m).

By the end of the day Dietl had lost Narvik. German losses amounted to 41 killed, 69 wounded, and 176 missing. It is clear that GJR 137 under Rieger and Schwaiger had seen the hardest of the fighting.

Fallschirmjäger commanded by Erich Walther attempt to defend the railway line between Narvik and the Swedish frontier at all costs. The defense of the railway tunnels during the last days of May cost the Germans heavy casualties. ("Fallschirmjäger Hier und Da")

29 May was to be another important day in the stabalization of the front. At 03:00 h Dietl received confirmation that Narvik had fallen. With the Allied advance threatening the railway line, so vital to German interests, Dietl ordered Walther to relieve von Freytag-Loringhoven's sailors and engage the advancing Allies.

Walther moved on the night of the 28th/29th with his available *Fallschirmjäger* to tunnels nº 3 and 4, intending to defend the railway line at all cost and link up with the left flank and the troops retiring from Narvik. The Allies attempted to force the Germans into a pocket (their intention was to reach Bjørnfjell by attacking from both the northeast and the south), but were unable to coordinate their movements.[106]

Walther took command of the railway line and Haussels' troops, trying to hold the attack of the Poles and the French Foreign Legion. The defense of the railway tunnels cost the Germans many casualties: among others *Oblt* Schwaiger (GJR 137), mortally wounded in the neck on the 28th while fighting in tunnel nº 1.

The "Walther Battalion" was hurriedly formed from *Fallschirmjäger* from the machine-gun platoon of the 3rd Company, under *Feldwebel* Rothärmel, with sailors and half of the I./FJR1 Signals Platoon, under *Stabsfeldwebel* Scheurig. The men travelled to

Above: *Fallschirmjäger* take up position along the railway line. These reinforcements were brought by train from Bjørnfjell to Hundalen. Once there they had to continue on foot, as the train was easy prey for the British naval guns in the Rombaks fjord. ("Fallschirmjäger Hier und Da") Below: *Fallschirmjäger* next to a sign marking the Arctic Circle. ("Fallschirmjäger Hier und Da")

Hundalen by train, in the south, in the Rombaken fjord, 3 km east of the Beis fjord. From here it was impossible to continue by train because the guns of the Royal Navy controlled the railway line as far as Narvik. The remaining distance to tunnel nº 4 was covered on foot. Their positions extended from the tunnel to Mount Rombakstötta. They also had units from 3./ and 4./ (4./FJR1 again moved from Sildvik) at their disposal, as well as newly arrived reinforcements (65 *Fallschirmjäger* from 3./FJR1,under *Leutnant* Rottke, who had landed in the early hours of that day). There were also reserve units in tunnels nº 5 and 6.

When he arrived at tunnel nº 4, Walther was informed that the front had been breached by the Poles. He sent Rothärmel's machine-gunners to spot height 1,400, south of Forneset. After several hours spent ascending the hill, the report was found to be false and the situation stable. The Platoon received new orders to transfer 6 km to tunnel nº 4, on the shore of the Rombaksbotn fjord, and maintain defensive positions.

Leutnant Keuchel's *Fallschirmjäger* arrived at the end of the day to reinforce Walther. Deployed on the 27th and 28th on the orders of Haussels, they had relieved II./GJR 139. This time Keuchel's men were deployed in the area of Middagsfjell, 3 km southwest of the Straits of Straumen, to defend the railway line.

As soon as Rottke landed with his *Fallschirmjäger*, he received orders from Dietl to deploy with two platoons of his company, reinforced with *Gebirgsjäger* and sailors, to the southern sector and attack the Poles in Aksla, at spot height 961. They left from Bjørnfjell at 12:00 h by train to Hundalen, and from there on foot to their destination, just as Walther's men had done earlier. On arriving, they found no sign of the Poles and asked for new orders. They moved 2 km north towards Sildvik. Finally, 14 hours after starting out they reached their positions. 7./GJR 139 was located on the left of *Kampfgruppe Rottke*. They were attacked by the Poles at Hestefjell at 19:45 h.

The sailors in tunnel nº 3 mounted a tenacious defense of the railway line. Allied air attacks were continuous, but they could not break the defense of the tunnels. In the afternoon, the combined fire from a British destroyer 1.5 km away and a battery deployed in Troeldal harassed Walther's men defending tunnel nº 4. This was the preliminary bombardment for a large scale attack on the railway line scheduled to take place at 18:00 h..

Walther held tunnel nº 4 until midnight on the 29th/30th, receiving and covering the German troops retreating from Narvik. The left flank, defended by the remnants of three companies of *Fallschirmjäger*, sailors, and soldiers of II./GJR 139, were unable to resist the Allied attack, which directly threatened Walther. As a result of this attack, the Germans withdrew at 23:00 h to positions near the river Orneelven. The manoeuvre was a success, with Rothärmel's machine-gunners covering Walther and Haussels. Rottke, relieved from his initial objective, also joined this group at the end of the day. One of his platoons later relieved Keuchel on the heights of Middagsfjell. The other platoon was assigned to *Olt.* Götte, one of the heroes of Fornebu.[107]

Walther's intention was not to remain on the Orneelven, despite it being a "comfortable" position, but rather to gain time and recover and hold the Middagsfjell–Straumen line.

The day was also dramatic for Haussels, under continual attack from the south. Nevertheless, he managed to contain the attack. Paratroops, together with GJR 137 and 2./GJR 138, tried to retake positions in Durmaasfjell without success.

I./FJR1 losses reflect the intensity of the fighting. On 29 May the unit had suffered 220 casualties (6 officers and 214 men). At the end of the day fresh reinforcements were dropped over Dietl's Headquarters: 61 paratroops from the I./FJR1 HQ.[108]

All of them were anxious to join up with Walther in Sildvik.

On **30 May** 3./FJR1 were transported by train along with *Mar.Kp. Salzwedel* and *Pi.Zug Brandt* to Hundalen. They were reinforcements for the defense of the line between Hundalen and Sildvik. No more reinforcements could be flown in due to the bad weather.

During the day Walther lost Straumsnes, together with the railway line, 2 km southwest of the small Straumen peninsula. On the left flank, defended by II./GJR 139 from the eastern banks of the Beisfjordtötta, located in the center of the Narvik peninsula, as far as Durmaalsfjell (spot height 844, covering the Sildvik region) came under repeated attack by the Poles. Finally, the Poles managed to penetrate as far as 4 km in the direction of Aksla, aided by the fog. The Germans counter-attacked without success. The breakthrough posed a threat to Walther, as the German units fighting on the heights south of the railway line could be cut off.

Walther decided to concentrate on the railway line, ordering the defensive line located to the west of Straumen to withdraw. It was necessary to maintain control of the railway line and "block holes" at all costs.

The Poles, for unknown reasons, did not take advantage of the situation and penetrate to Sildvik.

In the northern sector, on the left flank of *Gruppe Windisch*, the French and Norwegians continued to pressure, causing many casualties amongst the German mountain troops, as well as losing positions. The *Fallschirmjäger* defended spot height 456, maintaining contact with III./GJR 139. In the center, I./GJR 139, on spot height 625, had a heavy machine-gun and a mortar. Finally, in the east, Braun's platoon of Sailors and a company of seamen under Steinecker held spot heights 620 and 698, next to the Swedish frontier.[109]

The following day (**31 May**), Allied attacks on Walther's positions continued (during this day his left flank was located on spot height 638, at Stroskaret, with hardly any changes since the previous day), as well as on those of Haussels. As if this was not enough, the union of the two sectors of the German front was still not consolidated. Given the desperate lack of artillery, the Germans loaded a wagon with explosives, sending it against the French and Polish troops. Even so, this day was quieter than those preceeding it, allowing for the line between Middagsfjell and Straumen to be stabilised.

At mid-day the Allied aircraft attacked ground targets with the *Luftwaffe* absent. Bombing along the railway line was especially heavy between Sildvik and Bjørnfjell. For the first time the British aircraft were joined by Norwegian planes, which harassed German positions from the south of Rundfjeldet to the north of Bjørnfjell, where the command post of I./GJR 139 was located.

Meanwhile, reinforcements were awaited from the air, which arrived at 20:00 h, despite the thick fog and snow. Thirty-seven men (1 platoon with mortars, a *Gr. Wf. Zug* from 4./FJR1, commanded by *Lt* Wendt) and paratroops from the battalion HQ, together with medical personnel led by *Unterarzt* Dr. Scheffler, were sent to Walther's sector, while Wendt's men were deployed in the area of *Gruppe Windisch* at spot height 698, in Von Schlebrügge's sector. There they helped the platoon from I./GJR 139 located next to the Swedish frontier.

The "odyssey" undergone by Wendt's platoon is an example of the hard conditions of the fighting during that May. Without a guide, they began a march lasting several hours over snowy ground covered in a dense fog while carrying their 80mm mortars and ammunition. They became lost, and until a German patrol signalled their position with a flare they could not reach their objective. On the way Wendt was wounded by machine-gun fire, and an NCO had to take command of the platoon: *Oberjäger* Käding. Once at spot height 698 they positioned their mortars behind some blocks of ice just 200 m from the enemy.

The satisfaction of the Allied command on knowing that Bodø had been held without suffering heavy casualties cannot be denied. *Luftflotte 5* had been concentrating in the town since the 27th, bombing the Allied positions. The Norwegians had confidence in their allies—the British and French—and looked to the capture of Mounts Rundfjeldet and Haugfjedet, north of Bjørnfjell. These were the last remaining positions at altitude held by Windisch's men. The Norwegians believed that the capture of these positions would lead to the capitulation of the German troops in that sector, although there also existed another alternative: that the German troops would cross into neutral Sweden, which would lead to them being interned, although this course of action had been considered by the Germans (Hitler had authorized Deitl to cross the frontier). Through diplomatic contacts they had arranged for the Swedes to transfer 4 trains to the frontier on 25 May, but Deitl maintained his position of resisting at all costs.

1 June. The Allies' attempt to surprise Walther by applying pressure against Hundalen. At the same time the left flank defended by the reinforced II./GJR 139 was attacked and positions were lost.

At this point in the battle, the composition of the "Walther Battalion" deployed from the Rombaken fjord to the Middagsfjell, passing along spot height 638, was as follows:

- "*Fallschirmjäger Kompanie Götte*" (2 officers and 94 men), led by *Oberleutnant* Wilhelm Götte, officer commanding a platoon of the 2./FJR1
- "*Mar. Kompanie Fuchs*" (2 officers and 72 men), formed from sailors from the sunken German ships.
- "*Mar. Kompanie Meissner, v. Freytag and v. Diest*" (13 officers and 270 men), same composition as the previous unit.
- "*Fallschirmjäger Zug Kersten,*" platoon composed of 1 officer and 45 men
- "*Falschirmjäger Zug Keuchel,*" platoon of 1 officer and 51 men.
- 45 men of the "*Stab*" (HQ) of the Sifnals Platoon ("*Nachrichten Zug*") from I./FJR1. There were also 9 heavy machine-guns and 5 mortars.

The men were hungry and exhausted after days of intense fighting. Supplies and food (hot rations in the central wagon) were sent by train from Sildvik.

That day the *Luftwaffe* accidently bombed the men in the positions in front of Walther. It would appear the flare sent up from the German lines had fallen in their own positions, and the planes bombed friendly forces. Despite the terrible mistake there were no serious casualties.

The pressure on Walther's left flank and the threat of an Allied frontal attack made gauranteed resistance impossible in the positions being occupied at that time. Therefore, on 1 June Dietl ordered Walther to withdraw his forces beyond the already arranged "Orneelven" line. The manoeuvre began at 03:30 h with the transfer of equipment, followed by the ordered withdrawl of the men: first, the companies of sailors, covered by the paratroops. The withdrawl was completed between 10:00 and 12:00 h, with the men occupying positions behind the river Orneelven. From its mouth in the Rombaksbotn to the south, Walther's troops occupied the following new positions:

- North of the railway line, a platoon of sailors acted as the vangaurd for Walther, occupying a house near Orneelven.
- "*Marine Kompanie Meissner*" between Rombaksbotn and the railway line.

- South of the rails, on a slope, were "*Marine Kompanie Fuchs*" and the "Kersten parachute platoon."
- To the left of these, to the southwest, was "*Marine Kompanie Von Freytag*."
- The left flank was covered by the "Keuchel parachute platoon."
- The paratroop company led by *Olt* Götte deployed to both sides of the railway line, near the most advanced positions, and was attached to Meissner's company.
- The machine-gun platoon from 3./FJR1, commanded by *Feldwebel* Rothärmel, was also spread among several positions, as was Von Diest's company of sailors.
- The command post and communications center (all the other positions were linked to this) was located in tunnel nº 10.
- The area just in front of the German lines, between the Rombaksbotn fjord and the railway line, was mined and explosive charges were hidden. It was planned that if necessary tunnel nº 8 would be destroyed.

However, the day was relatively tranquil for Walther's Group, in spite of everything. The enemy only made his presence felt in the sector—without any effect—of Keuchel's platoon.

While this was occurring on the southern front, on the northern front the exhausted units on the left flank of "*Gruppe Windisch*" came under constant attack in the area north and west of the Haugfjells massif, having to withdraw their positions after heavy fighting.

On the right flank, Von Schlebrügge's situation was no better. Renner's 2./GJR 138, under Von Schlebrügge's orders, received determined attacks—frontal ground assaults and from the air—and had to abandon their positions on spot height 620, east of Lake Holm—this was Von Schlebrügge's right flank—on 1 June after 15 hours of combat (which left 7 dead and 14 wounded).

The pressure on Walther was unceasing. They were bombarded by a British destroyer from the early hours of the morning. Artillery and mortar fire took over from the destroyer, punishing the new German defensive positions.

As no infantry attack came Walther sent out patrols, who reported back that the terrain ceded to the enemy remained unoccupied. The *Fallschirmjäger* deployed on the left flank had to abandon spot height 638 on **2 June** in the face of overwhelming attacks (2 battalions of the French Foreign Legion, 2 battalions of Poles, and a French alpine battalion who occupied positions just 800 m from them, according to Walther's report of 5 June).[110]

Fresh paratroop reinforcements arrived in Bjørnfjell on 2 June at 14:45 h aboard 6 Ju 52s from KGr zbV 107. These were two more platoons under *Leutnant* Spang and *Leutnant* Süttner. A heterogenous unit formed of 2 officers and 44 men (15 men from the mortar platoon and another 15 from the 3rd Platoon of 2./FJR1). Last of all were 16 men from the machine-gun platoon (also from the 2nd Company).

During the journey the escort fighters shot down two British planes, while one of the German transport aircraft (WNr. 6751 DC+SP) was shot down when it overflew Swedish air space east of Ricksgraensenfjellet. Eight men were killed in the crash, among them 6 *Fallschirmjäger* (Joachim Liskow from the 1st Company, as was *Jäger* Konrad Hof, plus *Jäger* Franz Langfeld, *Jäger* Hans Vorstoffel, *Jäger* Bodo Weskamp, and *Jäger* Arno Fischer from the 2nd Company). It is most likely that the crew members killed were *Oberfeldwebel* Bruno Hasse and Walter Schmutzler. Five paratroops and two other crew members were able to jump free as the plane fell in flames. The last to jump found his parachute on fire, and Hasse quickly took off his own and gave it to his comrade. Hasse died in the impact. This was undoubtedly a heroic act that inspired the German troops during those hard days. The Swedes handed over the bodies of the *Fallschirmjäger* three days later, on 5 June.[111]

Spang's unit immediately went to reinforce Von Schlebrügge's right flank in the Rundfjeldet sector, in support of the forces (*Gebirgsjäger* and sailors) holding spot heights 615 and 698. The latter and the eastern shore of Lake Holm came under continuous attack during the days that followed (mainly 4, 5, and 6 June). They were facing the Norwegian 14th Infantry Regiment.

In spite of the Allied activity, it was obvious that the situation was changing. Bodø had fallen into the hands of the German 2nd Mountain Division—an event that demoralised the Norwegian King and his government—and *Luftflotte 5* concentrated to attack the British ships near Narvik. Walther also benefited from the *Luftwaffe's* activity: 10 *Stukas*, 2 fighters, and 8 Me 110s attacked the Allies along the railway line. Planes of the British "*263 Squadron*" flying from the carriers *Ark Royal* and *Glorious*, as well as from Bardufoss airfield, were forced to pay a high price in the air fighting with the *Luftwaffe*.

On **3 June** the situation was relatively quiet on Walther's front, and he sent out several patrols to scout the enemy positions. One such patrol followed the length of the railway line in order to take prisoners, and also to capture a high point to the west of the front. They were discovered and fired on by French machine-gunners located on spot height 638. Another patrol led by an *Oberjäger*, and covered by the machine-guns of *Fw* Rothärmel, was able to attack the French positions, occasioning them some minor losses.

The reduction of Allied pressure allowed the Germans to relieve their units to the extent that up to a third of the men were able to enjoy a rest in Sildvik, in the rearguard. This "pause" also gave the troops the opportunity to change their wet clothes, while those showing signs of frostbite were attended to.

In the north versus the Norwegians the pressure did not abate. It remained particularly active in the central sector of Windisch. Holmelven Creek, the area east of Lake Jernas, and height 698 would be attacked. At this point the action of the *Fallschirmjäger* platoon would be critical to maintain the position.

During **4 June** there was continual fierce fighting on the extreme east of Windisch's right flank, where the Norwegians were attempting to break through with artillery and infantry attacks in the area of Rundfjeldet. Again, mortar fire from the paratroop positions proved decisive and the Norwegian attacks failed.

On Walther's front things remained calm; the only activity came from the guns of the *Royal Navy* and Allied aircraft and artillery, above all in the area between the Rombaken and Beis fjords. Their mission, however, was to keep the Allied beachhead clear and ready for the Allied withdrawl.

With the deteriorating situation in France, the Allies had decided to withdraw from Narvik during the first days of June. 4,700 had already been evacuated during the night of 3/4 June, and they planned to evcuate a further 4,900 the following night. The battle was decided, but the Germans did not know it yet. The German command were still not aware that the Allies had decided to leave Narvik.

To aid in the withdrawl the Allies had brought 15 transport ships that were waiting some 180 nautical miles off the Norwegian coast, protected by the Royal Navy. The first convoy evacuating troops left on 4 June from Scapa Flow without incident.

The general situation changed radically from **5 June**. Negotiations underway to determine the conditions of the Norwegian surrender influenced the fighting in Narvik, although the three sectors (Windisch, Walther, and Von Schlebrügge) were still attacked by the Allies.

Windisch's right flank continued to hold the constant Norwegian attacks. Counter-attacks from the German reserves continued to frustrate the Noregians. Nevertheless, the Germans feared the worst: an overwhelming frontal attack.

An unexpected event was to add to the problems of Walther and Dietl. During an Allied air attack, the wagon supplying Walther's HQ was taken to the protection of tunnel nº 8, but due to brake failure it began rolling towards the Allied positions. The personnel in the wagon were able to jump off in time, but nothing could be done to save the maps, reports, and other secret German documents on board. When a German patrol under *Olt* Götte located the wagon on the Straumen peninsula it was empty. This supposed a serious reverse for Dietl.

On the night of **5/6 June** 5,100 Allied soldiers were evacuated. The Norwegians occupied the positions vacated by the French alpine troops north of the Rombaken fjord. The Allied naval contingent continued its intense bombardment of the German positions on the southern front during the 6th and 7th. The Allies were covering their withdrawl, and Dietl discovered what was happening on the **7th**. The Allied air force was also bombing the German positions, including Walther's command post in Sildvik station. Walther and the Germans supposed the Allies were concentrating ships for a landing on the southern shore of the Rombaksbotn fjord. To confront this 2 *Pak*, 2 *Flak*, 1 machine-gun, and various *Panzerbüchsen* were moved to Walther's sector northeast of Sildvik. Dietl also ordered Walther's sector to link up with II./GJR 139 (protected in Hundalen), which was done the following day. On the 7th French troops could be seen moving from the railway line. Slowly the Germans began discounting the possibility of a new landing.

In Von Schlebrügge's sector, Norwgian attempts to overwhelm the exhausted Germans continued to yield no results. But the continual combat and bad weather conditions brought the German troops to the edge of collapse.

That same day, between 18:45 and 23:00 h, significant reinforcements of paratroops arrived, with the purpose of providing Dietl with a reserve force: 5 Ju 52 (one was shot down) arrived transporting *Oberst* Meindl, *Leutnant* Von Blücher, and 26 *Fallschirmjäger* from 2./FJR1). However, Von Blücher's men did not see combat.

The case of *Oberst* Eugen Meindl deserves more detailed comment. At that time he was in command of "*Gebirgsjäger Artillerie Regiment 112*." Unlike the other troops who jumped at Narvik, Meindl did so without prior training.[112] The *Fallschirmjäger* Willi Nollen recalled the details years later:

"*On the afternoon of 2 June,*[113] *the 2nd Company received the order to go to Narvik. Around 7 in the evening we were moving with our gear towards the transport aircraft. A little later our Platoon leader,* Lt *Graf von Blücher, arrived. He had recently been decorated with the Knight's Cross following the operation in Holland, and he surprised us with the following order: 'the leading aircraft in the formation must leave one man behind in Trondheim to make room for an* Oberst *of the* Gebirgsjäger. *' The* Oberst, *an experienced mountain artillery officer, had to report to General Dietl in Narvik.*

My Group leader, Oberjäger *Schneider, and I decided who would remain behind. Finally, we chose an* Obergefreiter *who had to bid us farewell with tears in his eyes and wishing us all the best.*

At around 19:15 h von Blücher arrived with the Oberst. *We were surprised to see that he was not prepared for the jump. He wore only a leather coat and an infantry helmet. What's more, he was missing the most important piece of equipment: the parachute! The* Obergefreiter *who was to remain behind could have given him his but he had already left (we later found out that he had managed to slip in with another group and participated in....). Finally, we managed to find a parachute for the* Oberst.

The air crew and Fallschirmjäger *prepared for take off. We were in a hurry. Our* Oberst *was equipped in an improvised manner. His leather coat tied tight with cord; Von Blücher found him a helmet and checked his harness. Soon we received the signal to board the aircraft.*

During the flight we joked with the Oberst. *Then, after a 4-hour-flight, we approached the drop zone. It was small and rocky. Flares signalled the moment for the jump. 'ready! ¡Containers out!' Von Blücher jumped. The* Oberst *approached the door. As he was about to jump he noticed that his parachute pack was snagged above the door, which supposed a serious problem.* Oberjäger *Schneider, aware of the situation, struck the parachute, and with it the* Oberst, *pushing him out of the plane. I also helped with my right foot, pushing as hard as I could, in response to the* Oberst's *appeals for help. Finally we watched him jump, his RZ 1 opening without problem. The* Oberst *glided to the ground without problems, much to our relief. We waited for the aircraft to make another pass to jump. At last our turn came and we jumped towards the snow. Before we reached the ground there was a sudden gust of wind that endangered our landing. However, in the end it all went well. Our loyal comrades in the* Kriegsmarine *grabbed our chutes so we were not dragged away by the wind.*

The other two aircraft in our formation could not reach the drop zone; they were forced to return to Trondheim because of the weather. The result of our drop was as follows: of the 10 Fallschirmjäger *who jumped 9 were slightly injured. Only the* Oberst *arrived without a scratch! And without any previous experience or training...with enthusiasm he confessed: 'I'm going to be a paratrooper.'"*

Meindl informed Deitl of the intention of the *Kriegsmarine* to attack the British fleet blockading Narvik.

But the Allies were under pressure to get their men out of Narvik. By 7 June 10,000 men had already been evacuated. On the same day the first Allied aircraft to leave the combat zone flew from Bardufoss to the carrier HMS *Glorious*. Also that same day the King, Haakon VII, and his government boarded the cruiser HMS *Devonshire* in Tromsø, with the intention of continuing the fight from Great Britain. The commander in chief of the Norwegian armed forces, *General* Ruge, remained behind. He had been given the necessary powers to demobilize Norwegian troops and negotiate the surrender with German troops once the Allies had left Narvik.

During the night of 7/8 June the last 4,600 Allied troops were evacuated. The last security measures were effected by the destroyers in the early hours of the 8th. While the aircraft from the carrier *Ark Royal* protected the embarkation and the convoy, the last 7 Hurricanes landed on the flight deck of the *Glorious* from Bardufoss, and the ship headed for Britain escorted by the destroyers. The *Glorious* and its escorts were attacked and sunk soon after by the German battleships *Scharnhorst* and *Gneisenau* with the loss of 1,400 men, including 28 of the 32 pilots aboard.

The following day, Walther took the initiative and advanced his positions towards Narvik, reaching the Straits of Straumen /Middagsfjord. At the same time various patrols (*Spähtruppen*) continued to scout along the railway. Haussels also collaborated in the offensive, attacking Beisfjord. Meindl took command of Walther and Haussels' troops. That same day, in the other German sector, Windisch assured control of the area next to the

Swedish frontier. Nevertheless, a German soldier from one of Von Schlebrügge's patrols was killed in a clash with the Norwegians, while others were taken prisoner.

At this time "*Gruppe Meindl*" was formed from the following units:

- II./GJR139, commanded by *Major* Haussels. This unit also contained sailors and soldiers from "*Kompanie Rieger*," GJR137, who had been dropped by parachute. There were only 4 mortars.
- The *Kriegsmarine* company "*Von Gaartzen.*"
- 2 companies of I./FJR1, under *Hauptmann* Walther.
- 2 companies of the *Kriegsmarine* battalion "*Holtorf.*"
- 1 platoon of "*Gebirgsjäger Pionier Btl. 83.*"

Once the surrender had been signed on 10 June Narvik became a meeting point for all the *Fallschirmjäger* who had participated in the battle. On the morning of 17 June all the parachute units were in the city. According to Albert Valjeur, "*All of us paratroopers were able to leave Narvik aboard the cruiser* Nürnberg *on 17 June. We arrived in Trondheim on the 18th at 11:00 h, where we joined the rest of our battalion. We were then taken to Oslo by train, and then to Ålborg on the steamer* Isar. *We arrived in Germany on the 24th at 01:00 h after covering the final stretch of the journey by train.*" (Óscar González)

Walther and Haussels advised Meindl that there were no longer any enemy to face. It was evident that Narvik was an open city for the Germans.

On **9 June** all the doubts over the end of the fighting had disappeared. Dietl received an official communiquè from *Gruppe XXI* at 01:15 h stating that the King and his government had left the country. At 01:30 h Meindl and Walther reported that Narvik had been occupied without a fight. The Allied troops had put the port installations out of action before departing. Haussels also advanced and took Beisfjord without oppositiona at 6 in the afternoon, later moving on to Narvik.[114]

Once the city had been occupied, Meindl deployed his forces in Øjord, all on the other side of the Rombaken fjord. His intention was to form a bridgehead and secure Gjeisvik, the Elvenes road, and the one supplying Bjerkvik, where the bulk of Windisch's units were located. Last of all, it was necessary to re-establish the flow of maritime traffic between Ankenes and Øjord, once the waters had been swept of mines. The Norwegian prisoners were to be concentrated in Hundalen and Bjørnfjell. The Allies had left a large quantity of weapons and supplies in the town, and Meindl had to coordinate all efforts to secure control of the town, a task which ended on 16 June.

The arrival of air-transportable units continued its rhythm. three Ju 52s arrived at Bjørnfjell with 20 men of I./FJR1, under *Hauptmann* Wilch, who were immediately sent to Narvik.

At the same time, fighting between Norwegians and troops of "*Btl. Schlebrügge*" continued, especially at spot height 620, near the Swedish frontier. Finally, negotiations began with the Norwegians in this sector at the end of the day on the 9th. Norway's fate had been sealed

On 10 June, after many days of fighting, Von Schlebrügge's men reached the east of Lake Hartvik. Albert Valjeur remebers: "*After 4 weeks of fighting over rocks, ice, and snow, 24 hours a day spent under the midnight sun, we reached first Kuberget, where we occupied the Norwegian positions, using their provisions and installations. Finally we reached Lake Hartvig, where for the first time in many days we saw the green of the trees. The Allies had withdrawn; the fighting was over.*" (Óscar González)

Fallschirmjäger in the port of Narvik about to embark for Germany. ("Himmel und Holle")

Tromsø also fell into German hands, and the pressure on the Norwegians increased in the conversations taking place in Oslo to negotiate the surrender. At 12:00 h on 10 June general Otto Ruge received an ultimatum, threatening a general all out attack on the remaining centers of resistance by the *Luftwaffe* if he had not capitulated by 4 o'clock that afternoon. The General signed the armistice. Norway had surrendered two months after being invaded.

The deployment at Narvik contiued, and by 10 June Bjerkvik had been occupied. Finally, Von Schlebrügge reached the eastern shore of Lake Hartvik. Albert Valjeur, of 1./FJR1, recalls events:

"*After 4 weeks of fighting amongst the rocks, ice, and snow, 24 hours a day beneath the midnight sun, we first reached Kuberget, where we occupied the Norwegian positions. We used their provisions and installations. Finally, we reached Lake Hartvik. There we saw for the first time in weeks the green of the trees. The Allies had withdrawn and the fighting was over. Eleven Ju 52s had landed on the frozen lake with supplies, but they had sunk when the ice suddenly thawed.*"

Narvik became the meeting point for all the *Fallschirmjäger* who had fought at Narvik. Von Blücher's platoon entered the city on 11 June. On 12 June, in the city's sports palace, Walther decorated 26 men of his command with the Iron Cross second class (EKII). On the morning of 17 June all of the paratroops were in Narvik.

Of the 760 *Fallschirmjäger* of I./FJR1 sent to Trondheim following the invasion of Holland, approximately 375 were dropped at Bjørnfjell. The rest (including the 1st Company that had been created to replace Schmidt!) could not enter in combat because it had beeen impossible to drop them, either due to the adverse weather conditions or the lack of available aircraft. Together with the 164 officers, NCOs, and men of the "old" 1st Company, the first paratroop unit to join the fighting at Narvik, there were 539 *Fallschirmjäger* who fought under Dietl. Two officers, 2 NCOs, and 24 men died in shot down aircraft, while 2 officers, 16 NCOs, and 23 were wounded due to the same cause. Three NCOs and 2 soldiers were taken prisoner by the Allies and 4 disappeared in combat. Total losses for the 1st Company during the Narvik operation were 36 men killed and 41 wounded.

Valjeur describes the last days in Norway as follows:

"All of us paratroops weighed anchor from Narvik aboard the cruiser Nürnberg *on 17 June. We arrived inTrondheim at 11:00 h on the 18th, where we rejoined the rest of our battalion. I remember that we were later transferred to Oslo by train, where we embarked on the steam ship* Isar *bound for Ålborg. We were back in Germany on the 24th at 01:00 h after completing the last part of the journey by train."*

Final Airborne Operations

Two more jumps were made following the occupation of Narvik once Norway had capitulated. These were not carried out by *Fallschirmjäger*, but by mountain troops of GJR 136. This detail, added to the fact they were not "combat" jumps, has led to them being little known. It is necessary to underline the fact that as had happened with the *Gebirgsjäger* of GJR 137, the men of the two companies who made the jump obtained the official "qualification" and the paratroop insignia of the *Luftwaffe* in an "accelerated course,"[115] the only difference being they did not receive the Narvik Shield.

Fallschirmjäger of the 8th Company, 1st Regiment (8./FJR 1) walking through the streets of Oslo at the end of the Narvik operation. They are wearing army caps (*Bergmutze*). (Simon Orchard)

Leutnant Siefen's men jumping at Tromsø at 01:30 h on 13 June 1940 (in the midnight sun). The drop went off without difficulties, and the *Gebirgsjäger* soon took control of the town. (Simon Orchard)

Several *Gebirgsjäger* of GJR 136 showing off their *Luftwaffe* parachute insignia, awarded following their training and jump at Tromsø. (Eric Queen)

Gebirgsjäger of GJR 136 showing off their *Luftwaffe* parachute insignia, awarded following their training and jump at Tromsø. (Eric Queen)

Gebirgsjäger from GJR 136 before heading for Tromsø. 127 soldiers from this regiment, under command of *Leutnant* Siefen, jumped at the city's airfield on 13 June 1940. Note the two-buttoned cap typical of the *Gebirgsjäger*, as well as the M 38 jump suits (although the second soldier standing at left is wearing the earlier model, the M 36). (Eric Queen)

At 00:15 h on 12 June, 13 Ju 52s carried 137 men of GJR 136, commanded by *Leutnant* Brandner, to Bardufoss. Their mission was to secure the airfield, which had been defended by a company of French alpine troops during the Allied occupation. The following day, at 01:30 h, 127 men from the same regiment, commanded by *Leutnant* Siefen, were taken to Tromsø by Ju 52s of KG zbV 106, where they remained until the 21st, when they were relieved by troops from GJR 138, which had arrived by sea. Neither of the two drops met resistance, as there were no Allied forces left in the area, and British troops had already evacuated the town. The King, Haakon VII, and his government had already left from Tromsø six days earlier on their way to Britain where they would set up a government in exile.

Regarding Narvik (Final Considerations)

Narvik was the first time during the war that the *Fallschirmjäger* came to the support of troops already engaging the enemy. This was something that was to become more frequent as the war progressed, especially following the "disaster" of Crete and the strategic U-turn in the employment of airborne troops that came after.

Although the invasion of Norway was an example of the cooperation between air, sea, and land forces in achieving an objective, in Narvik, the *7. Fliegerdivision* was outside the operational decision making and planning process, lacking any influence on the orders. "Other officers"—as had occurred with Dombås—were those dictating orders, in many cases guided by personal interest and not from experience.

The number of Junkers Ju 52s lost is a clear indication in this respect. Around 28 *Fallschirmjäger* died in these circumstances. This was too high a price for the paratroops to pay.

Narvik also demonstrated that the paratroops' heavy armament was insufficient. Communications between the ground forces and the air force were also deficient (something which was also apparent during the Dombås operation). On many occasions the *Luftwaffe's* aircraft were not only expected to deal with the Royal Navy ships, but also Allied artillery and mortar positions. This was frequently a vain hope, and often left the *Fallschirmjäger* to protect themselves from the naval gunfire with their own insufficient means. The mortar platoons (*sGrWf Zug*) showed themselves to be a basic necessity as a result of Narvik.

Another serious mistake in the German deployment at Narvik, and one which specifically affected the *Fallschirmjäger*, was the lack of appropriate equipment for the troops. Being a soldier in an elite formation is of no use without the necessary equipment.

On 3 June Dietl wrote in his diary: "*The men are living in a desert with useless equipment and inadequate clothing.*"[116] On 4 June identical reflexions were written in the campaign diary of the 3rd Mountain Division:

"*The paratroops' rubber-soled boots are useless for walking over icy rocks and become unservicable in no time. For this reason they requested some time ago to be supplied with mountain boots and tents, which have yet to arrive. The weather is worsening; fog, heavy rain, and the biting wind are making it almost impossible to remain in the positions on the heights. What the men are putting up with is superhuman. They have nothing to protect them from the wind and there is no way to supply them. The distribution of hot rations is impossible because there is no field kitchen, and only those in the rearguard,in case of necessity, can prepare hot water for tea or coffee. There is no firewood, nor decent accommodation. The troops are living in a desolate landscape where the wind cuts like a knife. They are permanently exhausted, and their positions are known to the enemy. The worst equipped are the sailors.*"[117]

The last issue was related to another problem which arose in Norway: the vulnerability of the paratroops once they were on the ground. This was another of the fundamental lessons learned during the first airborne operations. It was clear that the first units on the ground had to be immediately combat ready. The *Fallschirmjäger* only had their pistols and a couple of hand grenades; the rest of their weapons were in containers. In spite of this changes only occurred after Crete, in May 1941—a year later. Even so, despite being rehearsed and trained for in the special "*Lehr*" units, it never became generalized, judging from what happened during the few combat jumps made after operation *Merkur* on the Greek island.

For all intents and purposes, and leaving aside the mistakes, it is obvious that the *Fallschirmjäger* faced an enemy unprepared for an airborne attack,[118] as was the case in Holland and Belgium. Although they suffered in order to hold their assigned positions, they were effective. Something else related to their excellent performance was the high degree of "readiness for the attack" that these men showed at all times, without sufficient time to recover from previous operations (Holland or Dombås). They were well trained and led troops capable of improvising when necessary, with quick withdrawls and breaking and holding the lines; in all, actions which benefited the Germans. An example of this attitude was the following case of II./FJR2.

Following the conclusion of the campaign in Holland the unit was rapidly reinforced specifically with the intention of supporting Dietl. Therefore, it can be said that soon after Holland it was ready for another airborne mission. After travelling overland to Frederikshaven and then by sea to Oslo, they were transported by train to Trondheim, arriving on 8 June. The Allied retreat from Narvik made their intervention unnecessary. Soon after the unit returned to their base in Berlin-Reinickendorf.

The key to understanding German success at Narvik revolves around Dietl's leadership, which kept the hope of victory alive when all seemed lost. Inferior in both numbers and armament, the Germans held their positions because, essentially, they believed in the end they would win. It was a question of will. Paratroops, mountain troops, and sailors were effectively commanded by a good leader. Dietl, a "product" of a traditional German military education, demonstrated a superior attitude and a desire for victory, something his counterparts in the Allied camp lacked, and something of invaluable help in avoiding a disaster.

Possesion of the approaches to the Baltic and effective control of the Scandinavian peninsula garanteed Germany security from an attack from the north for the rest of the war. As well as this, German submarines and aircraft obtained bases from which to attack the British, and later, Allied convoys taking war materiel to Murmansk. Finally, Germany was able to support Finland in its second war with the Soviet Union (1941-1944), which tied down large numbers of Red Army troops at minimum cost to the Germans.

However, the price Germany paid was high (although expected): she lost half of her destroyers in the Norwegian campaign, faced the need to maintain a large occupation force in Scandinavia, and the total ineffectiveness of air and maritime operations launched from Scandinavia against Britain.

In conclusion, it can be said that these reflexions confirm that, in spite of the human and materiel cost, the airborne operations carried out against Denmark and Norway were extraordinarily advantageous.

First of all, they allowed the invader to develop an enveloping "vertical attack," simultaneously penetrating enemy lines while they protected their own flanks. In this way the Germans were able to overcome obstacles that could have seriously interfered in the movements of their ground troops. This was the case at Dombås and Narvik.

Secondly, airborne assaults could be launched from inside the area dominated by the Germans. They were deployed with speed and were supported by an exceptional weapon: surprise. These characteristics allowed them to neutralize enemy counter-attacks to a great extent. Generally speaking, the attack on Denmark was supported in this way. The capture of the Norwegian airfields was as well, but with added difficulties.

Finally, the psychological effect of the "vertical attack" should not be discounted. Its effect could be said to be superior to the "horizontal" envelopment. Unpredictable, surprise attacks have a negative effect on the morale of enemy troops, the chain of command, and even on the morale of the civilian population. Even in the role of infantry, as was the case of the airborne "raid" on Elverum to capture the Norwegian King.

However, "*Eben Emael eclipsed Norway.*" Our last reflexion, expressed in concise terms, explains why so little attention has been paid to the first German airborne operations of the war. Without doubt, the assault on the Belgian fort and bridges over the Albert Canal on 10 May 1940 exhibited all the advantages already mentioned. The secret when preparing the attack with gliders and hollow-point charges and the almost total success with almost minimal cost in casualties converted the operation into a paradigm for airborne operations. However, the *Fallschirmjäger*, as a unit, already had a considerable "history" of several combat jumps and incursions into enemy territory before 10 May, all of which were carried out during *Weserübung*.

Even so, the "aura" of success gradually disappeared; the protaganism lasting only a short time. Only a year later, in May 1941, Crete became the "tomb" of the *Fallschirmjäger*. The days of glory for the German paratroops came to an end. The experience acquired during the Norwegian campaign nor the success at the Albert canal was not enough to avoid disaster. From then on, the key to the German advance ceased to pivot on the "vertical attack."

---

78 Rombaksfjord, also Rombakenfjord.

79 1,750 on 13 May, according to Buchner (1977), p. 199. Dietl had the following units at his disposal: the three battalions of GJR 139; a platoon from GebPiBtl 83; a battalion of *Marine-Artillerie*; and units from I./FlakRgt 32 and the HQ of 3.GJD (3rd Mountain Division).

80 Mabire (2007), pp. 69 and 167.

81 Alois Windisch, born 3 February 1892 in Bad Fischau, Austria, died on 28 December 1958 in Wiener-Neustadt. Had fought in the First World War and made an aristocrat from then on (*von Windisch*), received the highest Austro-Hungarian decoration, the Knight's Cross of the Order of Maria Theresa. Only one other *Wehrmacht* officer, Dr. Von Franek, held the same award. Windisch was decorated with the *Ritterkreuz* on 20 June 1940.

82 Mabire (2007), pp.161, 169, and 175.

83 Kurt Barank's complete account is included in: Barank, K.: *Fallschirmjäger vom Ersten Regiment. Mit der 1. Kompanie/FschJägerRgt 1 am 12. Mai 1940 nach Narvik*, DDF, 4/1990.

84 The question arises as to why they were not taken back to Germany after their liberation from captivity. Their participation in operation *Fall Gelb* would have helped Student, who was short on reserves (he tried to form a unit from trainees at the jump school). Mössinger and Valjeur agree that by agreeing to their intervention in Narvik "*Student wanted to avoid any negative effect on the morale of the* Fallschirmjäger *based in Germany just days before the drop in Holland.*" The High Command had decided to "draw a veil" over the failure of Dombås. A significant detail is that Student, in his memoirs, dedicates just sentences to the *Fallschirmjäger* in Narvik. (Götzel, H., *Generaloberst Kurt Student und seine Fallschirmjäger*, pp. 164 and 165.)

85 The left wing was defended by 3./GJR 138, 3./GJR 139, and Company "Müller" holding the French 13a semi-brigade. This area was located south of Lake Hartvik.

86 Mabire (2007), p. 185.

87 Mabire (2007), p. 293.

88 "*Die Landung von 600 Gebirgsjägern mit Segelflugzeugen wird für morgen angekundigt*" [Cf. *Kriegstagebuch Nr. 2 der 3.Geb.Div. (Gruppe Narvik), 19.5*]. The plan had foreseen 1,800 paratroops, and even a thousand *Gebirgsjäger* were to be dropped or flown in on gliders. [Mabire (2007), p. 462]

89 On the same line entered on the 22nd is the following: "*There are problems with the landing zone (...). The task of reinforcing must fall on the* Fallschirmjäger," according to the *Lageberichte*

des Wehrmachtführungsstabes während der Besetzung von Dänemark und Norwegen, in Hubatsch (1952), p. 355.

90 The order in the drop at Bjørnfjell was as follows: the weapons container and two paratroops were dropped on the first pass. In the second, two more containers from the bomb bay and four paratroops. Finally, on the 3rd, the remaining paratroops (normally four) and containers were dropped. According to paratrooper Gerhard Broder, "*We had to remove the four bombs in order to fit the reserve fuel tanks. We had to launch the heavy containers of weapons and ammunition by hand.*"

91 The exact composition and unit identification of the *Gebirgsjäger* who "jumped" at Bjørnfjell is one of the most confusing aspects and most difficult to clarify in an analysis of the Narvik operation. It is usually accepted that the 1./GJR 137 and the 2./GJR 137 were the companies that parachuted in to support Dietl. Buchner (1977), p. 70, cites the 1st Company as being formed of 108 men, commanded by *Oblt.* Schweiger, and the 2nd of 118 men under *Oblt.* Riegler. Golla (2006), p. 268, uses identical criteria. However, as shall be seen, things would not appear to be so straightforward.

First of all, it is necessary to correct Buchner, as he has made a mistake regarding the number of officers. It was not *Riegler*, but rather Hermann Rieger, and neither was it *Schweiger*, but Erich Schwaiger (born 31 January 1914 and killed in action on 28 May 1940, according to the register in the "*Volksbund Deutsche Kriegsgräberfürsorge e.V.*"). However, when checking the order in the jump proposed by Buchner against the diary of 3rd *Gebirgsjäger* Division (*Kriegstagebuch Nr.2 3.Geb.Div.*), significant differences appear.

According to Buchner (1977), p. 212, the 1st Company jumped on the 23rd, while Golla (2006), p. 268, claims that it was the 2nd that jumped. The diary of 3.GJD states that on the 23rd 65 *Gebirgsjäger* of 2./GJR 137 made the drop, but at no time does it specify who was in command. Continuing with the diary, it also relates that of the 24th Schweiger's men (sic) went to defend tunnel nº 4 at 19:00 h: "*Kp. Oblt. Schweiger (GJR 137) Richtung Tunnel 4 in Marsch gesetzt. Die Kp. Wird im Bahntransport in Gegend westl. Rundalen gebracht und sückt von da in den Abschnitt d.Kp.Freytag bei Djupvik* (...)". Therefore, Schwaiger had already landed, but at this time only one jump by mountain troops had been made: that of the 23rd. Did Schwaiger command the 1st or 2nd Company?

This apparent confusion is confirmed by other entries in the 3.GJD diary. For example, on the 25th "*1 officer and 53 men of* Oblt *Riegler's company jumped at 10:00 h* (sic) ***1./GJR 137*** (...) *so did the rest of Schweiger's company* (sic). *At 19:00 h, 4 Ju 52 brought more* Gebirgsjäger—*the rest of Riegler's company* (sic)—."

One theory could be as follows. The nomenclature "*1./GJR 137 and 2./GJR 137*" did not in reality correspond to the 1st and 2nd Companies of the Regiment. The *Gebirgsjäger* trained as paratroops on the 7-10-day intensive course came from the 1st and 3rd Battalions of the GJR 137 Regiment. Perhaps, then, these were "*ad hoc*" companies. One of these volunteers was *Gefreiter* Ernst Hölzl (born in Salzburg on 26/01/1917 and killed in action at Murmansk on 2/02/1943). He wrote to a friend, Richard Kloes, in a letter dated 10 July 1940:

"*...I took part in the occupation of Denmark and later Norway. In Trondheim I volunteered to be a paratrooper, as our comrades were in a desperate situation in Narvik. I flew to Germany and underwent a brief training course near Berlin. On 24 May I jumped at Narvik....*" The "*Feldpost*" of the letter is 09079C, which belonged to 12./GJR 137. That is to say, the 3rd Battalion.

With him also jumped *Gefreiter* Felix Holzermayr of 2./GJR 137. According to Holzermayr, they were already on the ground when **two companies** of volunteers were formed from men of *Rieger's* company: "*On 26 May our company was divided in two, one under* Oblt *Schweiger* (sic)*, with the mission to reinforce the northern front at Narvik, and the other under* Oblt *Rieger, defending the port and the south of the city.* (...) *Schweiger's company was seperated* (sic) *from that of Rieger.*" [Holzermayr (1996), pp. 169 and 170]. Without doubt, Holzermayr gives us the key to understanding the discrepancies ivolved when consulting the other accounts. It is also important to add a further

detail: many of the drops, in spite of being "nocturnal," were made in the mid-night sun of northern Scandinavia, making it sometimes difficult, especially for the person writing up the official report, to be always precise in the referral to the days and times.
It can be concluded, therefore, that from 23 to 25 May volunteers from *Rieger's company were dropped*, along with *Oblt*. Schwaiger.
92 "*Um 22.15 Uhr sollen 7 Ju 52 mit Fallschirmspringer kommen.*"
93 They were intercepted by a squadron of *Gladiators* of "*263 Squadron*" that had taken off from HMS *Furious* heading for Bardufoss. One of the Bf 110s was hit by shots from the aircraft piloted by Herman Francis Grant Ede (1917-1940). The German plane had to make an emergency landing on Lake Upmasjaure, in Sweden, at 13:00 h. This was Bf 110C-1 "M8+NK," piloted by *Feldwebel* Neureuter. The crew were rescued by a He 59 and taken to Trondheim. Grant Ede died in the sinking of the carrier HMS *Glorious* on 8 June 1940.
94 Ernst Graf von Strachwitz was born on 22 December 1919 in Wöbling, near Graz (Austria). He enlisted in the mountain troops in 1938, joining GJR 137. He took part in the invasion of Poland as a *Fahnenjunker-Oberjäger Gruppenführer* in the 6./GJR 99, and was later promoted to *Leutnant*. This was at the beginning of April 1940, just before the invasion of Denmark and Norway. In this operation he was the leader of a platoon of 14./GJR 137, jumping at Bjørnfjell with elements of the company (part of *III. Bataillon*) on 24 May 1940. He obtained his parachute insignia and, in June that same year, the EKII and Narvik Shield. He later took part in the Russian campaign, winning the EKI on the first day of the invasion. He commanded a platoon of 15./GJR 137 in the Murmansk offensive and was wounded in August 1941. He continued to be posted in the north of Finland commanding different units, and was promoted to *Hauptmann* in February 1944. In August the same year he was appointed commander of *II. Bataillon*. He was awarded the *Ritterkreuz* on 26 November 1944 for his actions in defense of the bridge at Titowa, where he was wounded. Once the German surrender had been signed he was (by then a *Major*) taken prisoner by the British, and liberated soon after in July 1945. He became a lawyer after the war, dying in Vienna on 13 July 1998. Ernst von Stachwitz was a nephew of another well known military figure of the Second World War, *GenLt. d.R.* Hyazinth Graf Straschwitz.
One of the *Gebirgsjäger* under his command was Walter Ernst. He had come from 11./GJR 137, then commanded by a certain Bucher. He was injured in the jump at Bjørnfjell together with another three soldiers. Although he recovered from his injuries, he was captured soon after and spent six months as a prisoner of war.
Lastly, it is worth noting the case of another of the *Gebirgsjäger* paratroopers: Adam Ebner, of 3./GJR 137, who began training for the jump on the 16 May. Ebner had joined the mountain units in 1934. He was awarded the Knight's Cross (RK) on 19 November 1941, and was by then an *Oberfeldwebel*. Among other decorations he received the EKII on 10 June 1940, the EKI on 15 October 1940, and the Narvik Shield on 10 November the same year. He served in Poland, Norway, and Russia, dying after the war in 1975.
95 Designated "*Spezialisten*" in official reports [Cf. *Kriegstagebuch Nr. 2 der 3.Geb.Div. (Gruppe Narvik)]*. 40 arrived on 20 May (with machine-guns and mortars); another 40 on 25 May; 80 on the 31st, commanded by *St. Arzt* Dr. Feurle; and 40 more on 8 June. Even before May, on 23 April approximately 30 Signals soldiers, disguised as civilian personnel, arrived through Sweden.
Paratrooper Gerhard Broder also refers to the arrival of these "medics" through Sweden during the month of May: "*they always arrived in groups of 12, and were then quickly armed and assigned to one of the units.*"
96 The formation that was available for Norway was far from being the same as the Battalion had before the assault on Holland. Here there was a 4th company and a machine-gun platoon (*Schwerenzug*) in each company that had 26 to 40 men available. According to Golla (2006), p. 269, the overall total

did not reach 760 men. Regarding the units that provided replacements for the Battalion, it was not only the *FschJgErgBtl*, but also other paratroop units, such as FJR2. (Cf. Note 15 in the chapter dedicated to Stavanger-Sola).

97 This occurred on 26 May. *Oberleutnant* Eckleben had taken part in the capture of the airfields at Ålborg (commanding 4./FJR1), as well as the assault on Holland, as a member of I./FJR2. This is a clear example of how the replacements for the 1st Battalion of the 1st Regiment (I./FJR1) were drawn from other units. With him also died the *Reg.Inspektor* Richard Rasch, *Fw.* Hans Niemeyer, *OGfr.* Karl Klawitter, *OGfr.*Herbert Pawellek, *Gfr.* Hermann Kleinert, *Oberjäger* Joachim Matz, and *Jägers* Artur Meyer, Max Pangel, and Berthold Schmidt.

98 Although Golla (2006) states that there were "*66 paratroops transported to the objective aboard nine Ju 52s.*"

99 It was not the only plane shot down, as has already been explained in the footnotes regarding the aircraft lost on 28 May. Tyczka had also participated in the taking of Masnedø, in Denmark.

100 A "hardened" British officer who had fought in the Russian Civil War from 1919 to 1920, and later, in 1937, he commanded an infantry brigade in Palestine.

101 A veteran of Verdun and the Somme, and a specialist in mountain warfare. He was an officer who worried about his alpine troops. Before going to Norway he had trained Finnish troops in the 1920s and had been Military Attaché in Yugoslavia during the 1930s. According to his own words, the differences between Mackesy and Cork in regard to Narvik were such that 15 precious days were lost going over the plan time and again. [Cf. Mabire (2007), pp. 17 y 116]

102 25% of these foreign volunteers were Spanish, almost all of them former members of the Republican Army. Some of them were to serve with distinction at Narvik: legionnaires Dalmaso and Ganoso or Sergeant Pujol de Villalonga, for example. [Mabire (2007), pp. 241 and 387].

103 This was the name of the Podolia Light Infantry Brigade (*Samodzielna Brygada Strzelców Podhalanskich–SBSP*). The unit was rested on 10 May 1940 with the intention of fighting the Soviets in Finland. A large part of the Polish 1st Infantry Division was used to create this mountain unit. At first the idea was to send them to Tromsø, in the extreme north of the country, but this was rejected: the Norwegians did not want to have "problems" on their frontier with the USSR. The officers of the Brigade were mainly Polish, but approximately two thirds of the other ranks were Poles resident in France (miners, intellectuals, writers, or ex members of the International Brigades from the Spanish Civil War), with little experience of mountain operations. A member of the unit remebers, "*Only a few had seen real mountains before Narvik.*" A French Signals detatchment was added to the Brigade.

104 Transfer was extended to 20 May. These troops had to be evacuated between 29 and 31 May in the face of the advancing German troops and attacks by the *Luftwaffe*. It was the prologue to the general evacuation of Narvik.

105 The attack was attributed to *Flight Lieutenant* Caesar Barrand Hull. It would appear he brought down 3 Ju 52s in total. Although, according to the report of the RAF's "*263 Squadron*" and Thomas (2002), p. 30, this occurred on 26 May. Golla (2006), p. 270, draws hasty conclusions, indicating that the British registers are erroneous As has already been seen, German reports do not mention the loss of two planes shot down on the 26th, but they do for the 28th. The affair becomes more complicated, as Hull was shot down over Bodohalvoya on the 27th (in a dogfight with a Bf 110 flown by Helmut Lent). It is evident that this is another example of contradictory reports.

German reports date the shooting down of *Olt* Tyczka to the 26th, but it is also highly likely that other reports of aircraft shot down on the 28th should really be attributed to 26 May.

According to Musgrave (2004), on 26 May three *Gladiators*, among which was the aircraft piloted by Hull, were operational in the Bodø area, covering the Allied withdrawl. Soon after taking off Hull shot down a He 111. He later spotted and attacked a Ju 52 "*which hit the ground wrapped in flames.*"

He then unsuccessfully attacked another He 111. Finally, he downed two Junkers "*the first slipped away into the clouds and the other crashed in flames after six men had jumped clear.*" This version is accepted by Thomas (2002), pp. 30/31—based on Hull's diary—and in Derry, T. K. (1995), p. 192. At http://ktsorens.tihlde.org there is information which helps in reconstructing the sequence of events. Regarding the planes brought down by Hull on the 26th, the first (WNr. 5636) was shot down over Storfjellet, near Saltdal, at 16:18 h. The three crew members and a paratrooper, *Fw.* Kurt Zell (jumpmaster), died in the crash. The rest of the paratroopers were able to jump in time.

The second plane (BA+KH), which burst into flames after being hit in the fuel tank, crashed at Ekornes/Evensdal, also near Saltdal, at 16:30 h. As has already been mentioned, several *Fallschirmjäger* were able to jump free. The 3 crew plus *Gefr* Walter Bellmann, *Jg.* Werner Schemmel, *Jg.* Harry Ludeke, *OGfr.* Ernst Böttcher, and *Gfr.* Wilhelm Geiger, all from 4./FJR1, were all killed. *Fw.* Karl Linek, of *Fallschirmschule 1* (parachute school), was also killed. The third transport plane (WNr. 6713 CM+BU), which "*slipped away into the clouds,*" was shot down over Kvassteinheia, Saltdal, between 16:30-16:45 h. According to Musgrave (2004), the pilot made an emergency landing in territory occupied by the Germans, and there were no casualties. Other sources (http://ktsorens.tihlde.org) indicate 4 were killed, among them *Uffz.* Siegfried Vangerow, of the *Fallschirmschule 1* in Wittstock.

106 In contrast to what was happening along the railway line, in the northern sector (*Gruppe Windisch*) the situation had not worsened since the landing of the French Foreign Legion at Bjerkvik. On the 28th, Windisch withdrew the 3./ GJR 138 from the left flank in order to transfer them to the right of Von Schlebrügge. The main activity was on the left flank, defended by III./GJR 139. This sector came under attack from the French alpine troops and Norwegian infantry, supported by artillery. In the area defended by Von Schlebrügge (with men from 1./FJR1 and *Gebirgsjäger*), the most easterly part of the northern front, near the Swedish frontier, the Allies contented themselves with selective artillery barrages (which caused the death of a paratrooper amongst those on spot height 456 with four heavy machine-guns). Renner's air-transportable company (2./GJR 138) was also deployed on this northern front.

107 *Olt* Wilhelm Götte would command 2./FJR1 during the operations in Narvik. Nevertheless, it must be remembered that this unit was originally under command of *Olt* Tyczka, whose plane was shot down on the way to Bjørnfjell. Although it is not certain, before Narvik and after Holland Götte was either Walther's adjutant or replaced the deceased *Olt* Von Brandis as commander of the 3rd Company (he even replaced *Hptm* Gericke as commander of the 4th).

Götte was born in Omaruru, in the German colony of South West Africa on 11 August 1915. It was he who, commanding a handful of paratroops of the *Stab.*/FJR1, took Fornebu. He was one of the first *Fallschirmjäger* to land at 09:33 h on 9 April, when chaos reigned in the German ranks in the face of withering Norwegian fire. With a small group of around 30 men (from the *Stab.*/FJR1, together with troops from II./IR 324 and pilots) he engaged the Norwegians, enabling the later German landings to go ahead. After Fornebu he was involved in the fighting at Dordrecht, Holland, on 10 May. Finally, he returned to Narvik attached to "Gruppe Walther." Wilhelm Götte died in Crete on 20 May 1941, at the start of the Nazi invasion of the island, and he is buried in the cemetery at Maleme.

108 Although the *Lageberichte des Wehrmachtführungsstabes während der Besetzung von Dänemark und Norwegen*, in Hubatsch (1952), p. 361, affirms there were two on the 29th, each one with 6 Ju 52s. Nevertheless, this detail is imprecise and unreliable, as it refers to them as *Gebirgsjäger.*

109 Mabire (2007), p. 435.

110 *Kriegstagebuch Nr. 2 der 3. Geb. Div. (Gruppe Narvik).*

111 The number of deaths differs according to the source quoted. Golla (2006), p. 279, states that 6 paratroops and a member of the crew were able to get out in time, while 4 paratroops and 2 crewmen

died. This information is not confirmed by the *Kriegstagebuch Nr. 2 der 3. Geb. Div. (Gruppe Narvik)*, which notes that 7 jumped free, while another 7 were burned to death and 1 more was killed in the impact. Barank (1990) argues (in accordance with the *Kriegstagebuch*) that 7 men jumped (5 paratroops and 2 crewmen), while another 7 were killed.

If, to these varying figures, we add the interesting observation that the flights to Narvik, due to the duration of the flight, could only carry 10 *Fallschirmjäger* and a crew of 3 men, we have a puzzle that is difficult to solve, and the question arises, why was this aircraft in particular carrying 15 men?

It is reasonable to acept the version of the "Kriegstagebug Nr.2" complemented by another primary source, *Gefechtsbericht Narvik der I./FschJgRgt 1*, written in the autumn of 1940 by then *Leutnant* Ernst Mössinger. This relates that "*2 members of the crew and 6 paratroops died, while another 2 of the crew and 5 managed to jump free, although most of them suffered wounds of varying degrees.*" Based on Alexander Uhlig's account that paratroops died, and this is corroborated by the "*Volksbund Deutsche Kriegsgräberfürsorge e.V.*" Although secondary sources exist that state 6 *Fallschirmjäger* jumped (of 10) and another 4 paratroops and 2 crew members died, these versions do not contrast a great deal (Cf. http://surfcity.kund.dalnet.se/commonwealth_jacobsen.htm).

The aircraft was shot down by Swedish anti-aircraft batteries, but everything indicates that it was also attacked by a *Gladiator* (N5681) of "*263 Squadron" RAF*, flown by Louis Reginald Jakobsen. In regard to this, we can find in *Kriegstagebuch Nr. 2 der 3. Geb. Div. (Gruppe Narvik)*: "*Ursprünglich wurde vermutet, daß die Ju von einem engl. Jäger abgeschossen wurde, da man den Abschuß nicht beobachten konnte und die Leute sehr hoch absprangen*" *(first of all it was thought that the Ju had been brought down by a British fighter, as the event was not seen and the men jumped at a great height)*. Jakosen died on 8 June in the sinking of HMS *Glorious*.

This version is also confirmed by Kurt Barank (1990): "*We had almost reached the objective when a tragedy occurred with the aircraft following* Feldwebel *Bansen. A British fighter suddenly appeared and hit the Ju 52 in the fuel tank with its machine-guns.*" Curiously, Barank cites the action as having taken place on 14 May. It can be stated fairly surely that, in spite of how precisely he narrated events, he confused the date. The official date attributed to the deaths of these men is 2 June, which is what appears in the "*Volksbund Deutsche Kriegs*." Lastly, http://ktsorens.thilde.org/flyvrak/riksgrensen.html adds important details on the incident.

112 From then on the name of Meindl would be associated with the *Fallschirmjäger*. Eugen Meindl (1892-1951) was an artillery officer during the First World War. He later joined the *Reichswehr* and then the *Wehrmacht*. He took part in the Polish campaign as commander of *GebArtRgt 112*, and at the end of the campaign he was promoted to *Oberst*. Following the jump he made at Narvik he joined the paratroops, taking command of "*Luftlande-Sturmregiment*" in September 1940. He was awarded the *Ritterkreuz* on 14 June 1941 for his actions in Crete while a *Generalmajor* commanding "*Fallschirmjäger Luftlande Sturm Regiment 1*." He jumped at 07:15 h on 20 May 1941 west of the bridge over the river Tavronitis, next to Maleme airfield. He was wounded by machine-gun fire soon after landing, having to hand over command to *Major* Stenzler. After Crete he was transferred to Russia at the head of the "Meindl Division" (later designated the "*21st Luftwaffe Feld Division*") and the *XIII. Fliegerkorps*. In January 1943 he was promoted to *Generalleutnant*; from September that year he was appointed Inspector General of *Luftwaffe* ground troops (*Luftwaffe Feldtruppen*). At the end of 1943 he returned to the *Fallschirmjäger* to lead II. *Fallschirm Korps*. From April 1944 he became a *General*. Present on the battlefield during the Allied invasion of Normandy, he received the Oak Leaves to his Knight's Cross in August 1944, and in May 1945 he received the Swords to the same decoration. He was captured at the end of the war and remained a prisoner until 1947.

113 As has already been mentioned, the diary of the 3rd Mountain Division states that it was the 7th: "*18:45. 4 Ju 88 and 4 Ju 52 arrived. The Ju 52s brought paratroops and supplies* (…) *Entry:* Obst. *Meindl, Lt Grf. Blücher with 26 men (*Fallschirmjäger*).*" However, according to Willi Nollen, Meindl, Von Blücher, and 8 *Fallschirmjäger* arrived at Bjørnfjell on 2 June. His account also differs from the diary in reference to the number of men who jumped. According to him, his plane was the only one that could reach the objective because the others transporting the rest of the 2nd Platoon could not find the drop zone due to a snow storm and were forced to return. (Cf. Nollen, Willi: *Der erste Sprung des Generals Meindl*, DDF, 9/1956, p. 7.)
114 It is said that Lt Colonel von Hengl, who commanded the German troops who, with great difficulty, had advanced to relieve Narvik, sent Dietl a telegram, regretting not having arrived in time: "*We dirtied our pants with the toilet seat in our hands*," which expressed how close they actually had been.
115 The case, for example, of *Gefreiter* Hermann Bachhuber, from 9./GJR 136, who received his documentation of accreditation (nº 3159/40) dated 14 June 1940.
116 *Die Leute leben in eine Steinwüste bei schlechter Ausrüstung und ungenügender Bekleidung.*
117 Entry for 4 June 14:50 h in the *Kriegstagebuch Nr. 2 der 3. Geb. Div. (Gruppe Narvik)*.
118 Windish and Dietl refer to the lack of offensive spirit among the Allies. [Cf. Mabire (2007), p. 175.]

Fallschirmjäger in the area of Kuberget. Dietl wrote in his diary: "*The rubber-soled boots of the paratroops are useless for walking over the frozen rocks and are soon rendered unservicable. For this reason mountain boots and tents were requested some time ago, but nothing has been received so far. The weather is worsening; the fog, the heavy rain and biting wind make it almost impossible to remain in the positions on the heights. What the men are putting up with is superhuman.*" (Óscar González)

Appendix 1: Parachutes and Transport

The parachutes used by the *Falschirmjäger* were based on an Italian design known as the "*Salvatore*." The RZ series of parachutes ("*Rückenpackung Zwangauslosung*") began with the RZ-1, which was not used after 1939; then the RZ-16, in service until 1941; and from then on the RZ-20. The RZ-36 was issued at the end of the war, and had a "single cord" between the harness/belt of the paratrooper and the chute itself, above the head and shoulders of the soldier. This system resulted in the paratrooper leaning as he descended, almost face down, in such a way as to make the use of knee and elbow pads a necessity. The paratrooper also had to turn and face forwards while he was descendeng in order to avoid injury when he landed. In fact many injuries did occur. To enable the parachute to open properly, the soldier had to launch himself headfirst in a "cross" position. The parachute opened automatically by the use of a static line that was hooked onto a cable inside the aircraft's fuselage. The harness had to be securely strapped to the paratrooper in order to avoid injury when the chute opened with a strong pull. Controlling the chute on descent was almost impossible, except for those men who had received a high degree of training and could exercise a small amount of control. It was also difficult to descend with weapons or equipment, due to the tight fit of the harness and the need to have the hands free in order

Junkers Ju 52/3m dropping first model containers (*Waffenbehälter*) in a training exercise between 1938 and 1939. This versatile plane, nicknamed "Aunty Ju," was the aircraft most used by the Germans during the war for parachute drops. (Óscar González)

to cushion the landing. Only pistols, SMGs, and hand grenades could be carried at most, and so the German paratroops relied on containers to carry their main armament.

The parachute was connected to the harness by four hooks, which were difficult to unhook if the soldier was under fire or had jumped in adverse weather conditions, such as a strong wind. This hook system was nothing like the quick release mechanism developed by the Allies. This was to have serious consequences in Norway, where many *Fallschirmjäger* were killed or seriously injured when strong winds, especially at Dombås, dragged them along the ground. The Germans, therefore, provided the *Fallschirmjäger* (and all their air crew) with a "gravity knife" to cut the cords in case of emergency.

It is curious that the *Fallschirmjäger* used this type of parachute, as the *Luftwaffe's* air crews used a type similar to that of the British and Americans with shoulder straps. The "*Salvatore*" option has been justified as allowing for drops at lower altitude, which meant less time in the air at the mercy of enemy fire.

Airborne operations in Norway led to reflexions on the disadavantages of deploying the *Fallschirmjäger*. The type of parachute harness was the main problem. It was based on the "*Irvin*" design, with fixed hooks on the belt, chest, and thighs. Other vertical straps between the horizontal straps across the chest and around the waist, and crossed at the back, gave the design consistancy. As has already been mentioned, German paratroops could not control their chutes during the descent. To jump with the RZ parachute in windy conditions, over unknown terrain and without any control, was extremely risky. All paratroops were prone to injury during the drop or dispertion on landing, but the Germans suffered more than the Allies in this regard.

All of these problems were known before the war began, but the operations in Norway highlighted the fact that many men died because of the RZ. However this design, with minor adjustments, remained in service throughout the war.

Another of the issues brought to the fore in Norway was that of the weapons containers (*Waffenbehälter*). Again, as has already been mentioned, the *Fallschirmjäger* did not jump with their weapons; instead these were dropped, together with the ammunition, in containers. The difficulty of recovering these containers under fire became something of a feat. At Sola airfield, for example, the paratroops were pinned down for several hours before they could retrieve their weapons. Finding and recovering their weapons was a vital task for the *Fallschirmjäger* in order for them to be ready for the attack. This problem was not satisfactorily resolved after Norway, except for the case of glider-born troops.

The transport aircraft used by the paratroops, the Ju 52, demonstrated its disadvantages in Norway. It was a versatile aircraft, in service since 1930; its construction made it secure, and it could absorb a lot of punishment and still keep flying. It could also land on a runway or in a field. However, its disadvantages were significant. It was slow, its fuel tanks were not armoured, and although relatively few were lost in Norway, it was clear that if faced with heavy anti-aircraft fire or troops who were well prepared to repel an air landing losses among the aircraft would be serious. It was necessary to dominate the enemy's air space, as only air superiority could guarantee the passage of these aircraft .

The Germans did not have "ideal" transport, and this was to hinder many operations during the war. Following this early campaign several aircraft were tested for dropping paratroops, but none proved as well suited as the veteran Junkers 52. In the hands of a good pilot the Ju 52 was an excellent, although not ideal, aircraft.

Appendix 2: The Narvik Shield (*Narvikschild*)

The Narvik Shield was the first of a series of "campaign insignias" instituted by the *Führer*. Article 1 of the regulation (dated 19 August 1940) regarding the creation of the Narvik Shield states that "*I institute the Narvik Shield in memory of the heroic and victorious fight by troops of the* Luftwaffe, Heer, *and* Kriegsmarine *in Narvik, in close collaboration and brotherhood.*"

Article 3 of the same established that "*The Narvik Shield will be bestowed on all members of the armed forces who participated in the landing at Narvik or in the fighting involving* "Gruppe Narvik." *The decoration will be awarded in my name by the commander in chief of this group, General of Mountain Troops Dietl.*"

Finally, an administrative order dated 9 September 1940, written by the commander of the *Gebirgskorp* in Norway, established the definitive conditions for the concession of the award. Those receiving the award would in all cases belong to the circle of those who had fought at Narvik: "*He, who from 9 April to the 24 hours of 9 June 1940, fought on land, sea, or in the air under the command of the then commander in chief of* Gruppe Narvik, *between Riksgränsen-Oalge-Pass-Gratangsbotn, including the Ofoten-zona east of Skjomen-Norddalen; or whomever fought in the air in this same area. Those engaged in scouting and resupply tasks are included.*" The deadline for requesting the award was constantly put back, finally ending in January 1942.

Supplying sufficient Shields met with problems. The *Gebirgskorp* asked for 10,000 silver Shields on 21 November 1940, which had still not been received by 15 March 1941. The reason for this was that the ship transporting them had to wait six weeks where it was anchored in the port of Stettin for the waters to thaw.

After Hitler had personally decorated *Gebirgsjäger* General Dietl on 21 March 1941, the award was conceded to the rest of those who had accumulated sufficient merits. The following were awarded up to 15 June 1941:

Heer

2. *Gebirgsdivision*	206
3. *Gebirgsdivision*	2338
Other units	59
Posthumous	152
TOTAL	2755

Kriegsmarine

Destroyer crews	2621
Other units	115
Merchant Marine	442
Kriegsmarine Posthumous	411
Merchant Marine Posthumous	22
TOTAL	3661

Luftwaffe

Air crew	1309
Fallschirmjäger	756
Posthumous and missing	96
TOTAL	2161

The insignia was worn on the upper arm of the left sleeve of the uniform and was designed by Richard Klein of Munich. The insignia was gold for the *Kriegsmarine* and silver for the *Luftwaffe* and *Heer*.

Bibliography

Books

Bekker, C.: *Angriffshöhe 4000. Ein Kriegstagebuch der deutschen Luftwaffe*, Oldenburg und Hamburg, Gerhard Stalling Verlag, 1964.

Böttger, G.: *Narvik im Bild*, Oldenburg-Berlin, Gerhard Stalling Verlag, 1941.

Broder, G.: *Guerre mondiale contre moi. 1938-1948 : Weltkrieg gegen mich. Norwegen-Kreta-Rußland-Italien*, Herausgegeben von Paul Bernhard, Ulm, Dieter Frieß Verlag, 2007.

Buchner, A.: *Narvik. Tatsachenbericht*, München, Wilhelm Heyne Verlag, 1977.

Busch, E.: *Die Fallschirmjäger Chronik 1935-1945*, Friedberg, Podzun-Pallas Verlag, 1983.

Derry, T.K.: *The campaign in Norway*, United Kingdom Military Series, Imperial War Museum, 1995.

Dildy, D.: *Denmark and Norway 1940. Hitler's boldest operation*, Oxford, Osprey Publishing, 2007.

Ellis, C.:*7th Flieger Division. Student's Fallschirmjäger Elite*, Hersham, Ian Allan Publishing, 2002.

Ettrup, E.; Ritterbach, E.; Schellenberger, D.: *Der Atlantikwall in Norwegen. Festung Stavanger. 1940-1945 und heute,* edición del autor/Mails and More, 2005.

Fowler, W.: *Poland and Scandinavia 1939-1940*, Surrey, Ian Allan Publishing, 2002

Gericke, W.: *Fallschirmjäger hier und da*. Berlin, Schützen Verlag, 1941.

Gericke, W.: *Soldaten fallen vom Himmel*, Berlin, Schützen Verlag, 1940.

Golla, K.-H.: *Die deutsche Fallschirmtruppe 1936-1941*, Hamburg, Mittler & Sohn, 2006

González, O.: *Fallschirmjäger sobre el Gran Sasso*, Valladolid, Quirón, 2006.

Götzel, H., *Generaloberst Kurt Student und seine Fallschirmjäger*, Friedberg, Podzun-Pallas Verlag, 1980.

Guhnfeldt, C.: *Fornebu 9. April*. Oslo, Wings Forlag A/S, 1990.

Hauge, A.: *Kampen på Midtskogen*, 1995.

Hauge, A.: *Kampene i Norge 1940 (Bind 1)*, Sandefjord, Krigshistorisk Forlag A.S., 1978

Holzermayr, F.: *Vom Ersten bis zum Letzten Tag 1938/1945. Ein Soldat aus Österreich erzählt*. Berg am Starnberger See, Druffel-Verlag, 1996.

Hooton, E. R.: *Luftwaffe at war. Blitzkrieg in the West 1939-1940 (Volume 2)*, Surrey, Ian Allan Publishing, 2007.

Hubatsch, W.:*Die deutsche Besatzung von Dänemark und Norwegen 1940*, Göttingen, Wissenschaftlicher Verlag, 1952.

Jochim, B.: *Luftlandung in Dombas*. Fallschirmjäger in Einsatz während des Norwegen-Feldzugs, Rastatt, Erich Pabel Verlag.

Jowett, P.; Snodgrass, B.: *Finland at war 1939-1945*, Oxford, Osprey Publishing, 2006.

Klietmann, K-G.: *Auszeichnungen des Deutschen Reiches 1936-1945*, Stuttgart, Motorbuch Verlag, 2004.

Kollatz, K.: *Die Fallschirmjäger von Dombas*, Rastatt, Pabel Moewig KG, 1997.

Leroux, R.: *Le Morbihan en Guerre 1939-1945*, Mayenne, Joseph Floch, 1979.

Mabire, J.: *La batalla de Narvik*, Barcelona, editors, 2007 (translated by Miquel Salarich).

Mølmen, Ø.: *Krigen 1940-1945*, Lesjaskog, 1996.

Poll, H.: *Das Land der Mitternachtssonne*, Oslo, Haraldssøn, 1940.

Pöppel, M.: *Himmel und Hölle*, München, Internationaler Kulturdienst, 1985.

Quarrie, B.: *German Airborne Divisions. Blitzkrieg 1940-41*, Oxford, Osprey Publishing, 2004.

Ramcke, B.: *Fallschirmjäger damals und danach*, Frankfurt am Main, Lorch-Verlag, 1951.

Recio Cardona, R.: *Blitzkrieg. Guerra Relámpago (1939-1941)*, Madrid, Acción Press, 2006.

Richards, G.: *World War II Troop Type Parachutes. Axis. Germany, Italy, Japan*, Atglen PA, Schiffer Publishing, 2000.

Riste, O.; Nökleby, B.: *Norway 1940-1945. The Resistance Movement*, Oslo, Johan Grundt Tanum Forlag, 1970.

Schlaug, G.: *Die deutschen Lastensegler-Verbände 1937-1945. Eine Chronik aus Berichten, Tagebüchern, Dokumenten*. Stuttgart, Motorbuch Verlag, 1985.

Schmidt, H.: *Die Fallschirmjäger von Dombas*, Berlin, Schützen Verlag, 1941.

Solvik, Ø.: *Dombås April 1940,* author's edition, 2006.

Thomas, A.: *Gloster Gladiator Aces*, Oxford, Osprey Publishing, 2002.

Thomas, F.; Wegmann, G.: *Die Ritterkreuzträger der Deutschen Wehrmacht 1939-1945. Teil II: Fallschirmjäger*, Osnabrück, Biblio-Verlag, 1986.

Von Hove, A.: *Achtung Fallschirmjäger. Eine Idee bricht sich Bahn*, Leoni Starnberger See, Druffel-Verlag,1954.

Von Roon, A.: *Die Bildchronik der Fallschirmtruppe 1935-1945*. Friedberg, Podzun-Pallas, 1986.

Von Roon, A.: *Zwischen Freiheit und Pflicht*. Geschichten aus der Fallschirmtruppe, Friedberg, Podzun-Pallas, 1989.

Williamson, G.: *Gebirgsjäger. German Mountain Trooper 1939-1945*, Oxford, Osprey Publishing, 2003.

Williamson, G.: *German Mountain & Ski Troops 1939-1945*, Oxford, Osprey Publishing, 1996.

Articles

AA.VV, *Kaptein som døde to ganger,* en *Aftenposten,* 25th February 2001.

Barank, K., *Fallschirmjäger vom Ersten Regiment. Mit der 1. Kompanie/FschJägerRgt 1 am 12. Mai 1940 nach Narvik*. DDF, 4/1990.

Bernhardt, G.: *Kritischer und treuer Fallschirminfanterist-Ernst Mössinger*, DDF, 2/2004.

Broder, G.: *Fallskjermhopping*, en „Kroppsøving", 5/2003.

Delgado, E.: *Operación Weserübung. La carrera por Narvik*, en "Serga", nº 7, septiembre/octubre 2000.

Eriksen, A.: *Dovrebygda 14.-19. april 1940*, en Dovrevygde, Dovre Historielag, 1994.

Gericke, W.:*Stoßtrupp übers Meer,* DDF, Abril 1953

Hooke, R.; Coglianese, C.: *Operation Weserübung and the origins of Joint Warfare*, JFQ, Summer 1993.
Le Berre, A.: *L'embuscade du 15 juin 1944 à Pluméliau ou les malheurs du général Ramcke*, en "Magazine 39 45", nº 203, July/August 2003.
Melchior, B.: *Oslo Einsatz 1940*, DDF, 4/1997.
Mössinger, E.: *14. April 1940: Vor 60 Jahren Dombas-Einsatz*, DDF, 2/2000.
Mössinger, E.: *Fallschirmjäger vom Ersten Regiment. Einsatz der 1.Kp/FschJgRgt 1 am 14. April 1940 in Dombas/Norwegen*, DDF, 3/1990.
Musgrave, B.: *Squadron Leader Caesar B. Hull, DFC. A Rhodesian born fighter pilot who fought and died in the Battle of Britain*, in "Annual Magazine of The Battle of Britain Historical Society", 2004.
Nollen, W.: *Der erste Sprung des Generals Meindl*, DDF, 9/1956
Renisch, P.: *Fallschirmjäger vom Ersten Regiment. Einsatz des I./FschJgRgt 1 am 9. April 1940 in Dänemark und Norwegen*, DDF, 2/1990.
Vázquez, J.: *"Weserübung Nord": assault on the fjords*, in "Revista de Historia Militar", nº 2, March-April 2000; nº 3, May-June 2000; nº4, July-August 2000.
Weiland, G.: *Deutsche Fallschirmjäger in Dombaas*, DDF, 3/2005.

Documents

Airborne operations. A German Appraisal. CMH Pub 104-13 U.S. Government Printing Office: 1989-247-384/00640.
Document: *Abschrift. Verbindungsstab der Luftwaffe bei Gruppe XXI. Oslo 14.4.1940.*
Document: *Befehl der Gruppe XXI (BA-MA RH 24-21/17)*
Document: *Kriegstagebuch Nr. 2 der 3. Geb. Div. (Gruppe Narvik).*
Einsatz der verstärkten 1.Kompanie Fallschirmjägerregiment 1 bei Dombas und Narvik nach Gefechtsberichten I. Bataillon Fallschirmjägerregiment 1.

A paratrooper is aided by a *Kriegsmarine* sailor as he lands. Note that the *Fallschirmjäger* is not wearing the M 38 paratrooper helmet. ("Narvik im Bild")